MARGARET COLE 1893-1980

A POLITICAL BIOGRAPHY

BETTY D. VERNON

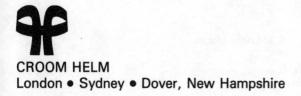

CROOM HELM
London • Sydney • Dover, New Hampshire

Croom Helm Ltd, Provident House, Burrell Row,
Beckenham, Kent BR3 1AT
Croom Helm Australia Pty Ltd, Suite 4, 6th Floor,
64–76 Kippax Street, Surry Hills, NSW 2010, Australia

British Library Cataloguing in Publication Data
Vernon, Betty D.
 Margaret Cole 1893–1980: a political biography.
 1. Cole, Margaret   2. Fabian Society — Biography
 3. Socialists — Great Britain — Biography
 I. Title
 335′.14′0924   HX243.C5

 ISBN 0-7099-2611-1

Croom Helm, 51 Washington Street,
Dover, New Hampshire 03820, USA

Library of Congress Cataloging in Publication Data
Vernon, Betty.
 Margaret Cole, 1893–1980.

 Bibliography: p.
 Includes index.
 1. Cole, Margaret, 1893–1980. 2. Socialists—
Great Britain—biography 3. Fabian society
(Great Britain)—history. I. Mitchison, Naomi,
1897–   . Margaret Cole, 1893–1980. II. Title.
HX244.7.C64V47   1986   335′.14′0924 (B)   85-29105
ISBN 0-7099-2611-1

Phototypeset by Patrick and Anne Murphy,
Highcliffe-on-Sea, Dorset

Printed and bound in Great Britain
by Billings Ltd, Worcester

CONTENTS

PLATES

1. Margaret Isabel Postgate, c. 1899
2. Margaret Isabel Postgate at university
3. Margaret Cole, c. 1922
4. Sidney and Beatrice Webb. Early days of The Partnership, 1894 (Courtesy of the British Library of Political and Economic Science)
5. Sidney and Beatrice Webb. Later days at Passfield Corner, c. 1940 (Courtesy of The British Library of Political and Economic Science)
6. Fabian Summer School at Dartington, 1941. (*Left to right*) Ruth Gollancz, Dr Stella Churchill, Margaret Cole, Victor Gollancz
7. G.D.H. Cole and Amber Blanco White. Dartington, 1941
8. Fabian window at Beatrice Webb House, Dorking. *Top:* Pease, Webb and Shaw. *Below:* members of the Fabian Executive, including (first left) H.G. Wells, (sixth) Amber Blanco White and (seventh) Mary Hankinson
9. Agnata Butler — *Punch* cartoon 2 July 1887
10. Raymond Postgate (with Mr White of J. Lyons), c. 1956
11. Chairman, Further Education Committee, LCC (c. 1958)
12. Dame Margaret with Michael Foot, MP, at the University of Sussex, April 1976 (Courtesy of the *Evening Argus*)
13. Margaret and G.D.H. Cole at Freeland. *The Bystander*, 20 April 1938 (photograph by Howard Coster)

TO JANE AND HUMPHREY

PREFACE

Margaret Cole believed with deep conviction that 'the poorest He that is in England hath as much a life to live as the greatest He'. As a socialist she strove by her teaching, her public activities and her pen to create a society in which hope, opportunity and equality would become the birthright of all. If her husband Professor G. D. H. Cole 'practically invented labour history' she, in her own right, was a distinguished chronicler of the Labour Movement.

Today when the quintessence of socialism is under continuous reappraisal and the course of its development is often misrepresented, it seems right to record the life and work of so scholarly and committed an exponent. This memoir, based upon Margaret's extensive publications and correspondence, on unpublished family papers, on the recollections of those who knew and worked with her and my own experience as a friend, an active Fabian and her vice chairman at London's County Hall, seeks to give permanent substance to her shade with accuracy and affection.

Betty D. Vernon

ACKNOWLEDGEMENTS

I am indebted to many people who, by sharing their memories and unearthing correspondence, have helped immeasurably in compiling this memoir: especially to Jane Abraham (née Cole), Will Abraham, Humphrey Cole, Naomi Mitchison and Richmond Postgate. They made available unpublished personal and family papers, and were infinitely patient with my questions. Together with Rosemary Beresford, Professor Lord Asa Briggs, Meredith Brown, Stanley Mayne, Lady Meynell, John Parker, Dr Lisanne Radice and Professor John Saville, they read my MS in whole or in part and offered wise advice. The conclusions drawn are, however, my own.

Sincere thanks go also to Mary, Oliver and Ormond Postgate, and to Margaret's numerous friends and colleagues — not all now alive — who helped by word or pen. These include Professor Brian Abel-Smith, C. Geoffrey Allen, Cis Amaral, Dr Robin Page Arnot, Irene Barclay, Molly Bolton, Noreen Branson, Rosamund Broadley, Mabel Bryant (Nanny Cole), Leila Campbell, Ina Chaplin, Lady Chorley, Professor Hugh Clegg, Peggy Crane, Professor Lionel Elvin, Lord Elwyn-Jones, Andrew Filson, Michael Foot MP, Val Arnold-Forster, Dorothy Fox, Eleanor Goodrich, Alec and Helen Grant, Charles Griffiths, Dr Bernice Hamilton, Dr Brian Harrison, Michael Holroyd, Beryl Hughes, H. D. Hughes, Hector Jelf, Jennifer Jenkins, Rashid Karen, S. F. Kissin, Dr D. M. Leggett, Ted Littlecott, Elizabeth Lloyd, Lady Longford, Professor Norman MacKenzie, Malcolm and Kitty Muggeridge, Sylvia Mulvey, Marjorie Nicholson, Olive Parsons, Nicolas Pease, Frank Pickstock, Ben Pimlott, Lord Ponsonby of Shulbrede, Patricia Pugh, E. A. Radice, W. T. Rodgers, C. H. Rolph, Rosemary Stanford, Elizabeth Thomas, Professor Peter Townsend, Colin Watson, Harold Wilson (Lord Wilson of Rievaulx), Professor Roger Wilson, G. D. N. Worswick and Michael Young (Lord Young of Dartington). Several other correspondents sent me unsolicited but enlightening material.

To Michael Foot, who also contributed the Introduction stamped with his unmistakable hallmark, goes my especial gratitude.

I have also had invaluable help from Colleen Saunders, who deciphered and typed my drafts with unfailing good humour, but above all my husband has sustained me throughout, as a tirelessly exacting — if unofficial — editor-adviser. He also compiled the Index, which, as Douglas Cole recognised, is an exasperating but essential chore. His work has made the book a joint tribute.

Librarians and archivists, as ever, have been generously resourceful, notably Dr Angela Raspin of the British Library of Political and Economic Science, Mr A. R. Neate of GLC Records and David Horsfield of Ruskin College Library, Oxford. Other invaluable sources have been the Bodleian, Oxford, the British Library (Newspaper Library) Colindale, Cambridge University Library, the Fabian Society, the Fawcett Library, Girton College Library, Hull University (Brymor Jones Library), Labour Research Department, Nuffield College Library, Sussex University Library and the University of Warwick Modern Records. Roy Smith and his staff at the Central Library, London Borough of Sutton, have been continuously co-operative.

In addition to Humphrey Cole, Lady Meynell, Naomi Mitchison, Lisanne Radice, John Parker and Anthony Wright, all of whom allowed the use of published writings, the author and publisher also thank the following for permission to reprint extracts from other copyright material, namely: The Bodley Head, Ford Madox Ford, *Parades' End*; William Collins, Harold Nicolson's *Diaries and Letters* (vol. 3); J. M. Dent & Sons Ltd, Maurice Reckitt, *As It Happened* and Rowland Kenney, *Westering*; Macmillan, Asa Briggs and John Saville (eds.), *Essays in Labour History*; Virago Press, Norman and Jeanne MacKenzie (eds.), *The Diary of Beatrice Webb* (4 vols.). David Higham Associates Ltd permitted extracts from Margery Todd, *Snakes and Ladders* (Longman's Green) and from Stella Bowen, *Drawn from Life* (Collins). Finally thanks are due to the British Library of Political and Economic Science and to T. M. Vyvyan (Literary Executor) for enabling me to quote from the Passfield Papers and from the papers of Professor R. H. Tawney.

ABBREVIATIONS

ABCA	Army Bureau of Current Affairs
CFP	Cole Family Papers (privately held)
DES	Department of Education and Science
FRD	Fabian Research Department
GLC	Greater London Council
ILEA	Inner London Education Authority
ILP	Independent Labour Party
LCC	London County Council
LEA	Local Education Authority
LRD	Labour Research Department
NEC	National Executive Committee of the Labour Party
NFRB	New Fabian Research Bureau
PLP	Parliamentary Labour Party
SSIP	Society for Socialist Inquiry and Propaganda
TULC	Trade Union Labour Co-operative Democratic History Society
WEA	Workers' Educational Association

INTRODUCTION

Rt. Hon. Michael Foot MP

One great partnership — between Beatrice Webb and Sidney Webb — placed its imprint on the history of the British Labour Movement, both the making and the writing of it. A long list of rebels, mostly on the left of the Labour Party, were inclined to chafe beneath the yoke, but often too they would stray back into the Fabian fold of their own free will. Whatever the arguments, few would or could deny the strength of the Webb tradition, and in recent years — thanks to the full, unexpected publication of the Beatrice Webb diaries — it has been given a fresh, almost unsuspected emotional force. Beatrice Webb has been winning for herself a whole new audience, and, I would guess, a young audience too.

A similar reawakening of interest should be achieved by the other great partnership which was modelled upon that of the Webbs, which deliberately strove to carry their tradition forward into new territory and toward new conquests. Douglas Cole and Margaret Cole believed in writing history and making history, and never striving to draw too sharp a distinction between the two: without them, the Fabian Society itself might have expired and the Fabian idea might never have been revitalised with some older and more refreshing streams.

Douglas Cole had learned his socialism in his schooldays from the blessed fount of William Morris, and he never would allow all the pressures and vicissitudes of politics to dilute it. He kept his faith through the darkest days, as when he had to endure Labour Governments, or in the darkest places, like the University of Oxford. However, without Margaret, it would have been a much more laborious and less effective affair; without her, even the inspiration of William Morris might never have held its own.

Almost single-handed at Oxford and setting the style in so many other universities and places of learning, Douglas revived interest in the history of the Labour Movement, and thereby helped to add a new dimension to the socialist idea. He poured into that study all his love of England and the English countryside and thereby, incidentally, brought forth the one masterpiece among his writings,

1

one of the great English biographies, his *Life of William Cobbett*. Margaret's part in this achievement is incontestable. She could often write more readily and sharply than he, and she in turn produced one masterpiece, her *Life of G. D. H. Cole*.

According to the legend, when Sidney Webb wooed Beatrice, he made the romantic claim: 'One and one, placed in a sufficiently integrated relationship, make not two but eleven.' Even bolder arithmetical calculations might have been apposite in the Margaret-Douglas match. Each without the other would have forfeited so much; each with the other could scale quite unexpected heights or circumvent the most awkward corners. Some of that story was most beautifully told in Margaret's *Life*. She was dealing with a saint, one who tried, according to his creed, to treat all men as equals, one who could be kindness and comradeship incarnate, as many of us who knew him less intimately could testify. But how to write a book on such a paragon?

Margaret knew: for the saint had another side to him. It was not that he had feet of clay, less still of course, a head of clay; he was a super-intellectual down to his eloquent, almost aristocratic, fingertips. But he did have eccentricities, and they transformed the cool, even slightly cold, exterior some of us used to see from the back of the lecture hall. He wrote a lot about education, but had hardly ever entered a state school. He was the model of steadfastness to the cause, but was often flouncing out of Fabian Society meetings or such-like places with the reproof: 'I withdraw the word Fools. I say Bloody Fools.' He had a splendid temper, which he could unloose on some of his comrades, such as the Webbs themselves, Kingsley Martin, Harold Laski and a host of other lesser and dimmer lights.

He liked to treat men as equals, but not so much women, and seemed to have been quite oblivious of the highly legitimate resentment of his wife against the offensive *maleness* of Oxford society — with its ineffable decree, for example, that when carol services were held in Magdalen Chapel 'the ladies' were allowed to listen only from a cold upper gallery. He was even conceivably a woman hater, had innocent little homosexual crushes on some of his students (one of them Hugh Gaitskell), and developed, as Margaret said, 'a disgust with sex almost equal to that of the early Christian fathers'. The courtship, as in the case of Beatrice and Sidney, had its most comical aspects, but Margaret recited them with honesty, taste and a real sense of humour. But why is it, I wonder, that a man's private defeats may hold as much interest as his most magnificent public conquests?

Thanks to Margaret's biography, thanks maybe also to the male-dominated atmosphere of socialist society in the 1920s and the 1930s, much more was known about Douglas than Margaret. But, as this book illustrates, that supposed balance was always misleading and unfair. Margaret's own autobiographical essays helped to readjust the picture. But there was always room for a fuller, richer portrait by someone who knew and loved her. Betty Vernon fulfils all these qualifications. Her biography of Ellen Wilkinson made one most notable addition to the literature of the Labour Movement, and here is another ready to set beside it.

There are three stages in the life of any woman with a public life. In the first she is 'that charming and intelligent girl'; in the second she becomes 'that rather frightful woman'; and in the third she is 'that very interesting old lady' — Susan Lawrence

He who would do good to another must do it in Minute Particulars. General Good is the plea of the scoundrel, the hypercritical flatterer. For Art and Science cannot exist but in minutely organised particulars — William Blake

Society we believe ought to pursue as its first object not the greatness of the State or Nation, but the happiness and well being of the greatest number of its citizens — Margaret and Douglas Cole, Introduction, The Condition of Britain

PART ONE:
MISS MARGARET POSTGATE

1 'THE WRONG SORT OF CUCKOO'

The Family

When Margaret Isabel Postgate, born on 6 May 1893, was six years old she asked in Latin at the family's Sunday lunch for *the* beef instead of *some* beef, whereupon her father, Dr (later Professor) John Percival Postgate, a keen practitioner of the direct method of teaching, 'pushed the whole sirloin on to my plate and I dissolved into tears'.[1]

This true anecdote is not to imply an unhappy childhood: far from that. It does, however, explain the development of two of Margaret's distinctive characteristics: a swift sensitivity to the feelings of others, and critical discernment over the nuances in the use of words.

In fact, Postgate family life, embracing six siblings — Margaret, Raymond, Esmond, Ethel, Ormond and Richmond — was lively, humorous and disciplined. Although Father was an authoritarian pedant, Mother — Edith Allen, affectionately known as Mrs P — was highly intelligent, practical, understanding and always accessible to her children.

The Professor's ancestry was 'reasonably mixed'. His forebears came from Yorkshire where there are records of Postgates (the name supposedly means keeper of the postern gate) holding land in the sixteenth century. Great-grandfather Postgate was a small builder in Scarborough, but his son John, Margaret's grandfather, reached the dignity of inclusion in the *Dictionary of National Biography*.[2]

A good specimen of the selfless, difficult Victorian reformer he [grandfather] started life as a grocer's boy, grew outraged by the adulteration of goods practised by his masters — at the salt in the sugar, the mouse-dirt in the tea — and vowed to fight them.

He then worked as a surgeon's boy, studied in his spare time, passed his medical examinations, and ultimately became a member of the Royal College of Surgeons. Thereafter, this Dr Postgate (who also became a Professor) began his life's campaign against the adulteration of food. Through his 'tireless prodding' Birmingham MPs introduced numerous Bills on adulteration, and he lived to see his work crowned by the 1875 Sale of Food and Drugs Act, a landmark in consumer protection.

Dr Postgate's sense of purpose resulted in his caring little for those he offended or for the well-being of his seven children, whom he kept short of pocket money in the interests of his unpaid public work. This frugality rubbed off on his eldest son, John Percival, who never forgot the harsh conditions of his youth, had a panic fear of spending and kept his own children short of material things. 'If we put too much butter or jam on our bread he pounced on us and scraped it off,' Margaret recalled, which explains her inordinate fondness for butter in later life.[3]

For over a decade Margaret's father was classics lecturer at Trinity College Cambridge, and subsequently Professor of Greek at Liverpool University. He created the famous Postgate *Latin Grammar* and edited various books of poetry which contained in his daughter's opinion 'some of the least interesting' of the Roman poets.

Like his father, Professor Postgate was also a crusader, but in the linguistic field. He was a protagonist of the modern pronunciation of Latin, and believed that children should talk Latin as if it were a modern language. Thus Margaret, with her beloved brother Raymond, and the next sibling, Esmond, had frequently to translate everyday situations into the Roman tongue. Over the years, however, Father modified his theories and by the time Richmond, fifteen years younger than Margaret, to whom she was also deeply attached, was old enough to participate, Latin was no longer the Postgates' *lingua franca*. The children had, however, created their own family vocabulary of eccentric words and phrases which 'just grew'.[4] To an outsider it sounded pure gobbledy gook, but it survived at least into the third generation!

Professor Postgate could be an 'exacting and irritable teacher' but he did believe in girls being as well educated as their brothers. He therefore continued to teach Margaret Latin long after she had gone to school, but failed to convey the beauties of either its ideas or its language. 'I hated Latin all through my childhood as bitterly as anyone can ever have hated it,' she wrote. 'It was not until I had ceased to be his pupil that I found any beauty in it at all.'[5]

Nevertheless, the seeds had been sown, and as an adult Margaret cherished classical literature, scattering Greek and Latin references in her poetry and correspondence with scholarly friends. Once, when lunching with Lord Hailsham to discuss affairs of the Central London Polytechnic, of which they were both governors, the purpose of their meeting was nearly vitiated by their spending most of the meal capping each other's classical quotations.[6]

Margaret considered her father a disappointed man. Although well regarded academically, he never achieved his ambition of becoming Classics Professor at Cambridge — the post went instead to A. E. Housman — and was not an endearing personality. He left a sizeable estate yet had a pathological fear of poverty, and an irritable temper — a trait more easily pardoned than his general illiberality. Apart from a conviction that 'the world was marching into political damnation', the Professor felt overburdened with a pack of children whom he tended to find 'exasperating, noisy, destructive and unfilial', an attitude Margaret, the eldest, regarded as understandable if not defensible.

'The first three children were not, I think, at all nice in their earlier years,' she wrote. 'They quarrelled and fought on the slightest provocation in real, if not constant, dislike of each other,' and she, on her own admission, 'was a young bully'. Raymond too was 'one of the most obstinate little boys ever born', while Esmond (Mondie), with his golden curls and pink cheeks, was 'a grizzling baby . . . we cannot have been a nice lot of offspring'. Happily, these three brown-eyed squabblers were succeeded by a blue-eyed trio — Ethel, Ormond and Richmond — 'whose temperaments by contrast were angelic'. The contrast did not, however, noticeably reduce the quarrels. Mrs P used jokingly to say that she had to go for six separate walks a day because of the family rows!

On the whole Professor Postgate, to his children, was 'a rather natural, hostile force, apt to erupt, and when in eruption best avoided'. In no way, however, were Freudian shadows cast. 'I do love you,' Esmond told his mother, 'and I don't mind Dadda.' And that, his elder sister laconically concluded, 'was about the size of it'. On Bastille Day in 1926 poor Dadda was run down by a steam wagon near the family home in Cambridge and died soon afterwards. It was an unworthy and untimely end.[7]

Edith Postgate, née Allen, was clearly the more endearing parent. 'We were not an adoring tribe, but what we should have done without her was unconceivable,' Margaret wrote. Perceptive and witty, she was an early Girton graduate, and to her eldest daughter 'the most individual person I have ever known'.

Her family were of trading stock: one side from the West Country, the other — the Le Lacheurs — from Guernsey, where their ancestry can be traced back to the seventeenth century. All — and especially the Guernsey side — were highly individualistic, not to say egocentric at times.

> When anyone says of my family, as they do, that the Postgates are all mad, it is the Le Lacheur strain they are observing . . . they have queer bits of private knowledge: they enjoy life and are resentful of being bored and are liable to utter disconcerting comments in very audible voices

Margaret wrote in unconscious self-parody.[8]

The Allens were a large and extremely handsome family. Edith, born 'five years before *Alice in Wonderland* came out in 1868', was beautiful, and her brother Tom, an Homeric Scholar of Queens, was voted the Adonis of the year at Oxford.

With her sisters, Edith attended the embryo of what became the distinguished North London Collegiate School.

> We used a house and stables in the Camden Road, and a house in Sandall Road where the first school was eventually built. I once had the unique privilege of helping Miss Buss [the joint Founder] scramble in at a school window . . . She was short and solid and very dignified with ample skirts . . . white hair, a cap and several shawls. What she did for girls' education is wonderful . . . The new school [now relocated in Cannons Park, Edgware] was opened by the Prince of Wales and Princess Alexandra. We had one really lovely girl, tall and swaying . . . it was amusing to see how the Prince came to life when she came up for her prize.[9]

With several friends from school Edith went on to Girton. In those days the college was smaller than it is today. 'There were no buses and no bicycles . . . so it always meant a walk in and out of Cambridge,' she wrote, 'but it was a delight to be really out of town.'

Originally Edith had intended to read Mathematics, but switched to Classics during her first term, undeterred by having heard that Dr Postgate, one of her preceptors, was 'awfully disagreeable'. He, ten years older, was not impervious to feminine charm, and invited

Edith and a friend to dine at the end of their last term:

> It was the lovliest of evenings . . . and I shall never forget the
> lilac at the bottom of the steps leading into the cloistered court
> . . . Mr Gill took me into dinner; he was afterwards our best
> man, and Margaret's godfather.[10]

They had, however, a long wait. Edith taught Classics for five
years at Norwich House, Cambridge, and then at South Hampstead High School. The wedding took place in 1891, soon after the
ban on Fellows marrying had been lifted.

For some fifteen years the family lived in Cambridge, but moved
north when Father became Professor of Classics at Liverpool
University. Mrs P hated the city for its dirt, sunlessness and bitter
winds. She delighted, however, in the teeming, colourful, multi-
religious population around the port, and when she discovered the
number of different consuls resident in the city was 'astounded'.
She had had 'no idea there were so many countries in the world'.

> While we were there, there was a dock strike . . . seven miles of
> docks lying idle — and the smell of rotting fruit and vegetables
> . . . A regulation was passed forbidding crowds to assemble, and
> defined a crowd as any number above three. So when I went out
> with my six children we had to walk in different companies and
> pretend we did not belong to each other.[11]

Her dislike of the city was unassuaged, for even though they had
'the most beautiful house at the top of nearly the highest hill in
Liverpool' overlooking the Mersey and the Dee, with the Welsh
hills in the background, near to where Turner reputedly painted
many of his sunsets, Mrs P never wanted to revisit Liverpool.
Indeed, the evening she returned to Cambridge 'the quiet made me
feel I had had a headache for ten years and when I smelt the lime
blossom in Newton Road and walked between the lavender and
rosemary hedges I felt I had come back to an earthly paradise'.[12]

Cambridge Childhood

Margaret, too, adored Cambridge. In the late spring she considered
it was the most satisfying place in the world in spite of exposure to

'winds from the Urals' and the unrelieved flatness of the fens:

> I have seen many parts of England and the world which are more
> beautiful in any accepted sense of the word . . . but this is merely
> irrelevant . . . As soon as I get on the raised highway with the
> white posts marking its corners that run through Hereward's
> country . . . see the huge expanse of sky with fat Queen Victoria
> clouds processing solemnly through the blue or the sun drawing
> water in long silvery shafts, something moves in me that is as old
> as my birth, and my senses recognise that I have come home . . .
> the place where my ghost will walk is Cambridge and the Fens

she wrote in an outburst of rare sentimentality.[13]

The abiding love for Cambridge implies a secure, happy childhood. And indeed, writing with graphic recall in her autobiography, Margaret confirmed it as such. The Postgate family were
assuredly middle class and 'belonged to a special group of the professional academic, living in a university town', she wrote.

> The importance of this is that we were brought up in an atmos-
> phere of comparative equality . . . although our family was
> rather on the low side as regards expenditure. Other children had
> more, or more expensive clothes and holidays than we had; and I
> vividly remember my mother explaining to me when I was eight
> that I could not have a rocking horse because we couldn't afford
> both a rocking horse and little brothers. I was furiously angry: I
> had never been consulted and would much have preferred the toy
> to horrible little brothers. But the difference lay in the frills, not
> the essentials . . . none of us was in a position to exploit or to
> despise socially any of the others, and I think this early
> experience of an equalitarian society, even within so narrow a
> compass, has given me a natural bent towards equality, ante-
> dating any socialist conviction, which will never be eradicated.[14]

Until Margaret was sixteen the Postgates lived at 54 Bateman
Street, Cambridge, in an unattractive four-storeyed house. Its chief
characteristic seems, like many Victorian homes, to have been cold-
ness and ugliness — but it was an ugliness redeemed by a small,
joyous garden, with an enormous mulberry tree 'which became a
friend as soon as we could climb', surrounded by 32 pear trees. The
surfeit of fruit was such that for years Margaret could never abide

pears or bear to pay for one! Her most vivid recollection of the garden, however, was of its aromatic plants, mingled with certain roses, white Nephetos and Pink Cabbage, of which she wrote most nostalgically in a letter to *The Times* decades later. Her sense of smell, 'the most atavistic and long-remembering of all our senses', was such that 'it annihilated fifty years' when it detected the aroma of one of those shrubs.[15]

In spite of her squabbling little brothers, Margaret found Cambridge a good place in which to be young. It was of manageable size, 'through which a nine-year-old could traverse comfortably'; there were plentiful open spaces — 'those who created the Botanic Gardens shall be remembered in heaven for providing small children with so much enjoyment' — and it was beautiful.

> You cannot be brought up within a mile of the Backs and the Bridges, seeing the weeping willows year by year coming into leaf and the spring flowers waking in St Johns Wilderness, or walk to school along the gracious curve of Trumpington Street, without some sense of beauty seeping into you.

It was also alive and amusing: there were Mays Week, Christmas parties, pageants and plays 'which gave me an illusion I could act, not dissipated for years'.[16]

Curiously, the Postgates were not a markedly bookish household: 'I never remember hearing any literary discussion at all, and when we played talking or writing games, as we often did, they tested general knowledge and spelling, never literary matters.' But there were, of course, 'a good few' books about. Margaret became an insatiable reader, ranging through Lewis Carroll, Edward Lear, Mrs Ewing and E. Nesbitt to Dickens, Thackeray, Kipling and Arthur Mee's splendidly omniscient *Children's Encyclopedia*.

> I cannot remember when I was not reading Kipling . . . and I still think he was a very good writer until nearly the end, when he got tangled up in verbiage. And some of his poetry, much of it in the *Songs from Books* is the real stuff

she told Robin Page Arnot.[17]

From her earliest years Margaret read with enormous voracity — 'while eating, minding the baby, washing, or lacing my boots for skating' — unguided and almost uncensored, although her parents forbade *Dracula* and Edgar Allen Poe. She loved 'any sort of history, though not historical novels which seemed to me neither one thing nor the other until I found *The Cloister and the Hearth*'. She read everything over and over again and was well on the way to becoming the compulsive reader of later life. Ideas were less prolific:

> There was very little either of politics or religion in our youthful lives. Our household was non-political. That is to say, Tory. My father's strong views did not impose upon us, until his opinions clashed violently with [Raymond] his eldest son's.[18]

Certainly, Margaret's philosophy was in no way hewn from the rock of any personal suffering or emotional introspection. It was largely intellectual, emerging in time from her reading, her own observations and the undoubted influence of G. D. H. Cole.

Similarly, religion was not forced upon the children. They were brought up orthodox Church of England, had prayers, and attended church regularly. At one time Margaret showed eagerness to become a 'Golden Sunbeam' by joining a band of children to 'bring the work of God to their contemporaries'. This, however, was firmly discouraged, and her enthusiasm waned: 'my father, I discovered long afterwards was an unbeliever who thought religion good for women; I suspect my mother's faith was not strong'.[19]

As was then expected of a child from an academic household, Margaret attended a small private school run by the wife of a don, a formidable lady but a good teacher. Pupils attended only half days, so Margaret could spend much time playing hospitals and ill-nesses. 'Psychologists will no doubt say that this was an early outlet for sexual feelings,' she wrote, but years later she admitted to a long-cherished desire to become a surgeon, and with her clear head and long, sensitive hands, might well have succeeded.[20]

The pen, however, superseded the scalpel, and much of her early school life Margaret spent 'somewhere where I could not be seen', telling herself endless stories 'which I sometimes wrote down'. In fact she 'commenced author' very young, before she could really write. Regretfully there was no one to record these efforts: 'I wish there had been, for the title of one that survives, *The Melon Who Drove too Fast*, excites my curiosity!' She did, however, act as amanuensis to her youngest brother Richmond, who followed in her footsteps and produced 'pithy masterpieces!'[21] Later Margaret did record her own works, 'writing quantities of stories on the backs of the London Matriculation papers' her father had for correction. Aspirations to be a novelist, however, abated, 'choked by a surfeit of other people's fiction', although in time that particular ambition was fulfilled by some thirty detective novels she wrote jointly with her husband 'as a mere relaxation'.

Roedean

Reality, however, had to be faced, and a formal education acquired. At fourteen Margaret was sent to a select, expensive girl's boarding school, Roedean in Sussex, which she entered by winning the sole annual scholarship.

Boarding school was selected because Mrs P did not want her eldest daughter to be overwhelmed by demands of family domesticity. 'I didn't know anything about the Misses Lawrence' (the heads of Roedean), she wrote to Margaret years later. 'But I insisted on your leaving home: we were making too much use of you.'[22] Nevertheless, Margaret loathed Roedean with all the intensity of sensitive adolescence, and initially was so unpopular that the early terms were 'almost pure misery'. She just could not fit into the pattern of a conforming community, and hated the lack of privacy communal living entailed. 'What I did specifically to turn me into a pariah dog I am not very sure. I was a bit unintentionally uppish.' She had, after all, won the scholarship.

I spoke before I was spoken to, and had the temerity to ask for a part in the school play . . . but the main cause was simple general distaste: I was the wrong sort of cuckoo in a horribly alien nest.[23]

The school, founded by the Misses Lawrence, was not geared to academic excellence. At that time few pupils went on to universities, and the standards of scholarship 'would have shocked Miss Buss and Miss Beale, and the founders of the GPDST [Girls' Public Day School Trust]'. Discipline and religious observance were all-important, and pupils became obsessed by games, which reinforced the compulsive, competitive element Margaret abhorred. Equally obnoxious she found the prefectorial system, which maintained discipline through endless petty restrictions, censorship and punishment. Christian principles, spelt out in a surfeit of scripture lessons and excessive chapel going 'left the girls in no doubt but that God was a kind of Super Senior Prefect'.[24]

Margaret's overriding criticism of Roedean concerned the lack of intellectual stimulus verging on philistinism. On one occasion, having finished her French 'prep', she was found reading Macaulay's *Essays* in the time assigned to French, a sin which resulted in her being barred from the library for the rest of the term. Further, no one 'ever discussed a cognate subject'; there was no debating society, and rarely were politics ever referred to save in a joke about the suffragettes. On the other hand Margaret did learn to appreciate the beauty of Virgil and Lucretius, was encouraged to write and acquired a broad knowledge of literature. She would smuggle Hazlitt and other books up to her bedroom in a large embroidery bag, for while 'reading in one's bedroom was prohibited, sewing was not'. She also discovered poets, whose works were 'free of notes to be memorised for examination purposes' and learnt a great deal of them by heart.[25] This skill she long prized in her maturity, and would spontaneously recite the verses of such poets as G. K. Chesterton and John Masefield with obvious delight.

For all its shortcomings, Roedean bestowed on Margaret three positive benefits: a life-long friendship with fellow pupil Phyllis Reid, a very real understanding — acquired from acute unhappiness — of 'what it is like to be well and truly pecked' which proved of inestimable value to her in human relationships, and, thirdly, a 'middling' scholarship to Girton. With this triumph, fresh fields and pastures new lay before Margaret, and entering them she blossomed.

Notes

1. M. I. Cole, *Growing Up into Revolution* (Longmans Green, London, 1949), p. 6.
2. Ibid., p. 3.
3. Jane Abraham, letter to author, and ibid., p. 4.
4. T. P. R. Layng and Richmond Postgate, letters to author.
5. Cole, *Growing Up*, p. 6.
6. M. I. Cole to Robin Page Arnot, 31 October 1974 (CFP). The Cole/Robin Page Arnot papers are also held by Hull University (Brymor Jones Library).
7. Cole, *Growing Up*, pp. 6–7, and CFP.
8. Cole, *Growing Up*, p. 8.

9. Mrs Postgate, unpublished reminiscences (CFP).
10. Ibid.
11. Ibid.
12. Ibid.
13. Cole, *Growing Up*, pp. 2–3.
14. Ibid., pp. 8–9.
15. Ibid., p. 14, and *The Times*, letter, 27 July 1971.
16. Cole, *Growing Up*, p. 16.
17. Ibid., pp. 11–12, and letter to Robin Page Arnot, 4 September 1974 (CFP).
Margaret was an addict of Charlotte Yonge's novels. Her friend Bernice Hamilton
remembered her meeting Helen Cam, the distinguished Cambridge medievalist, and
their discussing Charlotte's books. 'Both knew them from cover to cover and Helen
made a genealogical tree of the characters, while Margaret pointed out how various
people had improbably inconsistent ages in different novels!'
18. Cole, *Growing Up*, p. 17.
19. Ibid., pp. 21–2.
20. Mrs Bryant ('Nanny'), interview, and M. I. Cole to author.
21. Cole, *Growing Up*, p. 18.
22. Mrs Postgate to M. I. Cole, 11 November 1949 (CFP).
23. Cole, *Growing Up*, p. 26.
24. Ibid., p. 31.
25. Ibid., p. 30–2.

2   SLIPPING INTO SOCIALISM

Girton

When she left school in 1911, Margaret admitted to having been 'the most ignorant greenhorn in the world, totally unprepared for living and wholly ignorant of public affairs'. She knew nothing of the reforming Liberal Government, of its introducing rudimentary old age pensions, minimum wage rates and 'a little feeding for school children', while the Taff Vale judgement, which had so greatly weakened trade unions, was a total mystery to her.

Soon after the family's move to Liverpool, however, she became aware of dock strikes, and

> in a boiling August remembered the truck loads of rotting vegetables, the stench of unscavenged streets, tramless and silent through which soldiers marched . . . I gathered from my father's thunderous noises that it was the end of the world . . . but as to what the strike was all about I had to read my husband's first book [*The World of Labour*, 1913, a seminal publication] some years later to understand.[1]

If Girton did little to deepen Margaret's political awareness, it developed her self-confidence. Although one contemporary recalls her as being 'rather pathetic — she was so clever she didn't really fit in'[2] — she was highly respected for that cleverness. After the claustrophobic restraints of Roedean, Margaret found the friendships, social activities and above all the intellectual freedom that Girton offered exhilarating:

> To work when you liked, to cut lectures, to be where you liked, when you liked and with whom you liked . . . to go on reading, writing or talking till dawn, made it bliss to be alive . . . How often drunk with talk or poetry had I crept to my room for two hours' sleep before a new day . . . And even if we lived within a framework of regulations which modern undergraduates might regard as stifling, to creatures fresh from school it was Utopia.[3]

Only a few college friends remained important after she went down, but Margaret retained a lasting affection for her university, and in later years frequently attended Girton Roll Dinners — often with Helen Grant — until she became too deaf to enjoy them. Mrs Grant, an old friend and a Fabian, was a Fellow of Girton and a former lecturer in Spanish.

As an undergraduate her Thespian ambitions were realised through the Girton Dramatic Society, and she appeared with mild success in *Prunella*. Of her minor role the *Girton Review* noted: 'M. Postgate is to be congratulated for a spirited rendering of the general stupidity and vacuity of the attendant gardener's boy as bird scarer.'[4]

In the Debating Society she made less impact. Speaking, for example, in defence of the insularity of Englishmen, she argued that patriotism was more inspiring than cosmopolitanism because 'the latter led to loss of individuality'. Her 'forcible' speech was dismissed, again by the *Girton Review*, as 'a trifle aggressive, occasionally sinking to triviality'.[5]

If, as Margaret once admitted, she was 'a slow starter', at college she made Olympian strides. Girton led her to discover that she possessed 'book brains better than average . . . from my father I had always gathered that I was a semi-imbecile . . . and Roedean provided no-one to measure oneself against'. The classics captured her lively mind and she came to relish their history and literature, almost learning by heart Alfred Zimmern's *The Greek Commonwealth* and many of Gilbert Murray's translations. To those two scholars 'who both loved the civilisation of Greece as if it were a new discovery, I owe more than I can say'. She acquired other intellectual debts, particularly to Dr Terrot Reaveley Glover, whose lectures on Roman history she found 'a revelation . . . he related his lectures to whatever interested him at the moment . . . he was a great teacher'.[6]

Under the guidance of distinguished scholars Margaret became a 'good classicist', learning to enjoy and understand Greek and Roman civilisation at leisure. This was all-important in her development; since the range of classical literature was limited, and there could be no more of it, 'anyone with a reasonable brain and a good grounding', she argued, 'could acquire an appreciation of the whole of the civilisation under study', from architecture to philosophy, and still have the mental leisure to think about it. 'We classicists had a limited subject, but the whole of human life was its province . . . it dealt with human beings dead long ago, but it dealt with them as human beings in the round.'[7]

This breadth of vision was important to her personal growth. It was expressed in a tolerance and objectivity which came to characterise both her literary and administrative work as well as her human relationships, and her excellent judgement. Nevertherless, even into old age she could be explosively unwilling to suffer fools gladly.

In the Classics Tripos, Margaret gained a First, and also twice won the Agnata Butler Prize for classical excellence.[8] On graduation Margaret as a mere female received only a Degree Certificate — Cambridge did not admit women as full members of the university until 1947, although Oxford had first conferred full degrees some 25 years earlier.

Greatly to Professor Postgate's credit, he suggested that his daughter should acquire a degree by additional study at Liverpool University.[9] Typically, however, she refused and instead secured an appointment as classics mistress at St Paul's Girls' School just after the outbreak of the First World War.

Teaching at St Paul's

Margaret grew to like teaching 'very much indeed', and came to respect the school's high academic standards. Initially, she was 'slightly alarmed' at having to discipline girls so close to her own age, but soon discovered in herself 'an incurable didacticism' which she never lost. From being a promising starter she became in time a provoking and interesting lecturer of which adult education — and the Labour Movement — were the beneficiaries.

At St Paul's she acquired skill and understanding. So much so that Bernard Shaw covered her 'with blushing pride' when, having heard her speak at a discussion about education at a Fabian meeting, he told Margaret that she was the only speaker who seemed to understand what teaching was all about.

The staff room at St Paul's made Margaret feel 'so young and coltish' that she often landed herself in mild trouble for such behaviour as actually *sitting* on desks while talking to the girls! Not all her colleagues, however, were the fuddy-duddies of first impression. One, Edith Moor, a Fabian and a Free Thinker, invited Margaret to her Oxfordshire cottage. There, from her and a friend

Mary Hankinson — well known at Fabian summer schools — Margaret heard for the first time of a wickedly subversive young man who was attempting to ruin the Fabian Society by defying the great Sidney and Beatrice Webb, namely G. D. H. Cole.[10]

During the autumn of 1914, Margaret shared rooms in Kensington with a college friend and fellow teacher, a daughter of Elizabeth von Arnim, the author of *Elizabeth and her German Garden*. In view of the prevalent anti-German sentiment, Margaret considered it 'greatly to the credit of St Paul's that they took a German girl onto the staff that September'.[11] At this time, she herself had few friends, save for Phyllis Reid and Stella Bowen, the talented Australian artist, fewer social commitments and 'no understanding' with any young man in the Forces. Margaret had not yet become the extrovert of later years, and, for someone so able, she was curiously lacking in self-confidence and social charm. Partly this was due, she felt in retrospect, to a female-dominated education, and partly to the fact that Phyllis 'of the immense green eyes and massive light brown hair with curly edges' was so full of sex appeal that Margaret got dates mainly only with her rejects!

Stella Bowen, whose portraits in words were as vivid as her portraits in oils, described her first impression of Margaret:

> I thought her the most uncivilised girl I had ever met, as well as the cleverest. She was shy, untidy and wild, with a little square face under an immense mop of dark hair, small shoulders hunched, long arms held in at the elbows and narrow hands with long, gesticulating fingers. A high forehead, a wide humorous mouth and a very short chin. However much she might edge away from strangers and despise the small change of mannerly greetings, no bushel capable of hiding her light has ever been discovered![12]

The First World War

In a curious way Margaret was isolated intellectually from the war until 1916, when her brother Raymond was called up and the direction of her life changed suddenly. She walked into 'a new world of doubters and protesters'.

Ray, a scholar in his first year at Oxford, was a conscientious objector, who defied his order for call-up and thus reduced his father to 'apoplectic fury'. When Ray was charged with 'being a mutinous soldier' Margaret went to Oxford to give him moral support. Professing to be a 'conchie' in the First World War demanded great courage, and as an admitted non-Christian, Internationalist and Socialist, Ray was deemed a traitor who could expect little mercy from authority. In the event, he was committed to prison, fell ill, was released unconditionally, and not called up again for another two years. The whole event, however, had a profound effect upon his politically unsophisticated sister:

> I did not realise until I heard the sentence pronounced and had seen Ray disappear through a kind of pantomime trap-door in the floor, what a large slice of England there was that was either actively opposed to the war, or very doubtful about its conduct; but it is almost literally true that when I walked away from the Oxford court room with Gilbert Murray . . . I walked into a new world, a world of doubters and protesters — and into a new war — this time against the ruling classes and the government which represented them, and *with* the working classes, the Trade Unionists, the Irish rebels of Easter Week, and all those who resisted their governments or other governments which held them down.[13]

Ray's arrest made Margaret into an active socialist. Hitherto her commitment had been intellectual only, and she had not joined the university Fabian Society or any other political body. She did, however, discover at Cambridge that she was both an atheist and a socialist — 'two intellectual faiths from which I have never wavered' — and slipped into both with 'incredible ease'. Not for her the searing self-analysis which so wracked Beatrice Webb in her intellectual search for an ethical creed. When Margaret discovered that it was not imperative to accept certain Christian tenets, and that there were many intelligent people who did not, 'I felt the burden of religion slip from my shoulders exactly as Christian's slipped from his.'

And in much the same way she came to socialism, 'the non-dogmatic idealistic socialism of the early twentieth century'. A profound influence upon Margaret's thinking was J. A. Hobson's *Science of Wealth*, for

> When I read in it the statement, almost casually thrown out, that

a certain number of unemployed without wages, living in the last resort on charity and the Poor Law were a necessary condition of capitalist society, I was outraged.[14]

It was, however, H. G. Wells, with his vision, his optimism and his sympathy with the young, who built constructively upon that anger. Margaret was just one of the many young who

over three generations at least took their hope of the world from that vivid, generous, cantankerous personality . . . accepting again and again . . . his eager conviction that the ideal of socialism, which included world government, the abolition of all authority not based on reason, and of all inequality based on pre-judice or privilege of any kind, of complete freedom of associa-tion, speech and movement and of an immense increase of human welfare and material resources achieved by an all-wise, non-profit-making organisation of economic life, both could and would save humanity within a measurable space of time.[15]

Wells it was, Margaret wrote shortly after his death, who was 'the leaven — the anarchic leaven' who prevented 'our Labour Movement from becoming a soulless organisation'.[16] Others whose writings she absorbed included Norman Angell, author of *The Great Illusion*, Noel Brailsford, C. E. Montague of the *Manchester Guardian*, Lowes Dickinson of Kings, E. M. Forster, whose *Howard's End* was a best seller among undergraduates, and, of course, George Bernard Shaw: but Wells was the seminal influence.

Notes

1. M. I. Cole, *Growing Up into Revolution* (Longmans Green, London, 1949), pp. 34−5.
2. Olive Parsons (née Franklin), interview.
3. Cole, *Growing Up*, pp. 37−8.
4. *Girton Review* (Michaelmas Term, 1912).
5. Ibid. (Lent Term, 1913).
6. Cole, *Growing Up*, pp. 39−40.
7. Ibid., pp. 41−2.
8. This award, instituted by Montague Butler, the Master of Trinity, was a tribute to Agnata, his second wife, who in 1887 was the only student of her year to gain an Upper First in the Classics Tripos, so outstripping all the male undergraduates — an achievement immortalised by a Cartoon in *Punch*. The award operated from 1893 to 1917.

9. Cole, *Growing Up*, p. 43 n. 1.

10. Ibid., p. 57.

11. M. I. Cole to Dr S. F. Kissin, 5 August 1976 (CFP).

12. Stella Bowen, *Drawn from Life* (Collins, London, 1940), pp. 52–3; reprint (Virago, London, 1984).

13. Cole, *Growing Up*, p. 58.

14. Ibid., pp. 41–2.

15. Ibid., p. 42.

16. M. I. Cole, *Makers of the Labour Movement* (Longmans Green, London, 1948), p. 288.

3

'A WORLD OF DOUBTERS AND PROTESTERS'

Socialist Volunteer

If H. G. Wells convinced Margaret intellectually that Socialism
had a human face, it was Ray's sentence that led her directly into
active political work. Determined to uphold their joint socialist
beliefs after the state had taken her brother, she sought out Ray's
Oxford friend, Alan Kaye. He was working in the Fabian Research
Department, which had been founded by Sidney and Beatrice
Webb as an adjunct to the Fabian Society, then committed to
achieving socialism through state collectivism, but staffed almost
entirely by (volunteer) Guild Socialists to whom centralised bureaucracy was anathema.

Alan Kaye, 'the ugliest little man I had ever set eyes on, but kind
and friendly', drew Margaret into FRD activities. So it was one
September evening after school she arrived at a dingy house in
Tothill Street, Westminster, then the Fabian Society office. Tenta-
tively entering the smoke-filled room she found 'several very tall
men and one small man who said in a strong Scottish accent, "Will
ye come in or will ye go out — don't stand there like a Peri at the
gate o' paradise."'[1]

The 'small' man was (Dr) Robin Page Arnot, then paid secretary
of FRD; the others included William Mellor, a future editor of the
Daily Herald, and the extraordinarily handsome honorary secretary, then adviser to the Amalgamated Society of Engineers and a
Fellow of Magdalen College, Oxford, G. D. H. Cole. This was
Margaret's first formal introduction to her future husband and to
The Movement. Previously she had met Douglas briefly with her
brother in the rooms of a friend at St John's, Oxford, before Ray's
call-up. From then on she clearly had an eye on Douglas and
admitted thinking to herself that 'his face and appearance were
exactly what I should most like to look at for the rest of my days'.[2]
Not surprisingly, therefore, as a new recruit, she found the work
enthralling.

She was set to work compiling a trade union *Gazeteer*, which
entailed laboriously copying out innumerable details of trade

unions and branches on to pages geographically arranged.[3] It sounds dull enough, but to Margaret, tired of teaching and still lonely in London, it was different, exciting, purposeful and made her part of a team. She worked long on these complications with other volunteers, and 'was immensely proud when, by discovering that Finsbury Park was not located in Finsbury, I caused the reorganisation of many sheets'.[4]

Sixty years later, Dr Robin Page Arnot recalled Margaret, Stella Bowen and Phyllis Reid

> toiling on the *Gazeteer* in the back room, and Stella asking Dr Jimmy Mallon of the Trade Board Movement [later Warden of Toynbee Hall Settlement] for a Gothic alphabet. Mallon, rapidly frisking his breast pocket in vain, explained that certainly he had had one, 'but must have mislaid it'.[5]

Shrewd Mrs P had already written her daughter asking, 'Who is Cole? I shall early expect to hear of your engagement by the next post if you keep on assuring me that you have no matrimonial projects.'[6] The family therefore were not wholly surprised when told of Margaret's intention to resign from St Paul's at the end of the year and to work for FRD full time. Her mother wrote again:

> You are flighty and the creature of impulse (sad in a fine character); you resent any restraint that is good discipline for you, and you have not the scholar's interest in working at what you don't like . . . but your decision didn't give me very much shock — you had seemed so out of sympathy with the general tone of St Paul's, I didn't see how you could combine outside work with your teaching: and I thought it [the outside work] would inevitably prove more attractive.[7]

When at Christmas Margaret did leave St Paul's, she received a warm note expressing 'regret at your departure' signed by 23 'well wishers' on the staff. One of these, when an octogenarian, wrote to her: 'I realised your devotion and dedication to certain principles, and I can remember your enthusiasm, which I used to watch with awe in the Common Room at St Paul's.'[8]

In January 1917, Miss Postgate, 'a member of the NUT', became a full-time employee of FRD at the princely salary of £2 a week.

The Movement

Even if there were no orchids in Tothill Street, as Stella Bowen wrote, FRD was a turning point in Margaret's life. Working under Robin Page Arnot, a scholar of exacting standards and author of a definitive history of the Mineworkers' Union, she absorbed the basics of research — accuracy and verification of sources. She first met Sidney and Beatrice Webb, and she entered The Movement, 'my second university', to become part of that world of dissenters and protesters in which her husband-to-be was a leading light.

The Movement, Francis Meynell wrote, 'covered a multitude of sincerities'. Its members, a 'Stage Army of the Good', were drawn from progressive bodies ranging from the ILP and the Herald League to the Union of Democratic Control and the Fabian Society. Almost every member at some time or another worked in FRD, was a Guild Socialist and in the National Guilds League.

FRD, which changed its name to the Labour Research Department (LRD) in 1918, embraced personalities of great talent, with many of whom Margaret retained life-long friendships. Apart from paid staff, there were Norman ('Trilby') Ewer, a distinguished journalist, his wife Monica, Maurice Reckitt, Christian theologian and writer of satirical verse whose sister, Eva, an LRD volunteer, founded Collett's bookshop, W. H. Thompson, the redoubtable trade union lawyer, pacifist Clifford Allen (Lord Allen of Hurtwood), founder of the No Conscription League, Ivor Brown of the *Observer*, littérateur and distinguished dramatic critic, Australian Will Dyson, the unique and searing political cartoonist, and George Lansbury, the life-long pacifist. Others included the poet Francis Meynell, founder of the Nonesuch Press, Mostyn Lloyd of the *New Statesman*, trade unionists Harold Clay, Mary MacArthur and Ellen Wilkinson, and, more peripherally, Clement Attlee, Arthur Greenwood and Jimmy Mallon, who comforted Margaret 'inexpressibly when I was taken with panic the night before I married'.[9]

Until after the war, Guild Socialism was very much the political gospel of these young enthusiasts. Originating from A. R. Orage, the brilliant journalist, and S. G. Hobson in the *New Age*, it was remoulded and expounded by William Mellor and G. D. H. Cole, notably in Cole's books *The World of Labour* and *Guild Socialism Re-Stated*. It sought to reorganise British economic life on 'functionalist' lines, establishing in each industry self-governing guilds based upon trade unions, and working on capital provided by a socialist state: great emphasis was placed on workers' consultation and participation. These ideals flourished during the First World War, which also saw the emergence of the Shop Stewards' movement, for the extensive growth of war industries had combined with the vast manpower losses to give workers a hitherto unknown importance in the country's economy: their leaders were actually *consulted* by government. When, however, the post-war boom collapsed, leaving over two million unemployed in its wake, Guild Socialism withered away and The Movement was torn asunder by political and tactical disagreement. Nevertheless, throughout his life, Douglas Cole retained a fierce faith in workers' control and participation. As his friend Maurice Reckitt wrote, 'It was Cole who to a pre-eminent degree made Guild Socialism, though to him the Socialism mattered more than the Guild.'[10]

The Fabian Society to which most Guild Socialists belonged was regarded in 1912 as very progressive and one of the devils likely to upset civilisation. During the war it, too, was rent by internal dissension, but firmly withstood disintegration. The Society, founded in 1884 as an educational and propaganda body, was composed mostly of middle-class intellectuals. It was committed to working for a just society and elimination of poverty, which were to be achieved by the gradual establishment of socialism through constitutional means. This, before and during the First World War, Beatrice and Sidney Webb (who with Bernard Shaw were then leading lights of the Fabian Society) believed could and should be effected through state collectivism — a policy vehemently opposed by the Guild Socialists. For whereas the Webbs firmly considered that workers' control was 'pernicious nonsense' and said so, the Guild Socialists thought the Webbs 'wicked old bureaucrats' and 'staged magnificent ideological battles'.[11]

LRD attracted the more vigorous of the younger Fabians, all of whom eagerly emulated the Webbs' example of hard work and the steady collection of facts. During the war, hostility to the Webbs and political disagreements were rife, yet although both parties worked under the same roof the feud remained gentlemanly. 'We abused but we did not hate,' Margaret recalled, and in March 1918 Beatrice referred gently to 'the circle of rebellious spirits and idealist intellectuals who have gathered round G. D. H. Cole and ourselves'. The angry feelings of earlier years did not long persist.[12]

The Movement was neither a party nor a definite organisation but a 'strange and live thing', Margaret wrote, 'not merely socialist but Guild Socialist'. It was spilling over with eager young people, most of whom had worked in FRD, possessed the minimum of worldly experience but had the maximum of idealism. Inside and outside Tothill Street they comprised an enthusiastic, high spirited band of the rebellious but extremely happy young. As a new, lowly employee of LRD, Margaret recalled chairman Beatrice Webb unexpectedly entering the office when she and another worker were playing tennis with two fly whisks and a biscuit! 'Nothing was said, but the atmospheric tension made it quite clear that this was not the sort of behaviour which the eminent lady expected from those privileged to work for the Socialist Cause.'[13]

At weekends, friends in The Movement enjoyed long country rambles reciting poetry and singing G. K. Chesterton's songs from *The Flying Inn* or ribald satires written by Cole and Reckitt. As Margaret wrote:

> We were very young, and we were as arrogant as we were young, and contemptuous of anyone with whom we disagreed . . . but we were arrogant because we were public spirited, deeply convinced that we were right, upholding a righteous cause against embattled might . . . and being so dedicated we were extraordinarily happy.[14]

Exuberant and self-willed, Miss Postgate was both defiant and different. Rowland Kenney (brother of suffragette Annie Kenney), a journalist, ex-navvy and 'the only genuine working class man to get into the Foreign Office', remembered Margaret at a meeting of the National Guilds League, probably around 1917:

> sitting on the floor . . . a slightly built girl who made an arresting picture. She was wearing a rough felt hat, from under which fell black locks, surrounding a vital, vivid face, out of which stabbed a pair of blazing eyes. Everything about her was intensely, exceedingly alive, ready for anything, particularly for a fight to the finish on any point about which her opinion differed from that of anyone else in the room. You felt she had no use for the velvet glove. And she looked like a provocative elfin-tigress . . . there seemed nothing incongruous in the fact that she was smoking a big cigar.[15]

In a photograph taken after her marriage, Margaret looked even more engaging. The dark, turbulent hair still justified her nickname, Mop, but it was cut short in a fringe, below which those brilliantly defiant eyes dominated the heart-shaped face with its sensitive nose and broad, mobile mouth. Happiness had made her blossom.

Stella Bowen, remembering the comrades of The Movement as 'a very good lot, cheerful, selfless and serious-minded', made a further point: 'Bound by a common faith they could relax easily into a happy intimacy which contained spontaneous, warm gaiety . . . their dedication to a cause seemed to make personal relationships unimportant.'[16]

G. D. H. Cole, 'Primus inter Pares'

Yet to Margaret, personal relationships were never, ever unimportant. She was a sensitive and passionate young woman, as her published and unpublished prose and poems testify, and even if 'preoccupation with our kind of politics' did seem to preserve most of The Movement from sex entanglements, for her an emotional entanglement certainly came to pass, and this in spite of Beatrice Webb's warning the male staff of LRD against any 'ensnarements'.

Since their first encounter at Oxford, Douglas had bewitched Margaret. 'I had been physically attracted to him from almost the first time I met him,' she confessed,[17] and admitted to 'writing Mrs G. D. H. Cole on a piece of paper in the St Paul's staff room and hastily crumpling it up!'[18] Douglas, as photographs prove, was arrestingly handsome, and in Beatrice Webb's view 'from the intricate convolutions of his subtle brain to the tips of his long fingers . . . an intellectual and an aristocrat'.[19] He was also immensely kind, wholly charming, yet could be explosively rude which in no way diminished his appeal to his future wife. More important, however, were his commitment to socialism and his powerful mind. Both he and Margaret shared a love for literature and the classics and if Margaret did not possess Douglas' encyclopaedic knowledge of history she was an intellectual touchstone: the only person who could equal his skill in capping quotations and in identifying recondite allusions.[20]

Until his engagement, Douglas, ascetic and undersexed — in Margaret's words 'low-powered'[21] — had been only mildly interested in women. He had a quality of sexlessness, and to dub someone a 'womaniser' was his ultimate epithet of disparagement.[22] Douglas, moreover, was no feminist. He tended to regard women as 'not good socialist material' and only grudgingly supported their enfranchisement because he considered that 'the immediate result would be disastrous for all good left-wing causes'.[23] Unlike Margaret, Douglas was cold rather than passionate. One old friend remarked that he should have been an archbishop![24] Even so, his charm captivated both friends and colleagues.

The Postgate-Cole engagement was plighted in Hampden Woods, Buckinghamshire, in May 1918. Margaret recorded the event — during which an 'indignant pigeon flew out from the log on which we were sitting'[25] — in a joyous poem, 'Beechwoods'. Her delight, however, must have been somewhat deflated by Douglas' falling soundly asleep on their homeward train journey. Touchingly, he did not forget their precious patch, for years afterwards 'when we were walking in the same woods I asked him why he was questing about instead of sitting down, "I'm trying to find our log," he said.'[26]

Ray, back at Oxford, when he heard the news was 'amazingly delighted', and wrote to Margaret that 'G. D. H. . . . was just idiotically happy . . . if you are anything like as happy as he is, or as much in love, you will burst between you'.[27]

Her parents were less responsive. Mrs P, trusting her daughter's judgement, was 'very much pleased. I can be nothing but glad at what you tell me,' she wrote:

> You have been bachelor long enough to know what company you do like . . . You know each other in your workday clothes and it isn't the charm of summer surroundings. A puss of strong affections like you, and with your vigour, ought to have someone to look after and care for.[28]

Predictably, Professor Postgate was less encouraging. He quizzed Douglas first by letter — to which Margaret's frivolous intervention elicited her father's solemn rebuke, 'Your answers are adequately explicit though the sense of the sentence "neither is he an hereditary drunkard nor a criminal" might have been less crudely expressed'[29] — and then by personal encounter. Having probed further into Douglas' beliefs on class war and the confiscation of capital, the Professor wrote:

> although the profound differences between us . . . do not at
> present make acquaintance of a friendly character impossible,
> they are nevertheless a bar to our close intimacy, which in dif-
> ferent circumstances I should have gladly welcomed, as from
> what I have both heard and seen I have conceived for you per-
> sonally both respect and esteem.[30]

Severely Victorian her father might be, but in a letter to Margaret
he announced a generous wedding gift and displayed unexpected
sensitivity: 'You are no doubt living days of exhilaration in aery
and faery heights above the perpetual snowline. Make the most of
them. They come but once in a lifetime.'[31]

In spite of his seeming amiability Professor Postgate made relationships with the young couple difficult and refused to let Mrs P
stay with them. He turned Ray out from home for his political
beliefs and later disinherited both him and Margaret. Thus, until
after her father's death, Margaret saw little of the family except
Ray, in marked contrast to Douglas' parents, from whom 'I never
received anything but great kindness'.

Friends everywhere agreed with Ray that the engagement 'was
very right altogether'. Good wishes from The Movement were
inscribed in an illuminated triptych devised by Alan Kaye and
Francis Meynell, which accompanied their present of William
Morris tapestry and cretonnes for the Coles' living room. 'It was a
nice warm feeling to come home and find visual evidence that 93
people wished you well,' Margaret wrote appreciatively.[32] That
triptych, which she cherished, still exists, a glowing reminder of
friendships past.

Margaret, a sentimental squirrel if ever there was one, preserved
not only the invitation to their engagement party (painted in the
form of a Call-up notice) but also congratulatory letters: 'I rejoice
in Cole's happiness,' wrote J. L. (Lawrence) Hammond, the social
historian, 'and also in the consternation of capitalists, militants
and bureaucrats, who will remind themselves of the saying of the
Greek poet about two being better — or worse — than one.'[33]

Beatrice Webb, with typical generosity (the Coles' curt, critical
antipathy was still evident), sent a cheque. 'I admire the Cole-
Postgate marriage,' she wrote: 'It has the characteristics that I
value highly — adventure, disinterestedness and intellect. There is

rough water ahead of the Rebels, but you have our best wishes.'[34]

George Lansbury, whose daughter Daisy later became Ray's wife, was affectionately paternal:

> You are both clever, uncommon people . . . But never forget that keeping a home and tending children is good, honourable work . . . Just as highly to be prized as hunting statistics and keeping us all straight on figures . . . You both have great gifts and if you use them wisely will help to make a great movement. But don't let anything spoil your own home life.[35]

Maurice Reckitt, Douglas' perceptive Oxford friend, offered Margaret sound advice:

> Cole has always seemed to me a very lonely person . . . and is so much more in need of being 'satisfactorily completed' than you are. Don't applaud him too often; don't let him sulk when his intellectual inferiors (we're most of us that!) prevent his getting his own way; don't let him get too Fabian in tactics or too 'reconstructed' in his policy. He'll always be a *'primus inter pares'* so long as he keeps the *'Pares'* with him, but that requires more doing than his impatient spirit always remembers.[36]

Margaret and Douglas were married on 14 August 1918, in a dingy St Pancras Registry Office, where 26 years earlier Beatrice and Sidney Webb had preceded them. To Margaret's intense amusement, the walls were plastered with notices saying 'No Confetti: Defence of the Realm Act'.

Notes

1. M. I. Cole, *Growing Up into Revolution* (Longmans Green, London, 1949), p. 60.
2. Ibid., p. 75.
3. The *Gazeteer* served a significant purpose, as for example when Beatrice Webb was urging the appointment of workers' representatives on to the local committees administering the Pensions for the Disabled Act. In 1916 this was a revolutionary suggestion, and hotly resisted by the Establishment. Its implementation depended upon the availability of appropriate details about trade unions, and these were exactly what LRD was able eventually to provide (M. I. Cole, *The Story of Fabian Socialism* (Heinemann, London, 1961), p. 178 n. 3.
4. Cole, *Growing Up*, p. 61.

5. Robin Page Arnot to M. I. Cole, 18 May 1978 (CFP).
6. Mrs Postgate to M. I. Cole, 13 November 1916 (CFP).
7. Mrs Postgate to M. I. Cole, 14 November 1916 (CFP).
8. Marcelle Carver to M. I. Cole 8 October 1976 (CFP).
9. Cole, *Growing Up*, pp. 68–70.
10. Maurice Reckitt, *As It Happened* (Dent, London, 1940), p. 124.
11. Cole, *Growing Up*, p. 64.
12. M. I. Cole, *Life of G. D. H. Cole* (Macmillan, London, 1971), p. 88.
13. M. I. Cole, *Beatrice Webb* (Longmans Green, London, 1945), p. 122, n. 1.
14. Cole, *Growing Up*, pp. 72–3.
15. Rowland Kenney, *Westering* (Dent, London, 1939), pp. 204–5.
16. Stella Bowen, *Drawn from Life* (Collins, London, 1940; reprint, Virago, London, 1984), pp. 52–4.
17. Cole, *Life*, p. 90.
18. Cole, *Growing Up*, p. 75.
19. *Beatrice Webb's Diaries (1912–24)*, vol. 1, ed. M. I. Cole (Longmans Green, London, 1952), p. 135.
20. Jane Abraham, letter to author.
21. Cole, *Life*, p. 91.
22. Rosamund Broadley, Sylvia Mulvey, interviews.
23. Cole, *Life*, pp. 92–3.
24. Molly Bolton, interview.
25. Cole, *Growing Up*, pp. 75–6.
26. Cole, *Life*, p. 92 no. 1.
27. Raymond Postgate to M. I. Postgate, 25 May 1918 (CFP).
28. Mrs Postgate to M. I. Postgate, 24 May 1918 (CFP).
29. Professor Postgate to M. I. Postgate, 30 June 1918 (CFP).
30. Professor Postgate to G. D. H. Cole, 19 July 1918 (CFP).
31. Professor Postgate to M. I. Postgate, 30 July 1918 (CFP).
32. Cole, *Growing Up*, p. 80.
33. J. L. and B. Hammond, 23 May 1918 (CFP).
34. Beatrice Webb, 9 June 1918 (CFP).
35. George Lansbury, 25 May 1918 (CFP).
36. Maurice Reckitt, 24 May 1918 (CFP).

4

POETRY, PROSE AND PEOPLE

Poems by Margaret Postgate

Long before her marriage, poetry for Margaret had become and remained an abiding joy. It was a medium for self-expression, a common thread in friendships, and between her and Douglas a close bond. He wrote sheafs of poems: his first volume, *New Beginnings*, appeared in 1914, his second, *The Crooked Billet*, in 1933, but many more remained in manuscript. Together they savoured traditional and modern poetry, and wrote satiric political verse which delighted The Movement. Of her own work Margaret confessed, 'I like what poetry I have written, but others, save a few friends, do not. Naomi Mitchison, who should know, once explained to me why it wasn't poetry at all. So I suppose it isn't.'[1] Some, however, may think otherwise.

Margaret's earliest traceable poetry appeared in *Bits and Things*, a symposium she edited at Girton, and in the *Saturday Westminster Gazette*. In the latter she won outright a prize for parodying A. E. Housman's *The Shropshire Lad*. Certain lines, including

> They'll crush the purple loosestrife
> The happy lads at play
> And trample down the brook lime
> Whose flowers are summer day

prompted the adjudicator to enquire whether the Professor might not actually think they were his own![2]

A selection of her verse appeared in *Margaret Postgate's Poems*. This elegant little book, her first ever, contains personal poetry both tough and charming, some of which as C. H. Rolph commented, 'is pure Herrick'. It was published for the *Herald* by Francis Meynell, who was 'much taken by her work . . . Margaret introduced me to the modern poets', he wrote. 'And I enveloped her with my favourites, the seventeenth century metaphysical poets.'

When they first met Margaret was

37

heart and head in The Movement . . . her looks were handsome, even intriguing, and next to politics her passion like mine was poetry . . . We went for country walks together, a political pamphlet in one pocket, a book of poems in the other . . . sometimes the two of us, more often in company. Margaret and I never went so far as to have an affair, though *affairés* we were indeed in our kisses and our contemplation. (Make what you like to that, Mrs. Grundy.)[3]

Francis, Margaret recalled, was 'my first love (not lover) before ever I had met Douglas in the flesh', and in her autobiography she gratefully acknowledged the socialist-pacifist hunger striker who later founded the beautiful Nonesuch Press as 'the first man who ever seemed attracted to me for myself alone'.[4]

When convalescing from severe pneumonia in Portofino years later, Margaret half apologetically sent Francis a long evocative poem, 'Lorelei', which cast back to their happy early days together. 'I can't', she wrote, 'tear the thing up or bury it — having once written it — it really seems to belong to you.'

Night has fallen on Rackham Hill, black and slow-moving,
Fallen even across the white thin road that scales it . . .
Come down into the valley, darling, darling,
The pool is dark with sunset, and your father
Will be asking what you did with that girl you brought from
    nowhere . . .
. . . Oh, dearest, gentlest, loveliest of lovers,
Is it hard, ungrateful so to write you verses?
. . . But how can one write till the spell be broken,
How make bare clumsy lines for you to read them?
They would not sound like Marvell or like Herbert,
They would not be fine art, or quaint, or special,
Or nice to put inside a Nonesuch cover . . .
. . .
You are not a Lorelei: you are not heartless.
You have a heart, a heart romantic, silly,
A heart that wants to do the childish things,
The gallant things, the things in story books —
To climb the Jungfrau at dawn, to bring the water
To the pent city, to believe in something
Besides fine printing — to die on a barricade somewhere.

Oh, Francis, Francis.
You do not break hearts, do you? You only put them
Feeling a little dusty, a little tarnished —
With cool, firm fingers, back on the shelf they came from.[5]

Within this long poem Margaret, musing upon a carefree happy
social life of parties and punting, of cricket matches and dancing,
had written

. . . add a party . . . a dawn on election night;
And to dance (or stand) on the roof by the cross of St Anne's
Where the sound floats up on velvet — or restaurants,
Fourteen *horse-dovers* served upon one plate only . . .

Years later she wrote Robin Page Arnot how she and Francis 'were
nearly turned out of a Soho restaurant for eating up all the hors
d'oeuvres . . . This was when you bought meals on a ration card!'[6]

Clearly Margaret had been more in love with Francis than he
with her. Yet on her engagement he wrote:

Make Douglas like me; and if ever you want me, use me as a
'stop gap' — remember . . . God love you both, as Ben Tillett
says . . . I wrote a slobbery letter to Phyllis [Reid] about you this
morning. I hope she won't mind being used as a kind of corkline
ooze mat.[7]

Their friendship spanned six decades, and Margaret used to visit
Sir Francis and his delightful third wife, Dame Alix (Bay) Meynell,
at their elegant eighteenth-century home in Suffolk. Bay remembers
how 'Margaret bridled delightfully, even though in her eighties and
then far from beautiful, when Francis praised her "pretty ankles",'
as indeed they were. After his death, Bay wrote her:

radical humanist, I so much like your words . . . I know how fond
he was of you, both in those early days long before I met him, and
later . . . I know you are right in thinking that he liked remembering past times and swapping poems with you.[8]

Margaret's poetry[9] was more than sentimental nostalgia: it also
illuminated her bitterness over the war. In, for example, 'The
Veteran':

We came upon him sitting in the sun
Blinded by war, and left. And past the fence
There came young soldiers from the *Hand and Flower*,
Asking advice of his experience . . .

And he said this, and that, and told them tales,
And all the nightmares of each empty head
Blew into air; then, hearing us beside,
'Poor chaps, how'd they know what it's like?' he said.

And we stood there, and watched him as he sat,
Turning his sockets where they went away,
Until it came to one of us to ask
'And you're — how old?'
'Nineteen, the third of May'.

Her anxiety over Ray's imprisonment for his pacifism was
expressed in 'Desmotes':

They have taken you into a timeless place . . .

But the incredible blossom will fall, and the woods darken,
And you won't know — how should you?
Stone walls don't generally burst into flower,
And hang themselves with trails of blackberries.
Nor do paved yards gape open with heather splitting the flags,
And turn to sudden purple and gold,
As though a drunken painter spilt his pots — or do they?
There are stranger things have happened.
How much, do you think, could one conjecture,
From a square blot of changing sky?
Well, I shall not know, nor will you.

All I can do
With eyes and mouth and brain choked full of the spring,
Is daily to send my brimming spirit southwards there,
    believing
My most uncensored thoughts will find you there.

Finally, her attitudes to Douglas, expressing — in 'The Stranger'
— uncertainty:

O why were you born of English speech,
Stranger, stranger I love?
I would in a tongue of the furthest folk
You made your wise lips move.
. . .
O would that you lived beyond man's ken
In a distant desolate place
— While each day and leagues away
I meet you face to face —

At least I would crush the mountains low,
And harrow the sea's grey field,
But here behind your open eyes
Lies fast your spirit sealed.

O dear dark-eyed! The door is wide,
But faster than hill or sea
Are planted the silent boundaries
That guard your soul from me

— reality, in an unpublished fragment:

The red sun laid long fingers on your face,
The evening crept about you, blue and sweet;
You shuffled leaflets in your bag and said,
My god, Kaye, hurry up, it starts at eight!

and yearning, in 'Wishing':

I wish I could stop remembering your face.
I wish you had a face that nobody could remember.
. . .
I wish you wouldn't say such unexpected things,
    and never know you've said them.
. . .
I wish you wouldn't go on holidays with deadly people,
    and be quite idiotically happy there.
I wish you'd always be alone.
I wish — Damn! I suppose I wish you loved me.

Finally there was happiness and triumph, in 'Beechwoods' (May 1918):

What would a gentleman do who kissed a girl in a
    beechwood?
O young beechwood, O green May beechwood.
Who kissed her quick and suddenly, so that a pigeon
Flew out from under a log, all shocked and fluffy?

Darling, O darling, underneath the beechtree,
Darling whose arms I loved, but never hoped for,
Keep close, keep holding; never mind the pigeon,
O dearest in all the world, your eyes, your lips, your kisses,
But what will a Socialist do who kisses a girl in a beechwood?
O green beechwood, O young May beechwood.
He may think all sorts of things; he mayn't hold with
    marriage;
He may be afraid — he knows he's always saying
That a stake in the country — that means a wife and
    children —
Is only a stick-in-the-mud. O God, suppose he means it.

Darling, O darling, kiss away the shadow,
Hold your eyes closed, forget the past and future,
Forget the thousand things that need reforming;
We'll talk about them in the train — hold closer,
O dearest in all the world, your eyes, your lips, your kisses!

It is arguable whether 'Beechwoods', 'this modern verse', is good
poetry. Indeed, Margaret much later sent revised, amplified
versions to both Francis Meynell and Maurice Reckitt: but the
joyful immediacy of the original did convey the elation she felt on
her engagement. As Maurice Reckitt observed, years later, 'she
stood at the heart of her theme'.[10]

Her happiness was finally transmuted into 'Envoy', perhaps the
best poem in her book:

Because I am happy,
You will get no set songs out of me.
When I was sad and lost,
Then desolation and shame held fast my tongue,
And I was silent before the eyes of men.
And all my heart I wrote upon scraps of paper
In brooded lines and sore poetic phrases.

But now
No one looks in my face but sees my gladness,
And no one hears me speak but knows it all.
I have proclaimed it in the streets
In the commonest of words;
I have made it plain in every movement,
And even in my silence there is something of a song.
What place is there then for music? what for rhymes?
All that I do is my song to you, my darling.

After this she 'sung but few set songs'; and all on serious themes. 'Gas' encapsulated sadness — 'One can't tell a ghost one is sorry' — at the joint suicide of colleagues Alan Kaye and Sadie Kaiser. There is strong evidence from the poem that Kaye, an intellectual and an idealist, was shattered by 'the fallibility of man':

There are other things than girls that break men's hearts;
Dear, gentle heart, boy's heart — I can't believe it . . .
There is faith and love and hope and trust in man,
There is fellowship and the excellent love of comrades.
And if that breaks, if those one trusted fail one,
Why not the gas pipe?

Margaret asked, in May 1919.

Later she wrote: 'Kaye's death, because he was literally too good for this (political) world, was the first great personal sorrow of my life.'[11]

Beatrice Webb showed less sensitivity. She described Kaye, whom she had long known, as 'an odd little mortal . . . wandering disconsolately between revolutionary opinions and Roman Catholic rites' and

who suffered imprisonment for distributing pamphlets to soldiers . . . He recently left the Department and the National Guilds League because the Coles and their followers had renounced immediate revolution . . . It is said that he came to the Research Department adoring Cole and left it loathing him. Whether Cole's marriage to the daring Margaret Postgate had anything to do with it, I know not,

she gossiped in her diary.[12] It is understandable why in her maturity Margaret sometimes considered Beatrice's judgement suspect!

Margaret wrote her last traceable poems, 'Epilogue' and 'Geometrician's Apology', while recovering from pneumonia in the thirties. The former concerned her relationship with Douglas, and the latter with their friend Dick Mitchison. These, together with the revised 'Lorelei', she explained to Francis Meynell, 'related to the different kinds of love which can co-exist, as I think the batch of poems proves'.[13] After that, poetically speaking, there was silence.

During the twenties the Coles directed their extensive knowledge of literature into pleasurably productive channels, and searching through the forests of English poetry together, they edited a series of 16 small anthologies, *The Ormond Poets* (1927–8) published by Noel Douglas. Other versifying ventures were in political parodies, for which Douglas especially had an inexhaustible facility. Such was his aptitude, Margaret wrote, that 'set him down anywhere and he immediately started to write; it was as though a plug had been pulled out'.[14] Verses, comic and satiric, often with content and lines suggested by Margaret, streamed from his pen; most are now dated, but in their day they were highly pertinent:

> There was a poor worker and what do you think?
> He claimed that the state owed him victuals and drink;
> And when work was scarce and no victuals about,
> He thought that the state would not let him peg out.
> The cause of his death, you will quite understand,
> The thing that he lacked was Effective Demand.

The best verses were gathered into the *Bolo Book*, which also included 'The Homeland of Mystery', edited jointly by the Coles, and Douglas' famous skit, the 'Striker Stricken', about the General Strike. These, all written to be sung to popular tunes, particularly those of Gilbert and Sullivan, have delighted generations of socialists. Margaret, too, kept their memory geeen. For even in her eighties, she would break out unpredictably into singing tunelessly but with nostalic panache these parodies written in the hopeful happy years of earlier socialism.

Literary Friends and Opinions

Not all Margaret's friends were humane politicals. Indeed before

her marriage, at Phyllis' and Stella's parties she met literary and
artistic luminaries, including G. B. Stern the novelist, Wyndham
Lewis the artist, and poets W. B. Yeats, T. S. Eliot and Ezra
Pound, among many. Ezra, who according to Stella had a face 'like
the ace of spades with a tuft on his chin and emitted hooting noises
that represented laughter', made overtures to Margaret which she
wittily, but positively, rebuffed.[15] He had been something of a 'boy
friend', Margaret told C. H. Rolph,

and when he wanted to go further than I did he called me a
Roman Matron and I asked him whether he meant Cornelia the
mother of the Gracchi, or Catullus' Clodia . . . but that was long
ago when Ezra was young and fun to be with. Since then acolytes
have made him a God of poetry, which emphatically he was
not.[16]

Through Stella, Margaret also came to know and admire Ford
Madox Ford. According to Naomi Mitchison, he based a major
character in his trilogy about the Great War, *Parades' End* (published 1924–6), upon Margaret in Valentine Wallop, 'a pug nosed
girl and a hot pacifist who hated any man's death'; and this internal
evidence substantiates. For the head of the school where Valentine
taught recalled

sitting at the feet of your father, a great teacher . . . we used to
hear how he spoke Latin with you and your brother . . . Miss
Hall says you are the most remarkable Latinist ever . . . 'It's not
true' Valentine said, 'I can't think in Latin. You cannot be a real
Latinist unless you do that. He did, of course.'[17]

Always a fair but generous critic of her friends' writing,
Margaret wrote exultantly to Stella, after Ford's death, about his
March of Literature, which she had

sat up for two nights galloping through . . . I don't agree with it
all — but I have not for years read anything that so really
breathed the spirit of literature . . . I do not think that Ford
could have closed his career better . . . I wish I could write and
tell him so; only a poet can really write about literature. PS. I'm
not drunk. I don't often write like this: it was a book I could
hardly put down. Tell Julie her father was a great writer who

cared for other writers.[18]

Margaret's taste generally in poetry was catholic. Tennyson she
loved because he was 'so mellifluous and easy to get by heart';
Swinburne whose *Songs before Sunrise* 'I discovered at just the
right moment' and Kipling for 'his rhythmic robustness and ability
to tell a good story'.[19] Douglas was shocked by Margaret's inability
to love William Morris' verses, which she regarded as 'definitely
second-rate', but they shared a deep admiration for Walt
Whitman, whom Margaret thought 'more than a democrat; he was
a philosopher, an optimist and a lover of life'. To her Whitman was
'a true poet, possibly the greatest America has produced'.[20]

For J. C. (Jack) Squire, sometime Literary Editor of the *New
Statesman*, she retained a 'specially soft spot'. A good poet in his
own right, he printed, at the end of the First World War 'a couple
of good things by me, and asked for more . . . but Douglas . . .
who had quarrelled with the *Nation*, sent a rejected article to the
New Statesman, which grabbed him. So', Margaret wrote regretfully, 'I lost my glimmer of a job . . . but shall always remember
Squire's encouragement to a great unknown.'[21]

Masefield's writing, too, she greatly enjoyed, especially *The
Midnight Folk*, which she considered 'the best modern children's
book I know',[22] remembering him from Oxford as being 'very kind
and not a bit superior'.

Although loyal to the old, Margaret was also observant about the
new and commented to Gilbert Murray that 'Day Lewis has it in
him to be good . . . the poems are forcible stuff and unexpectedly
hopeful in tone . . . but why do all young poets or young preachers
assume that either everything is sordid or nothing is?'[23] During the
war she sent her friend Bernice Hamilton a stanza from a poem in
French by Robert Desmos, who had died in a transit camp at
Teresin. 'I've never heard of him, but the lines seem to me
moving.'[24]

Of course Margaret had reservations: 'I do wish modern verses
had lines, rhythm and rhyme that one could remember,' she told
Robin Page Arnot, for she always delighted to quote. 'Concrete
poetry is beyond me — like modern music with great holes, or some
Hepworth sculpture — it makes me agonise.'[25]

Nevertheless, as with friends, so with poetry and prose. Affection forged was for ever. When during the mid-fifties Margaret was
in hospital, the book she took with her was Gibbon's *The Decline*

and Fall. Classical history, like the classics, remained a life-long love.

Notes

1. M. I. Cole, *Growing Up into Revolution* (Longmans Green, London, 1949), p. 47 n. 2.
2. *Saturday Westminster Gazette*, 23 May 1914.
3. Francis Meynell, *My Lives* (Bodley Head, London, 1971), pp. 132–4.
4. Cole, *Growing Up*, p. 68. Letters to Robin Page Arnot, 15 July 1975, and to C. H. Rolph, 2 November 1976 (CFP).
5. Parts of these stanza were abridged and so quoted in *My Lives* by Francis Meynell (with Margaret's permission), pp. 132–4. See also her letter to Francis Meynell, 31 March 1931, and further letter undated from Portofino. Meynell Papers, Cambridge University Library, Box XVIII.
6. M. I. Cole to Robin Page Arnot, July 1975 (CFP).
7. Francis Meynell to M. I. Cole, undated (CFP).
8. Dame Alix Meynell to M. I. Cole, 18 August 1975 (CFP).
9. All poems quoted are either from *Margaret Postgate's Poems* (Printed for the *Herald*, London, 1918) or unpublished poems among the Cole Family Papers.
10. Maurice Reckitt to M. I. Cole, 23 November 1960 (CFP).
11. Cole, *Growing Up*, p. 71.
12. Diaries of Beatrice Webb, 3 June 1919, British Library, vol. 35, fos. 3699–701.
13. M. I. Cole to Francis Meynell, undated (probably March 1931), Meynell Papers, Box XVIII.
14. M. I. Cole, *Life of G. D. H. Cole* (Macmillan, London, 1971), p. 31.
15. Stella Bowen, *Drawn from Life* (Collins, London, 1940), pp. 49–52; (reprint Virago, London, 1984).
16. M. I. Cole to C. H. Rolph, 11 November 1976 (CFP).
17. Ford Madox Ford, *Parades' End* (Bodley Head, London, 1963), vol. 4, p. 297.
18. M. I. Cole to Stella Bowen (probably March 1940), Cornell University Papers.
19. M. I. Cole to Robin Page Arnot, April 1975 (CFP).
20. *Books and Bookmen* (September 1976).
21. M. I. Cole to Robin Page Arnot, 31 October 1974 (CFP).
22. *The Author* (Spring 1979) and letter to C. H. Rolph, 23 April 1979 (CFP).
23. M. I. Cole to Gilbert Murray, 6 May 1933, Gilbert Murray Papers, Bodleian Library, Box 64 (19/21).
24. M. I. Cole to Bernice Hamilton (in possession of Dr Bernice Hamilton), and Bernice Hamilton, interview.
25. M. I. Cole, letter to Robin Page Arnot, 26 July 1968 (CFP).

PART TWO:
MRS G. D. H. COLE

5 SOCIALISTS IN HARNESS

Marriage

In marrying GDH, Margaret achieved what friends considered 'a terrific catch'[1] and Beatrice Webb applauded as 'a promising union of two devoted fellow workers'. There were difficulties and disagreements of course, inevitable between two such positive personalities, but 'neither of us could have possibly married anyone else', Margaret wrote thirty years later.[2] Happiness dissipated her shyness, and self-confidence began to bloom, albeit with an abrasive streak.

Visiting the Coles at 12 Bramerton Street, Chelsea, the first abode of their married life, Beatrice recalled how Margaret had

> formerly shocked us old folk with her daringly unconventional ways and rebellious attitude . . . She kept what hours she chose, smoked the most masculine pipe . . . but though her manners have been disorderly, her ways have been straight; she has wit and reasoning power of an unusual quality, and is fundamentally sweet tempered and kind . . . courtship and marriage have increased her womanliness and self restraint. She and Cole seem perfect intellectual companions. On both sides the marriage is an unworldly one . . . These two are now friendly with us, convinced that however we may differ from their vision of the future we mean to help, not to hinder, their career in the Labour Movement[3]

— a more sober assessment than that of Kingsley Martin, who when he first met the Coles together some years later, remembered them as 'a gay and pugnacious young couple'.

There is an amusing account by Margaret of a further visit from Mr and Mrs Sidney Webb

> bearing a codfish of moderate size. Mrs Webb explained that when invited to the houses of some of her more aristocratic friends they were expected to bring a salmon with them. Salmon however were nowadays costly, 'but I *have* brought you a fish'.[4]

Living in a whole house of her own was a new experience for

Margaret, accustomed to lodgings or a room in Mecklenburgh Square, Bloomsbury. Douglas, well off and 'born a burying beetle', was an accumulator of furniture, glass and books, which all demanded space, in contrast to his wife who could have 'existed in a suitcase' providing it too contained books. Years later Margaret wrote that accommodating Douglas' possessions had so dictated their decisions over a home that only when widowed had she really been able to choose freely.[5]

Nevertheless, 'the little house in a bye street off Chelsea, the interior of choice spirits, comfortable even luxurious in lounges, restful in colouring, full of outsize furniture — solid and old — with a plentitude of books', as Beatrice saw it,[6] pleased Margaret. She loved especially the Morris furnishings, their wedding present from friends in The Movement. Her delight in this belied the somewhat waspish comment of Hugh Dalton who, after visiting Chelsea, noted 'his [Cole's] wife I did not much like . . . a fine lot of black hair . . . poses for a William Morris type . . . the pair of them a little difficult!'[7]

Life was made easy for the Coles by dependable staff, who usually became personal friends. Partly this was due to Douglas' 'remarkable gift for getting himself adored' by nearly all who ever worked for him and partly to Margaret's own good judgement of people. It certainly enabled both to pursue, together and independently, their various activities; for Douglas, whose Fellowship at Magdalen ended in 1918, this was to be expected: for Margaret, a married woman, it was, in those days, unusual.

The Coles remained loyal to Guild Socialism, and continued editing *The Guildsman* together until its demise in 1923. They were also continuously involved with LRD. Its chairman Bernard Shaw wrote, when Douglas was vice chairman, that after seven years' growth LRD had taken 'its permanent form as a vital organisation of the Labour Movement and as a recognised department, closely linked with the Labour Party, trade unions and the Co-operative Movement'.[8]

Margaret worked with the LRD long after her marriage. Appointed acting secretary when Robin Page Arnot went to prison for his anti-war convictions, she held the post until his reinstatement, and then became correspondence secretary. In addition to extensive research, her outstanding contribution was editing for eight years the *Monthly Bulletin*. This, embracing Labour events and the movement of prices, wages and profits, was produced against a background of what Margaret called 'a growling class war'. From the first, as editor, probably assisted by Douglas, she had welcomed criticisms and suggestions about the *Bulletin*, which was typical of the Coles' approach, for 'unlike the Webbs they were essentially democratic, preferring to test out rather than to impose their ideas upon people'.[9] Such was its success that in a more sophisticated format, the publication flourishes still.

During the early autumn of 1920 Margaret became a 'half-time worker' and in February 1921 Jane, the Coles' elder daughter and the first of their 'three highly satisfactory' children, was born. Secure on the home front, Margaret continued working, and the advent of Anne in October 1922 did not noticeably reduce her commitments. On the contrary, she was writing (with and without Douglas) for both LRD and the Labour Party pamphlets on *Price Movements During the War, Whitley Councils: the Regulation of Wages*, syllabuses for LRD study circles, and articles for *The Nation* and *Labour Monthly*.

The Movement Crumbles

For many left wingers during the early twenties, political alignments were in a state of flux. Support for Guild Socialism plummeted as mass unemployment generated by the post-war slump brought defeat to trade unionism and saw the collapse of the Shop Stewards' Movement. The National Guilds League died and The Movement, riven by disagreement about and disillusion over the Russian Revolution which had once been welcomed so euphorically, disintegrated.

When the news about Russia had first broken, 'we danced round tables and sang', Margaret recalled: 'Everyone with an ounce of liberalism in his composition rejoiced that tyranny had fallen. Thousands gathered at the Albert Hall and wept unashamedly.'[10] At a stroke, it had seemed, Russia had reversed the social values and was blazing a trail for socialism.

Inevitably, a Communist Party of Great Britain was formed, and not only 'insurrectionists and Marxists believing in the class war' helped in that formation. For there were also in the Labour Movement, Margaret wrote,

those who were genuinely impatient and frustrated at the

slowness of the Labour Party in initiating action . . . [and who] . . . shared the desire for a plan and direction . . . of wanting to feel part of a society which was going somewhere.[11]

Many from The Movement therefore became founder members of the Communist Party, but many of those who were first in were also the first to withdraw, mainly in disagreement over the policy of democratic centralism. The Coles, who had not been invited at the outset, never joined, though more by accident than design. Douglas 'saw from the first that the Party was not for him' and Margaret, although not opposed to Communism, was apprehensive over the Party being formed as a branch of the new, Moscow-based Third International, the Comintern:

> Had it been the other way round, if the Communist Party had been the first-born, I think I might have joined it. But I did not feel I could take orders from foreigners, however much I might respect their achievements.[12]

She also distrusted the subsequent policy of 'Bolshevisation' on which an instruction allegedly from the Comintern ordered communists to capture organisations in which they were active by the formation of 'cells' in order to implement agreed policies and to replace 'non-believers'.

Ironically, these tactics of democratic centralism were directed against Douglas at a time when he had been working to reconcile revolutionary and evolutionary attitudes within the Labour Movement. Indeed, he greatly annoyed the Labour Establishment by supporting a proposal for LRD to accept 'Moscow Gold' in the form of a substantial subsidy from Arcos Ltd, a Soviet-orientated trading company. This stand lost LRD the support of Bernard Shaw and infuriated the Webbs, but it did not prevent Douglas being deliberately engineered out of office by communists within LRD.[13] At the time, he and Margaret were unaware of the machinations devised to 'vex Mr G. D. H. Cole into resigning'.[14] Only Raymond, then on the LRD Executive, was uneasily alerted.

As a paid employee Margaret continued working amicably in LRD until Douglas was appointed to a Readership in Economics at Oxford University (the first of its kind in the new school of Philosophy, Politics and Economics) and to a Fellowship at University College. In 1925 they moved from Hampstead to Holywell in the city of dreaming spires.

The Oxford Years and the Cole Group

Oxford never won Margaret's affection. She disliked it fiercely, both on environmental and intellectual grounds. In contrast to Cambridge, she found it a 'minor Detroit', hated the 'closed-in market day, smelling of butchery, slippery with slimey squashed vegetables', and considered that Oxford colleges, unlike Cambridge, 'neglected their river'. She did concede the city's beauty in late spring, but detested its 'dank, soggy miasmic, chill — like the bottom of a disused water tank'. To this pervasive dampness and to nearby New College which obscured most of the sun from their pretty, medieval oak-beamed house she attributed the reason for her and Anne never being 'really well so long as we lived in Oxford'.

Ill health, however, only partly explains her jaundiced view. Intellectual loneliness was the more potent factor. Margaret always needed congenial, stimulating friends, and because she had felt so acutely a 'dull and growing misery' at the break-up of The Movement, the maleness of adult life of intellectual Oxford hit her exceptionally hard. It also helped to convince her that she was 'not naturally cut out to be a don's wife'. In London she had had a job as well as family, and was 'sure of a place in the front row of whatever was going on'. In Oxford, she found that all of the really interesting discussions, or the occasions when something important was being done, took place in colleges which excluded women. Even when she entertained distinguished visitors like R. H. Tawney in her own home, she noted angrily that 'I was only expected to feed him, and after dinner he went down for talk in a male common-room.'[15] Nor did the 'routine' occupations of Oxford wives appeal, but the final indignity was attending a carol service at Magdalen in a loft reserved 'For Ladies Only'!

Life, however, was enriched by a friendship, which deepened over the years, with Lady Mary Murray, 'the kindest person at whatever cost to herself, I have ever known', and with her husband, Professor Gilbert Murray, the distinguished classicist. 'An intellectual and spiritual host in himself', he was the original of Shaw's Greek Professor in Major Barbara, a pillar of the League of Nations and a pioneer in international co-operation.[16] This did not, however, prevent him in old age from adopting authoritarian and undemocratic views over which Margaret would chide him in their correspondence.

With typical honesty, Margaret admitted that in posing as a 'disconsolate exile' she did behave 'rather badly'.[17] There was, however, one fact of life in Oxford which she valued highly: the cherishing of Douglas' students. Each week they invited batches to lunch, and also regularly had members of the Labour Club to coffee. Douglas considered it his duty to cosset, counsel and intellectually stimulate undergraduates; and from these Monday evenings developed, after the General Strike, the famous Cole Group. (Lord) Michael Stewart, (Dr) Colin Clark the economist, E. A. (Teddy) Radice, Robert Henriques the novelist, (Sir) John Betjeman and W. H. Auden (poets) were but some of the future famous who argued together and formulated ideas about socialism there. John Parker has related how each member of the Group was allocated a government post and had to propound positive policies for implementation by a Labour Government. He, together with other Cole Group members, praised Margaret's skill as a hostess, recalling 'the warmth with which she welcomed us undergraduates into her home, and the lively and stimulating influence she exercised in discussions'.[18] Elizabeth Lloyd, the daughter of Mostyn Lloyd, Douglas' friend and colleague on the *New Statesman*, remembered her at this time as 'an admirably kind hostess to the gauche adolescent . . . delicious Sunday luncheons to which I was invited while at school . . . The lively conversation made a lasting impression.'[19]

Margaret, like Beatrice Webb, delighted as much in identifying able minds and in encouraging the young to argue, as in applauding later their mature achievements. Professor Roger Wilson, who saw the Cole Group as 'essentially a joint operation', considered that Margaret and Douglas provided an ideal pattern of 'what should be the relationship between university teachers and their students'. When, after Douglas' death he wrote to Margaret saying just that, she explained that the meetings had had their origin in what she and Douglas had known in their undergraduate days.[20]

Inevitably members of the Labour Club became involved in the General Strike of 1926, channelling their loyalties through the Oxford University Strike Committee. This committee, which grew out of the 'collaboration between the Labour Club and G. D. H. Cole', Margaret wrote, 'had its headquarters and its inky duplicator in our home at Holywell'.[21] She acted as Liaison Officer between Oxford, the TUC and the Labour Party, and has delightedly described being driven frequently up to town during the

nine fateful days along 'curiously empty, silent roads' by undergraduates Hugh Gaitskell and John Dugdale, to collect instructions
and supplies for distribution of the *British Worker*. 'I retain to this
day a clear recollection of the contrast between the excited
solidarity of the Strike Committee in that improbable city and the
gloom and confusion at the Strike Headquarters in London.'[22] She
also gleefully remembered taking 'the enormous bulk' that was
Will Thorne MP of the General Workers to the House in their tiny
Morris: 'I looked at him and at the car, apprehensively comparing
their relative sizes; but he said cheerfully, "Never mind, I'll get in
back'ards, but you'll have to get me out wi'a shoehorn."'

The development of the General Strike, and the subsequent
courageous resistance for nine months of the miners and their
families, have been proudly and widely recorded. Margaret saw
nothing of the conditions in the Welsh valleys, but her conclusions
about the strike are important because they were based on first-
hand observations in London and the south of England:

> The solidarity of the workers astonished even their own leaders
> . . . In town after town where the labour movement was
> genuinely considered weak, reports of nearly a hundred percent
> response to the strike call were recorded . . . yet the whole brief
> war was extraordinarily peaceable . . . Such was the self-restraint
> and regard for public order shown that it might have caused one
> to hope that given reasonably favourable conditions a good deal
> of fundamental change might be carried out in Britain without
> civil war.

The most important fact, and — Margaret observed — the least
proclaimed, was

> the quantity of organising ability disclosed among rank and file
> trade unionists who manned local Trades Councils and Strike
> Committees . . . Since their national leaders had made no plans
> at all, they were responsible for transport, the movement of food
> and of coal, and this they did extremely well, showing plenty of
> initiative and decision.[23]

Adult Education

The most permanently rewarding work that Margaret undertook

during her Oxford years was as a tutor for the Workers' Educational Association, and there is little doubt that it was this experience that sparked off her long burning commitment to adult education. The WEA, founded in 1903 by Albert Mansbridge to bring educational benefit and enjoyment to the working classes and closely associated with extra-mural university courses, became deeply important to the Coles. They saw adult education as a fundamental part of the Good Society and firmly believed that 'working men and women had a disinterested desire for seeking knowledge of and understanding about the world in which they were living'.[24] Their approach to teaching was fundamentally democratic. 'We do not have to force our own theories . . . upon our students,' Douglas wrote, 'but have to give them what they are acutely conscious of desiring for themselves,'[25] a view with which his wife wholly concurred.

As Director of tutorial classes in London University for three years prior to his appointment at Oxford, Douglas exhibited, Margaret wrote, 'all the characteristics of an electric eel' in his efforts to effect the development of workers' classes. He succeeded in linking the adult education movement firmly with the trades union movement, founded the Tutors' Association and its back-up the *Tutors' Bulletin* — which Margaret edited for some years — and managed, after a prolonged battle, to convince the LCC that it should increase financial assistance to the WEA.

Helping to fill the educational vacuum which men and women faced who had left school at twelve (or earlier) delighted Margaret as much as the spontaneity of her students. She began lecturing for the WEA in 1925 and continued, with breaks, until 1944, giving her final classes at Morley College during the war on 'Economics in the Modern World' (1942/3) and on 'Post-War Reconstruction' with Oliver Gollancz (1943/4).[26] She and Douglas would travel up weekly from Oxford for their classes, staying in London with Amyas Ross, a fellow tutor.

Margaret relished her teaching commitments, initially in Croydon and Deptford, in spite of tedious journeys, humping bags of heavy books, and teaching under difficult physical conditions. 'I have lectured to the accompaniment of a shunting yard, a choral class, and underneath the meeting place of a remarkable religious sect which registered inspiration by collectively jumping up and down on the floor,' she wrote,[27] but these diversions did not deter. Heartened by the enthusiasm of her students, who ranged from teachers and trade unionists to public sewermen and a grave-digger ('appropriately named Elms'), Margaret really understood how much they needed individual help. Her students often possessed great ability, and for many the WEA opened doors of opportunity. Apart from classes there were WEA summer schools, evocatively described by a former student, Margery Todd:

> Our tutors included Cyril Joad, Professor G. D. H. Cole, Margaret Cole, Barbara Wootton . . . and Amyas Ross . . . all of us students — miners, clerks or mill workers . . . felt it was a holiday to be able to work in seminars in the morning . . . and spend the rest of the day in the country . . . or just loafing in the grounds of Easton Lodge, taking out a pile of books, not reading them but lying in the sunshine and talking . . . We were all serious minded people . . . but there was a great deal of donnish wit . . . [and] plenty of more robust fun.[28]

Hugh Gaitskell, a former extra-mural lecturer himself, observed: 'as well as wanting to bring non-vocational education to those who had badly missed out, Margaret and Douglas were also moved by the need to educate and train men and women as future leaders of the Labour Movement'.[29] And indeed, in 1945, after the General Election, Margaret delightedly identified 'over 100 Labour MPs who had been students or tutors in the adult education movement'.[30]

Not all the Coles' ewe-lambs matured into practising politicians, but they often became thoughtful socialists. The experience of Ted Littlecott, a former WEA working-class Ruskin College student and Cole Group member, a future Deputy Education Officer in Hampshire, was not untypical. 'Douglas and you', he wrote to Margaret, 'made us see adult education as an armoury in which we could equip ourselves to join issue with the social and economic evils that prevented us and our kind from sharing in the good things of life' — a memory he later amplified by recalling in lighter vein how 'they both loved to cock a snook at the pompous, the smug and the complacent. Stained glass windows were always in danger when the Coles were around!'[31]

WEA involvement, conferences, syllabus writing and agitation for better training conditions helped to fill the gap left for Margaret by the break-up of The Movement, for she found many friends, old and new, among fellow tutors. These included R. S. Lambert, editor of *The Listener* and hero of the famous 'Mongoose' libel case;[32] H. L. (Lance) Beales, later Reader in Economic History at LSE; and Amyas Ross, 'the most original and wayward of all my friends'.

Amyas, affectionately sketched by Margery Todd in *Snakes and Ladders*, deserves mention, because to Margaret he was ' a friend whose legend I had hoped one day to write'. She had known him since as a Repton schoolboy he had irrupted into LRD, and she had followed with interested his 'chameleon career', from being 'the most intemperate and shocking of tutors' to a successful fine-art importer and wartime civil servant. In her estimation he was 'more personally unaccountable, honest, disconcerting and entertaining than most people put together'.[33] Amyas died young, as a result of a motor accident, but characteristically Margaret in her desire to put the record straight out of loyalty to a friend remonstrated with Victor Gollancz over his reference to Amyas' 'death by self-neglect' in his book, *More for Timothy*. 'I think', she wrote to the distinguished publisher, 'your reference is unkind to his memory, comparable with the people who determinedly say that Ellen Wilkinson committed suicide, which she did not'. Subsequently, though not without protest, Victor Gollancz modified his conclusion.[34]

As a lecturer in English social and industrial history Margaret was hard-working and provocative; she was less fluent than Douglas, with her slight speech impediment, but, like him, had infinite patience to listen, and the priceless capacity to evoke in her students — each of whom was individually important to her — a desire to find out more. The basic techniques of WEA work, and the satisfaction of its work being collaborative, were never forgotten. 'It is no use talking over the heads of your class,' Margaret said. 'When you are a teacher, as distinct from propagandist, you've got to be honest.'[35] Undeterred by deafness, she participated when well over eighty in several forums on education, organised in Ealing, where she was then living. Although she tended to mumble, her wit was undimmed, and she was singularly pleased to have been invited.

Notes

1. Molly Bolton, Olive Parsons, interviews.
2. M. I. Cole, *Growing Up into Revolution* (Longmans Green, London, 1949), p. 77.

3. *The Diary of Beatrice Webb*, 7 November 1918, ed. Norman and Jeanne MacKenzie (Virago, London, 1984), vol. 3, pp. 317–18.

4. M. I. Cole, *Life of G. D. H. Cole* (Macmillan, London, 1971), p. 98.

5. M. I. Cole to Agnes Murray, 27 January 1959 (in the possession of Beryl Hughes).

6. Diaries of Beatrice Webb, 7 November 1918, British Library, vol. 35, fos. 3638–9.

7. Dalton Papers, 16 February 1919, British Library, Box 1, fo. 51.

8. Labour Research Department, *Annual Report* (1918–19).

9. Noreen Branson, interview.

10. Cole, *Growing Up*, p. 86.

11. Ibid., pp. 96–8.

12. Ibid., pp. 96–7.

13. Cole, *Life*, p. 126.

14. Ibid., p. 127.

15. Cole, *Growing Up*, p. 110.

16. Ibid., pp. 111–12.

17. Ibid., p. 113.

18. John Parker, *Father of the House* (Routledge and Kegan Paul, London, 1982), pp. 169–88, and Professor James Meade and Professor Roger Wilson, letters to author.

19. Elizabeth Lloyd, 28 April 1982, letter to author.

20. M. I. Cole to Professor Roger Wilson, 4 July 1983, letter to author.

21. M. I. Cole, letter, *New Statesman*, 19 November 1971.

22. *Books and Bookmen* (April 1975).

23. Cole, *Growing Up*, pp. 121–3.

24. Frank Pickstock, interview and letters.

25. Cole, *Life*, pp. 104–13.

26. John Burrows, *University Adult Education in London* (University of London, Senate House, London, 1972), p. 56.

27. Cole, *Growing Up*, pp. 116–17.

28. Margery Todd, *Snakes and Ladders* (Longmans Green, London, 1960), pp. 139–42.

29. Hugh Gaitskell in Asa Briggs and John Saville (eds.), *Essays in Labour History* (Macmillan, London, 1960).

30. Cole, *Growing Up*, pp. 118–19.

31. Ted Littlecott to M. I. Cole, 5 January 1971 and 13 March 1983, letter to author.

32. Cole, *Growing Up*, p. 118. Subsequently Lambert 'retreated triumphant' to Canada, having received £7,500 damages, to work for the Canadian Broadcasting Company.

33. Ibid., p. 118 n. 1.

34. M. I. Cole to Victor Gollancz, 18 March 1954, University of Warwick Modern Records Centre, MS 157/3 LI MFT 4/274.

35. M. I. Cole to Andrea Hirsch, interview, 1977 (CFP).

6 RETURN TO LONDON

Joint Ventures

Commitment to adult education and to Douglas' students was not enough to tether Margaret to Oxford. Her own restlessness, hostility to the University's male-dominated society, health factors and, above all, Douglas' mounting involvement with the Labour Party, encouraged by the Webbs and Arthur Henderson, prompted their decision in 1929 to move back to London. Douglas, who had rooms in University College, returned home at weekends.

Prior to Oxford, the Coles had lived in Thurlow Road, Hampstead, in a large, ugly, square, grey house next to Mostyn Lloyd. Margaret has described its 'Victorian-style speaking tube through which the odours of kippers and onions frying were diffused strongly through the upper rooms', and the plumbing system which 'emitted groaning noises'.[1] To Hampstead they returned, but this time to 'a red brick, bow windowed house with a ramshackle garden in Parsifal Road'.[2] Margaret found it 'unglamorous' and for Douglas 'it had no soul'; but from here the little girls went to school, Humphrey the baby, born in 1928, grew apace, and for a while it served well enough.

Margaret once diffidently admitted that until the early twenties The Movement meant more to her than her two young daughters — she had modified her original intention, confided to Mrs P when very young, of having eight children: 'one a year, not oftener'. But nevertheless, with her friends Phyllis and Stella, she happily savoured the anxieties and delights of parenthood. Stella has described an occasion when, at her Sussex cottage, 'Margaret's pram ran downhill by itself and baby Jane was found pitched on top of the hedge below. Margaret was dreadfully shaken: Jane not at all.'[3]

Margaret would undoubtedly have been bored and frustrated by a life of pure domesticity. She wanted, she admitted, 'public work — paid or unpaid', and was able to pursue this aim because her domestic front was so well covered. The household rarely lacked a children's nurse — of whom Nanny Cole (Mrs Bryant) was certainly the most loved — and a husband and wife housekeeper-handyman team. Not surprisingly the nursery had an Edwardian aura. Jane remembers her mother as 'a tremendously busy, awesome figure with whom one daily spent a ritual half hour', but she was, however, 'good at reading aloud and at devising games from the sofa cushions and small tables . . . On Sundays my father played the pianola to which we would dance as rather clumsy goblins.'[4]

If Margaret was a somewhat aloof parent, willing to delegate domestic obligations, she never abrogated maternal responsibilities and would drop everything to assist in nursing the children through their inevitable youthful infections. She watched astutely over their physical development and was always alert to their intellectual needs. The psychological effect upon the family of having high-powered intellectual parents, keenly interested in public affairs and with mounting reputations, must have been somewhat cramping. There is indication that the girls at least felt they never quite measured up to their parents' expectations. Yet relationships, if not demonstrably affectionate, deepened over the years, to the extent that Margaret could reasonably observe, 'I do not feel that adolescents who addressed their mother as "IOG" (Inebriated Old Goat) can claim they were unduly repressed!'[5]

In 1935 the family moved to Freeland, in Hendon, north-west London. The house once belonged to John Galsworthy and stood in large grounds, through which the river Brent wandered; it had tennis and badminton courts and a large garden crowned by a great copper beech which offered plentiful scope for parties. There was a handsome studio room and much space, but even so an extension was added partly to meet the needs of Douglas' ever expanding library and partly for him to escape from his children's loud radio! For over twenty years Freeland was the family home of great happiness, of generous entertainment, lively intellectual dispute, and in spite of suffering severe damage in the Blitz 'was ours in a way no other home had ever been or ever would be'.[6] Stella Bowen embodied its charm in a painting which Margaret cherished.

Even before Oxford, Margaret's horizons were widening. How far this was Douglas' influence, how far due to her own enthusiasm, is conjectural, but their mutual enjoyment over joint ventures is indisputable. They watched cricket, visited parish churches — there were few in the south of England they had not explored — and indulged their delight in wandering, pack on back, over Morris' Cotswolds and through Cobbett's counties.

I believe that in the twenties, one way or another, we covered nearly all the ground which Cobbett had ridden on horseback a hundred years before. We were a good team for this kind of exploration . . . Douglas loved one-inch Ordnance Surveys, and I had a useful sense of direction.

These experiences were distilled into Douglas' *Life of Cobbett* (1924) which Michael Foot, Professor John Saville and Margaret, among many, considered his best work, and later used in the three jointly edited volumes of *Rural Rides* with maps and notes. These works were very much a labour of love, for Cobbett was Douglas' hero, and one of the happiest periods of his later years was, Margaret recalled, when 'he and I were jointly making a selection called *The Opinions of William Cobbett* (1944) and he read aloud with enormous pleasure Cobbett's fiercest tirades and his most eloquent eulogies'.[7]

The year 1923 heralded a new departure. The publication of a mystery tale, *The Brooklyn Murders*, by G. D. H. Cole, was followed by *Death of a Millionaire* (1925) and *The Blatchington Triangle* (1926), both by G. D. H. and M. I. Cole. After this they wrote together some thirty detective novels 'for fun'. The actual process of creation, described by their son, was one whereby each book was written wholly by either Margaret or by Douglas, 'but there was full collaboration in plot formulation, and each would later critically review the other's drafts'.[8] Margaret was well aware that the critics used to say 'we put in too much politics, but the books gave us something to talk about'.[9] So, with occasional breaks, at least one Cole detective novel appeared annually until the early forties, when they suddenly ceased 'because we got bored'.

The novels may have lacked the lasting distinction of Raymond Postgate's most original *Verdict of Twelve* (1940), but several are notable for reflecting critically how certain social institutions work and for analysing aspects of capitalist society. If the books were sometimes thought to be too political, they rarely failed to garner favourable mention from *The Times*, whose critic approved of the Coles' stolid sleuth Superintendent Wilson. Moreover, of *The Brothers Sackville*, he wrote, 'although a trifle conventional . . . the construction with . . . its lucid interpretation of detail should be studied by anyone with an urge to write a detective story!'[10]

The earlier novels, always 'carefully planned and thought

through', were regarded as the more readable, and 'at their best they were a credit to the avocation; at their least they represented the British police novel at its most British and dullest. Generally, however, the writers' joint skill placed their collaboration high up among crime novelists.'[11] Today the books still seem well contrived but somewhat slow.

The Coles did not take their detective novels seriously, but found the writing pleasurable, chiefly because 'it could be done any time, in any place, without research, providing that caution was exercised in dealing with subjects on which our readers — such as members of University Common Rooms — were often embarrassingly well-informed'.[12] The books never became best sellers because, as Margaret admitted, 'they were not good enough . . . competent, but no more'. Nevertheless, writing them was a source of mutual enjoyment and relaxation, and not unlucrative.

As an amusing spin-off, Margaret and Douglas became founder members of the Detection Club. This was a private association of writers of detective fiction in Great Britain, which existed 'chiefly for the purpose of eating dinners together . . . and of talking illimitable shop'.[13] Membership was confined to those who had written genuine detective stories and 'embraced the cream of the crime-writing fraternity', of which the Coles' old friend, G. K. Chesterton, was the first chairman. Members included Antony Berkley, Dorothy Sayers and E. C. Bentley, and everyone had to swear upon a skull to refrain from using in their books 'untraceable poison, unscrupulous Chinamen, or to keep clues concealed from their readers'. 'Rules', Margaret caustically commented, 'which Agatha Christie, a founder member, appeared to have forgotten all about.'[14]

Travel

Although both loved exploring the British countryside, Douglas, unlike his wife, disliked foreign travel. He detested visiting other European countries and long remained a 'Little Englander'. Elizabeth Lloyd recalled how on a family holiday in Spain with the Coles her mother commented upon a spectacular view, to which Douglas replied, 'I'd much rather be at home'.[15] There were nevertheless various family holidays abroad — to Guernsey, Madeira, Spain — in which he did take part, interspersed with visits to their friends Naomi and Dick Mitchison in Scotland.

Margaret, on the contrary, delighted in being a 'truant matron'. She first went abroad without Douglas with Raymond and his wife Daisy (George Lansbury's daughter) to Italy in the early twenties, and long remembered the 'pure excitement' of her first approach to Dieppe on a 'decrepit cross-channel steamer', noting that 'one should always approach foreign countries gradually to get any savour out of them . . . if you want to appreciate the Pyramids or the Manhattan skyline, see them from eye level!'[16] Later she discovered the panoramic beauty of Provence, and its Roman cities, delighted in Portofino, and fell in love with the Left Bank while staying with Stella and Ford in Montparnasse.

These discoveries produced no traceable correspondence, but her cruise to Greece in 1937 did. She described evocatively to Gilbert Murray

> the incredible blue of the sea . . . olives and barley growing so high together at Delphi, and bright green bees with golden wings flying in and out of a mass of flowers which Persephone was plucking . . . and the Acropolis so much more beautiful than any description or painting — nothing can really show you that golden translucence unless you've seen it.
>
> I didn't find in it so much of the compost of history as I expected . . . the sense of generation upon generation . . . not so much as in Provence or Verona . . . I don't know whether it is something in the Roman stamp on fertile land that seems to preserve, like a mammoth in an ice block something of *everything* that has lived there.
>
> Greece and the Islands seem to me so much more unchanging, that one might have seen Pythagoras any moment coming round the corner . . . This is a monstrous letter . . . [but] . . . I had to talk nonsense about Greece to someone.[17]

In retrospect Margaret found that places visited purely for holidaymaking 'left far less impression than those where I managed to feel part of the community', either because 'I was doing some work, or because I was living with friends'. Certainly her letters to Douglas when she was investigating the USSR with colleagues from the New Fabian Research Bureau in 1932 bear this out.

Just before the Second World War Margaret visited Mrs P in Cairo, where she was living with her headmaster son, Ormond. It was a city Margaret loved, and afterwards she wrote 'what I thought was a nice book of travellers' tales — reminiscences of Egypt ancient, medieval and modern. But the war hit the poor thing on the head, so it sits in typescript' — and thus it remained, one of her few unpublished manuscripts.[18]

The Mitchisons

Socially, Margaret was always far more outgoing than Douglas, though she could be fierce, and on occasion formidable. Yet, whereas Douglas, apart from his students, gained little from social contacts with 'outside people', friends were important to Margaret who was always

> interested in individuals, in what they do and think, and in their companionship. If I cannot revitalise myself in having friends and meeting people . . . I become miserable and eventually of no use to myself or anyone. I have the kind of mind which seems to require frequent stimulation from outside sources.[19]

As participants in various enterprises, Margaret and Douglas shared broadly the same friends, and after the demise of the Guild Socialist movement again collected a host of like-minded colleagues. As well as Francis Meynell, Maurice Reckitt and 'Trilby' Ewer, their circle encompassed WEA students and tutors, *New Statesman* writers, Labour Party pundits and socialist intellectuals including Kingsley Martin, Dr Ernest Green of the WEA, Lance and Taffy Beales and the Webbs — for whom initial hostility had blossomed into deeply affectionate regard.

And then there were the Mitchisons, Naomi (Nou) of the great Haldane tribe, and Gilbert (Dick), later a QC and enobled. Between the two families and their able offspring, shared holidays and social occasions became expected and accepted. It was the Mitchisons 'who first introduced us to the semi-baronial life', Margaret wrote, warmly admiring 'their openhanded hospitality [for] they were among the most generous people alive in giving entertainment or presents or in helping friends'.[20]

Whether at boat race or bonfire night parties at River Court, the Mitchisons' handsome Thames-side home, now long demolished, or at Carradale House on the Mull of Kintyre which, during the war, became a haven for people of all kinds and conditions,

Margaret found in their generosity and friendship both balm and ballast. Carradale was a 'wonderfully beautiful place', infinitely soothing in the relief it offered both her and Douglas from London's bombing, and in the kindness of both Naomi and Dick. 'I tried to look after them both,' Naomi recalled, 'though I got cross with Douglas for being so unsympathetic to Scottish Nationalism. Margaret was nearer to understanding it!'[21]

After Beatrice Webb, Naomi, 'one of the most original and gifted people I have ever known', was the woman for whom Margaret had the deepest regard. Her personal friends over the years — Taffy Beales, Helen Bentwich, Rosemary Beresford, Dorothy Fox, Agnes Murray — and former secretaries of Douglas — Sylvia Mulvey, Rosamund Broadley and Bernice Hamilton, who later became Provost of Alcuin College, York University — represented different facets of Margaret's various interests; but with Nou the friendship was all-embracing.

Naomi, a considerable poet and fervent Scottish Nationalist, had an extraordinary capacity for work, both physical and intellectual. With her catholic curiosity, diversity of experience and magical imagination, she wrote prolifically for young and old. Her love of art and literature often took precedence over the formalities of politics; but her husband's parliamentary candidatures and her active involvement as a public figure in both Scottish and, later, African affairs, also claimed much time. Like Margaret, causes held her loyalty.

Naomi's *Vienna Diary* (1934), a moving book even today, reflected a concern which she and Margaret shared: refugee relief. Based on Naomi's reports from Vienna to the British press, it described the agony of Austria under Nazi persecution and her own underground work with Hugh Gaitskell and (Lord) Elwyn-Jones to aid the victims of fascism. It still stands as an honourable monument to courage and grief.

Dick Mitchison, who had been converted to socialism mainly by Margaret, became a close friend of both her and Douglas and was actively involved with several of their political projects. An able, conscientious barrister and later an MP 'who should have had a ministerial post in which undoubtedly he would have attained judicial distinction',[22] he was knowledgeable, intensely committed to socialism and generous with his expertise. He willingly helped colleagues and organisations by examining draft legislation clause by clause with infinite care, and even when a busy QC and MP his readiness to undertake the 'nitty gritty of alteration and correction' is still gratefully remembered.[23]

Dependable and loyal, he was indefatigable in helping with time and money anyone in trouble, or any cause to which his support had been pledged. A large, self-effacing, gentle and humorous man, Dick Mitchison possessed an awkward charm and generosity of spirit; he enjoyed good living and was an unrepentant gourmet. He wined, dined and entertained his friends with an openhandedness in which Margaret delighted, and generally exuded 'a geniality and sociability which Douglas undeniably lacked'.[24] Her husband, as Margaret once observed, was 'a far more Unsocial Socialist than ever Bernard Shaw created'. Whereas she constantly needed outside contacts and was continuously interested in people, Douglas tended to seek personal association only for the purpose of obtaining information, 'and even then I think he would rather they wrote it down on an envelope!'[25]

Diabetes

To be fair, Douglas' asceticism and social aloofness were reinforced by his diabetes, diagnosed in the summer of 1931. Thereafter he 'changed from a normal person, not very robust . . . to a man who was never for long out of doctors' hands'.[26] Even before his illness, however, Douglas was sexually low-powered. 'Physically he was always undersexed,' Margaret wrote,

> and after he was diagnosed as a diabetic, this asexuality was greatly increased. If he had not married I doubt very much whether he would have had any sex life at all in the ordinary sense . . . [although] he often said that he could not have married any woman but his wife, and I never saw any reason to doubt this.[27]

By reason of his illness Margaret firmly yet unobtrusively tended to cosset and protect her husband. Her concern essentially was unfussy, but 'always at the back of one's mind all the time was his diabetes — seeing he didn't collapse and that he got his food at the proper time'.[28]

Soon after the diagnosis Beatrice Webb noted how Margaret 'regulates his diet, he submitting with many half comic protests of disgust at the choicelessness of his four solid meals a day', and, with less approval, how 'they both stayed indoors continuously at work, enveloped in tobacco smoke, writing, writing . . . they both drink heavily of whiskey — their one relaxation from timeless work . . . [though] reserved for before bed-going'.[29]

Douglas' illness presented many problems, physical and psychological, but Margaret learnt stoically to cope. 'Douglas, thank goodness,' she wrote to Gilbert Murray, 'is better under insulin, and has stopped being convinced he's ruined. It's really rather hard. He's too young to develop an incurable disease and it makes him talk nonsense about people being fit for lethal chambers at forty.'[30]

In addition to physical discomfort and the necessity for dietary control, the diabetes had curious psychological repercussions. It produced, Margaret explained, 'a kind of black cloud upon the spirit with which it was hopeless to reason . . . and — more difficult to face — a certain feverish activity which could affect both work and judgement'.[31]

So it was that Douglas' well-being and preferences became Margaret's prime concern. Gone now were opportunities for joint walking tours, for theatre-going together or for their frequent dinner parties and Douglas, always a 'loner', became yet more withdrawn.

It is wholly understandable therefore why Margaret, the lively enquiring extrovert, was buoyed up by, indeed grateful for, Dick Mitchison's affectionate companionship. 'At this time she was still both attractive and charming,' Malcolm Muggeridge recalled, 'and made you conscious of her womanliness.'[32] Both family and friends were well aware of the mutual enjoyment Dick and she had in the other's company, and of how deeply Margaret, 'one of the warmest hearted people ever', appreciated the extended social life Dick in his generosity opened up for her: self-confidence radiated from her happiness.[33]

His, however, was a generosity of doing as well as of giving. For when Douglas had to shed certain physically demanding commitments on health grounds, Dick, who shared the Coles' socialist beliefs, took over Douglas' parliamentary constituency at King's Norton, Birmingham, where he was the prospective Labour candidate, and fought two unsuccessful elections there. Eventually he won Kettering (Yorkshire) in 1945; and held the seat for nineteen years, until created a Lord.[34]

Although Naomi and Douglas were aware of the close relationship between Margaret and Dick, the quartet of friendship was not undermined. On the contrary, over the years the four grew even closer as the stability of both partnerships strengthened, and the bonds of affection between Naomi and Margaret deepened.

In no way was the Coles' work, literary or political, curtailed by Douglas' illness. On the contrary, during the thirties their output was prodigious. Both possessed driving energy — Douglas seemed galvanised into yet more frenetic activity. In addition to much joint organisational effort in the 'political and near-political world, for which we felt deeply committed', Douglas produced no less than 22 books between 1932 and the end of 1935, in some of which Margaret helped; and this as well as his tutoring and brilliant teaching. In Michael Foot's estimation Douglas was 'without doubt the most exciting lecturer in pre-war Oxford'. Ideas cascaded from Douglas' mind as rapidly as books from his pen, and Beatrice Webb regarded him as 'one of the few men in the Labour Movement who continues as a devoted propagandist and as the centre of groups of young intellectuals'.[35]

Partly because Douglas felt he was striving against time, partly because of their whole-hearted commitment to socialism, Margaret became the willing collaborator 'to the extent permitted by the very rapid pace set by the principal author'.[36] She also acted as a tireless agent in what Douglas described as 'the body-and-soul-destroying task of indexing'. During the thirties apart from their baker's dozen of detective novels and the various books on Cobbett, Margaret and Douglas wrote or jointly edited *The Intelligent Man's Guide through World Chaos* (1932), which, known cheerfully as 'Cole's Chaos', was a 'resounding success'; *The Intelligent Man's Guide to Europe Today* (1933), an encyclopaedic survey of contemporary Europe considered by *The Times* to be 'a very helpful piece of work',[37] the *Guide to Modern Politics* (1934), and *The Condition of Britain* (1937), a work of considerable importance which is still acclaimed. Additionally there were book reviews, articles and pamphlets from each, and several books by Margaret alone.

Hitherto Margaret had written mainly in co-operation with her husband — for Douglas had always taken precedence in her mind as The Authority, and she felt herself to be very much Mrs G. D. H. Cole. Gradually, however, she emerged as an editor and author in her own right. Among the first books she produced on her own were two symposia for the New Fabian Research Bureau (NFRB), *Twelve Studies on Soviet Russia* (1933) and, later, *Democratic Sweden* (with Charles Smith, 1938). The firmly feminist but unaggressive *Roads to Success* (1936) identified career opportunities for young women and was prompted, as Margaret wrote in the Introduction, by her desire to gather advice for her own daughters as to what it really was like to hold certain specific jobs. She therefore approached a number of successful, mainly professional, women — often her own friends — and sought answers to 'earnest enquiries for guidance'. A lively book resulted, based on the practical experiences of such achievers as (Dame) Evelyn Sharp and (Dame) Alix Kilroy (Civil Service), Irene Barclay (property management), Storm Jameson (writing) and Ellen Wilkinson MP. The editor herself discussed 'Running Two Jobs'.

Two years later Margaret produced a complementary volume, *Women of Today*, a collection of biographical vignettes ranging from Dame Ethel Smyth and Clare Sheridan to Elizabeth Garrett Anderson and Laura Knight. As she commented in the Introduction to a later edition, much of what women were able to attain in the post-war era was made possible by the achievements of those recorded in the book, 'when the dice was much more heavily loaded against them'.[38]

Marriage and Feminism

The first full-length book that Margaret wrote without Douglas, though to which indirectly he contributed a great deal, *Marriage*, appeared in 1938. Though in part outmoded, it is important for reflecting how she then felt about family life and her relationship with Douglas.

She accepted that the original purpose of marriage was the production and care of children, but argued that 'desire for companionship, for protection against loneliness and for partnership of long duration upon varying terms' were integral elements. Parents, needed by children while they were 'helpless and irrational', had one indispensable function, that of

the final protection . . . of loving children as nobody else will . . . You cannot however be expected to like all your children equally . . . but you can love them all equally, and your loving may be of considerably more importance in the case of the child you like less . . . Yet even so, parental love should not expect automatic reciprocity.[39]

Marriage also encompassed the job of home-keeping, which entailed being a 'kind of spiritual Selfridge'. This involved not only playing games with the children, helping with homework and listening to grievances, but also running the home and generally 'spinning the services into a cocoon of living for the family' which she relished far less; such work, she considered, was laborious, thoroughly unsatisfactory and wholly irrational.[40] 'Modern house-keeping is too like perpetually weeding a bed where ground elder flourishes and into which a steady supply of thistle, poppy and darnel seed is blown over the fence,' she wrote, in a metaphor probably culled from Douglas, who made weeding one of his few outside hobbies.[41]

Margaret's views on companionship and trust within marriage make the book an important personal testament.

Sex is not the only important thing in married life . . . for much happiness can be found in married lives which are not sexually adjusted . . . but to find mutual happiness under such circumstances calls for a fairly high degree of intelligence and control.

Freedom in sex relations could lead to trouble because of jealousy, which was simply hurt vanity. Some outbursts understandably reflected feelings of wounded proprietorship, but she conceded that this was not wholly fair, 'for you cannot call the cherishing of a life which two people have built up together and the fear lest new relationships may change it out of all recognition, merely a sense of property'. She recognised that 'one of the most indispensable requirements of successful marriage is loyalty between two partners and it would be ridiculous to deny that as things are, one-sided sex adventures are one of the most frequent threats to loyalty', but agreed that the 'eventual recognition by society of differences in sexual desire' might well make people realise that 'it was neither insulting nor disloyal if one partner seeks from outside, the pleasure or satisfaction which the other is unable or unwilling to give'. Since therefore the success of marriage seemed to depend upon 'the fitting together of the personalities of individuals, we should aim more and more to be tolerant of the arrangements adopted'.[42]

Margaret made some sharp comments about husbands who, like children, could not endure to be left out in the cold, 'contemplating their own insignificance and lack of charm'.

'The ordinary English male', she added with tongue in cheek

> is spiritually a frail and delicate creature, easily upset by breaths of external criticism, needing to be continually restored and encouraged . . . and it is often the most brilliant men whose life work is really of great value to the world who need such reassurance most.[43]

Some women found the job of cushioning their husbands completely satisfying; others, however, needed encouragement themselves, although too many men rarely appreciated this necessity. In fact, wives 'could often do with a good deal more reassurance than they get'. A really good marriage between people of personality had, in short, to be worked at. It must be based on mutual respect and recognition that 'the personality you married changes over the years'. Men tended 'to harden the arteries of their minds at an earlier age than their wives' and should not therefore resent their wives growing up 'out of the mental status of efficient subalterns'.[44]

Today thousands of wives in fact attain that maturity, partly through the opportunities for 'late' education for mature students which Margaret herself helped to develop through her work on the LCC.

The book concluded wisely and unpretentiously, revealing a great deal about the author, that

> the more women develop independent personalities, the more the need for loyalty grows . . . and the need for conscious adjustment and deeper mutual respect . . . to be able to count on loyalty is more than to be able to count on fidelity or even on truth. It is essentially to believe in the other person and to trust in the relationship you have both made, and in its being more precious to either of you in the long run, than anything which can happen to disturb it.[45]

No one could call Margaret sentimental — rather she was, in

Naomi's words, 'loving and astringent', but read carefully this book can be seen as a warm testimony of her deep, confident affection for Douglas, and of their jointly sane approach to a situation within their marriage which might have, but never did, become destructive. Although Margaret could write to Naomi that 'I was made monogamous, but not faithful,' and although her relationship with Dick mattered far more to her than to him,[46] there is little doubt from the prolific evidence of Margaret and Douglas' joint *useful* output that Douglas was her sheet anchor. Their marriage, on occasion stormy, proved lasting and secure. When in her eighties Naomi was asked how it was that her own marriage survived, since 'both you and your husband took lovers yet remained so close', she replied that the pattern had been less unusual than it sounded, but 'it did depend on our having total trust in one another, and in not being possessive',[47] a reply that precisely reflected the attitude Margaret had expressed in *Marriage* some forty years earlier. As Naomi herself had written (in *Tribune*) at the time of its publication, 'the book talks less nonsense about marriage than I should have thought possible!'

As her characteristically independent views of marriage suggest, Margaret was a firm feminist. Unlike her sister-in-law, Daisy Postgate, who had on occasion (when still Miss Lansbury) exchanged clothes with Sylvia Pankhurst to help her escape from political meetings and so evade arrest, Margaret was never a suffragette. She was, however, a pacifist until the Second World War and

> as a Wellsian Socialist naturally became a feminist, but I had no spur to become a militant . . . never in my life had I felt any acute sex disability, other than the youthful, inescapable one, of being a girl in petticoats.[48]

So, although both she and Ray were strong suffrage supporters, neither ever took part in violence. 'We both had hesitation in breaking the law, in view of father,' she told Dr Brian Harrison in an interview in 1975, 'but I never felt like demonstrating: politically I was very immature, and actively disliked a great deal of what the extreme suffrage people did'.

Of course she supported the enfranchisement of women, but was cautiously unenthusiastic when it became law in the twenties. She shared Douglas' scepticism, aware that 'if we had votes at once, most of those would be Tory'.[49]

After the vote had been won, Margaret continued to advocate equal work and press these views in the Fabian Women's Group. She believed firmly in equal opportunity and did her utmost to encourage young women to enter public life or to train for the professions, and would unhesitatingly expose and oppose any male chauvinism in small as well as in mighty issues. When, for example, it became known in the sixties that the Royal Horticultural Society had never appointed a woman to their Council, she wrote caustically to *The Times*, regretting that the Society's President had made it clear that 'the full Council had never been able to accept that any lady could ever reach the high standards of their august selves!'[50]

Margaret disliked the aggressive approach adopted by some in the feminist battle, and disapproved of the noisily assertive attitudes of certain colleagues on the LCC, which caused the Education Committee to be dubbed 'the Shrieking Sisterhood'! While acknowledging the absence of any overt anti-feminism at County Hall, she often regretted that generally the Labour Party had a poor record in assisting or encouraging women to enter public life. In a letter to Richmond, she put the women's movement in perspective.

> The pre-1914 suffragettes did have a hell of a time, though you don't have to take Vera Brittain *au pied de lettre*, because she's an emotional ass . . . but the whole revolt of women is historically and sociologically very interesting, for they were being double-crossed by a Parliament of males . . . it provided some of the clearest indications that the age-long conception of democracy was not working, and the sort of desperate, angry, semi-hysterical kicking that this produced was an indication of what happened later in Germany and Italy, when the democratic machinery had broken down much more seriously . . . but we haven't solved the problem . . . Now we have got to try again to make the forms fit the values.[51]

Change, she still firmly believed, was to be achieved through constitutional methods, a belief she tacitly expressed by accepting a vice presidency emeritus of the Fawcett Society. This organisation, which flourishes still, evolved from the London Society of Women's Suffrage, and is an all-party body in the non-militant tradition of the leading suffragist, Dame Millicent Fawcett. It eschewed violence and sought by constitutional methods to secure equality and social justice for all women. The Society's clutch of vice presidents are culled from the whole political spectrum. Margaret was but one of several.

She never denied the need for women to 'educate, agitate and organise' on behalf of their cause, and to seek equality of opportunity, and she would argue and write to that end, but Margaret never wanted to be a member exclusively of women's groupings. 'I did think that [some] women advocates talked an awful lot of rubbish,' she told Dr Brian Harrison,[52] but she lost no chance to promote opportunity for, or the placement of, women in professional and public life. Like her contemporary Ellen Wilkinson, for whom she had a warm if critical affection, Margaret recognised that the most effective way to plead women's case was by their demonstrating positive ability and personal achievement. And this, in her firm unflamboyant way, she unquestionably did.

Notes

1. M. I. Cole, *Life of G. D. H. Cole* (Macmillan, London, 1971), p. 105.
2. Sylvia Mulvey, interview.
3. Stella Bowen, *Drawn from Life* (Collins, London, 1940; reprint, Virago, London, 1984), pp. 80–2.
4. Jane Abraham, letter to author.
5. M. I. Cole, *Growing Up into Revolution* (Longmans Green, London, 1949), p. 107.
6. Cole, *Life*, p. 172.
7. Ibid., pp. 130–4.
8. Humphrey Cole, interview and letter to author.
9. M. I. Cole to Andrea Hirsch, interview, 1977.
10. *The Times*, 18 December 1930.
11. Howard Haycroft, *Murder for Pleasure* (Peter Davies, London, 1942), pp. 143–7.
12. Cole, *Life*, p. 136.
13. Dorothy Sayers, Introduction to *The Floating Admiral*, by members of the Detection Club, revised edition (Macmillan, London, 1981).
14. Julian Symons, 14 April 1982, letter to author, and M. I. Cole, *Books and Bookmen* (April 1978).
15. Elizabeth Lloyd, letter to author.
16. Cole, *Growing Up*, p. 126.
17. M. I. Cole to Gilbert Murray, 16 May 1937, Bodleian Library, Gilbert Murray Papers, Box 82, fos. 10–13.
18. M. I. Cole to Gilbert Murray, 30 December 1945, Gilbert Murray Papers, Box 96, fo. 206.
19. Cole, *Growing Up*, p. 79.
20. Ibid., pp. 139–41.

21. Naomi Mitchison, letter to author, 24 January 1985.
22. Lord Elwyn-Jones, interview.
23. Lord Elwyn-Jones, Dorothy Fox, Peggy Crane, interviews.
24. Lady Chorley, Bernice Hamilton, Rosamund Broadley, interviews.
25. Cole, *Growing Up*, pp. 77–8.
26. Cole, *Life*, p. 183.
27. Ibid., pp. 91–3.
28. M. I. Cole to Andrea Hirsch, interiew, 1977.
29. Diaries of Beatrice Webb, 10 December 1931, British Library, vol. 45, fos. 5220–2.
30. M. I. Cole to Gilbert Murray, Gilbert Murray Papers, Box 60, fos. 224–5.
31. Cole, *Life*, p. 186.
32. Malcolm Muggeridge, interview, 1 November 1982.
33. Lady Chorley, Naomi Mitchison, Jane Abraham, interviews.
34. 'Henderson suggested a peerage for Douglas, but Margaret strongly disapproved. As there were no Life Peers then, the children would have been involved.' John Parker, letter to author, 19 February 1985.
35. Diaries of Beatrice Webb, 10 December 1931, vol. 45, fo. 5221.
36. Cole, *Life*, pp. 198–200.
37. *The Times*, 15 September 1933.
38. M. I. Cole (ed.), *Women of Today*, Introduction to 1946 edition (Nelson, London, 1938).
39. M. I. Cole, *Marriage* (Dent, London, 1939), pp. 175–7.
40. Ibid., p. 213.
41. Ibid., p. 216, and Humphrey Cole, who commented, 'Douglas never planted anything in his life. But weed he would, patiently and persistently, though paying attention to only one kind of weed in any particular year!' (interview and letter to author).
42. Cole, *Marriage*, pp. 254–9.
43. Ibid., pp. 271–2.
44. Ibid., pp. 277–87.
45. Ibid., p. 298.
46. Humphrey Cole, interview.
47. *The Listener*, 12 July 1984.
48. Cole, *Growing Up*, p. 43.
49. *Hampstead and Highgate Express*, 19 June 1970.
50. *The Times*, 28 April 1967.
51. M. I. Cole to Richmond Postgate, 28 April 1945 (CFP).
52. Dr Brian Harrison, July 1975 (CFP).

The 1931 Crisis

When in 1929 the Coles re-based themselves in London, the political outlook had appeared buoyant. In his massive book, *The Next Ten Years* (1929), Douglas had outlined lists of achievements reasonably to be expected of a Labour Government, and was drawn closer into the Party's counsels. At Ramsay MacDonald's request he served on the large Economic Advisory Council, with R. H. Tawney and J. M. Keynes. Urged by Henderson and the Webbs, Douglas also agreed to become a parliamentary candidate, a move Margaret thoroughly approved. For engaged with, but not absorbed by, the demands of three small children, she was eager for action in a political situation which for a while seemed one of hope.

The second Labour Government which won the 1929 election primarily on the promise to cure unemployment was returned in a minority, but with a vote nearly double that at the dissolution. Briand of France and Stresemann of Germany seemed willing to make a durable peace with Arthur Henderson, the idealistic Foreign Secretary committed to the League of Nations. 'His patient labours for peace and understanding were', Margaret considered, 'in the very best tradition of English Nonconformity.'[1]

Had the Government not become enmeshed in the web of world depression, their innovatory legislation could have been welcomed as an encouraging if tentative approach to socialism. As it was, the Wall Street Crash annihilated optimism: 'America slid into panic and depression . . . ceased to lend, and scrambled to withdraw investments from Europe . . . While Britain's financiers, deeply involved with Germany and elsewhere, lent heavily to continental banks in desperate but unsuccessful attempts to avert collapse.'[2]

For a while the gravity of the situation was concealed from the British public, but when in 1931 the European banks and great industries began to fail it became obvious that Great Britain too was in crisis. Unemployment soared from 1.25 million in 1929 to 2.9 million in September 1931, as the Government's plans for public works and development schemes proved pitifully inadequate. This inadequacy was attributable partly to the Government's wrong analysis of economic forces and partly due to Labour's having no agreed plan for economic recovery. A Labour Government was thus led into accepting 'solutions' at the expense of the working class it had been elected to succour.

This conflict was exemplified in the detested 'Anomalies' Act which purported to deal with dole abuse, but which in effect withdrew or reduced benefits from many in great need. The Chancellor, Philip Snowden, anxious only for a balanced budget, and sympathetic to calls for retrenchment, set up the infamous (and 'loaded') May Committee. After Parliament had risen, it produced a report — damned by J. M. Keynes as the most foolish he had ever read — which precipitated a run on the pound by depicting Britain on the edge of bankruptcy and recommending swingeing economies. It urged that the budget be rebalanced by increasing taxation, but mainly by a 20 per cent cut in unemployment relief.

The Cabinet split over how May should be implemented. Unity was shattered and resignations followed. After much vacillating MacDonald as Prime Minister ('the Scottish neurotic with a lovely voice and accent', as Margaret described him) formed a temporary coalition to defend the gold standard of the pound. This decision startled Cabinet colleagues and disgusted the Parliamentary Labour Party which promptly expelled him and elected Henderson as Party Leader. Urged by Ernest Bevin and the TUC, the PLP resisted May's recommendations on the unemployment cuts as strongly as Bevin, advised by Cole and Keynes, opposed retention of the gold standard. In September, however, the Coalition Government was forced to abandon the gold standard and jettison the very principles it had been created to defend. Two months later MacDonald called a General Election in spite of having pledged that under no circumstances would his Government go to the country as a coalition.

In the face of confusion over the causes of the crisis, and a panic deliberately generated by allegations that a Labour victory would mean gross inflation and confiscation of Post Office savings to pay for the dole, Labour was routed. Its representation fell to below 50 MPs, with Attlee, Cripps and Lansbury among the chosen few. Clearly, before Labour could recover, it had somehow, as Margaret wrote, 'to recreate confidence in itself and its leadership, and that required rethinking policy'.[3]

MacDonald's tergiversation had angered many on the left, but surprised few. Well before the devastating events of 1931 Margaret had regarded him with profound distrust, and described sceptically her and Douglas' visit to Chequers at which MacDonald 'played the role of an inheritor of broad acres . . . the son of the people called by fate to emerge . . . a lonely leader, as their saviour'.[4]

Socialist Societies

Against this background of deep concern over mounting unemployment and the Labour Government's general ineptitude, but prior to the May Report, the Coles moved into action. The Society for Socialist Inquiry and Propaganda (SSIP) was formed 'to bring back into the Labour Movement a sense of Socialist Purpose and a programme of Socialist Action'.[5] Because members were to work only from within the Labour Party, they were dubbed by Francis Meynell 'the loyal grousers'.

SSIP was the brain-child of Lance Beales, Mostyn Lloyd and Margaret, who at a WEA Tutors' Conference late in 1930 were bemoaning their disappointment with the Government's lack of policy. 'We decided that we must get something going to get socialism re-stated,' Margaret wrote to Kingsley Martin, 'so we convinced Douglas, and the thinking began that autumn, with three weekends at Easton Lodge.'[6]

Easton Lodge, vast and rambling, was the home of Frances Lady Warwick, who over the years had hosted many seminars and conferences for the Labour Movement. An Edwardian beauty, beloved of Edward VII, Lady Warwick had been converted to socialism by Robert Blatchford, and had never wavered. She readily lent her mansion for, and would often preside over, Labour gatherings. This irked Beatrice Webb, for she thought that the Countess tended to 'disregard the freedom of personal opinions in others, and expect to be deferred to', although she did concede that Lady Warwick was a 'dignified, public spirited old woman whose socialist faith, uninformed and emotional, remained deep-rooted and persistent'.[7]

Margaret drew a more vivid picture of the aristocratic 'chatelaine', residing in decaying grandeur and with H. G. Wells living amid the neglected grounds in nearby Easton Glebe. She regarded Lady Warwick, with her faded Lily Langtry beauty, her electric smile switched on and off, and yapping Pekinese as 'a kind, emotional woman of purpose and principle'. She respected Lady

Warwick for spending her dwindling resources on good causes
rather than on her property, and in helping Conrad Noel — the red
parson of Thaxted — socialists, pacifists, internationalists and
'under dogs generally'.[8] Unlike Beatrice, Margaret did not consider
that 'working amid such decayed magnificence was out of keeping
with . . . discussions on the inevitability of gradualness in abolish-
ing poverty'.[9] Easton Lodge, now demolished, was once the nub of
socialist activity, and coupled with the warm hearted generosity of
its owner, remains memorable for its role in Labour history.

SSIP, formally created in January 1931, owed much to
Margaret's tenacity and organising skill. She and Douglas 'drew
upon comrades from all stages of their political lives, spanning
Guild Socialists to the PLP' and Margaret, who wrote 'dozens of
introductory letters and . . . received no refusals', felt that The
Movement really had been resurrected. Members eager to join and
willing to work included George Lansbury, Clement Attlee,
Stafford Cripps, Francis Meynell, J. F. Horrabin, D. N. Pritt,
Hugh Gaitskell, Raymond Postgate and Ellen Wilkinson. Ernest
Bevin, who sat on the Economic Advisory Council with Douglas,
was chairman of the Executive Committee; Douglas and Arthur
Pugh vice chairmen; the treasurer was Dick Mitchison, with Lance
Beales and Margaret as joint secretaries. The recruitment of
Oswald Mosley, then a prominent and vocal socialist, had also been
considered, but 'fortunately, he rushed out of the Labour Party
before we had time to become compromised'.[10]

Although SSIP had a membership of under six hundred and was
short-lived, it was singularly active. It spawned provincial branches
and study groups, organised lectures, held seminars at Easton
Lodge, and published numerous pamphlets. Issues tackled ranged
from the banks and socialist planning to Anglo-Soviet trade and
Facts for Socialists, and by the time of its dissolution in October
1932, SSIP had sold some 19,000 copies of its publications.
Douglas, who had plans for many more such, wrote to Beatrice
Webb that he was 'bubbling with ideas'. Certainly, as Margaret
noted, SSIP provided a sorely needed heartlift to socialists who had
been near to leaving the Labour Movement in despair at its
sterility.[11]

While SSIP was emerging, Douglas envisaged yet another organ-
isation to 'undertake solid Socialist research and to fill a gap in
Labour Party work'. After he had consulted the Webbs and Arthur
Henderson, Professor Harold Laski and William Robson, both of

LSE, and arranged further Easton Lodge gatherings, the New Fabian Research Bureau (NFRB) came into being, also in 1931, and was for a while his main interest. It followed the Fabian tradition of socialist research, but undertook no propaganda or political activities independent of the Labour Party; later it became singularly important in reviving the moribund Fabian Society.

The personnel of NFRB largely overlapped with that of SSIP; both were 'stage armies of the good', but fresh volunteers were also attracted, including Evan Durbin and Margaret's friend Dr Stella Churchill. They joined with old hands to work, by word and pen, in devising socialist policies.

When SSIP dissolved itself, and merged against Douglas' better judgement with the rump of the ILP, which had disaffiliated from the Labour Party to form the Socialist League, it chose Frank Wise and not Ernest Bevin as chairman. This was a cardinal mistake and not only lost Bevin from their ranks, but also 'deepened in his mind the conviction already implanted by the behaviour of MacDonald and Mosley, that intellectuals of the Left were people who stabbed honest working class trade unionists in the back'.[12]

'Cole and Mrs Cole' were active only briefly in the Socialist League. Douglas, presciently anticipating that it would soon cease to operate solely from within the Labour Party, resigned in 1933, and Margaret went with him.

In the initial formation of the NFRB Margaret played no part. She was desperately ill with pneumonia in early 1931, so much so that Beatrice Webb told Douglas, 'I hardly dared write you until I knew she was out of danger.'[13] Following a sunny convalescence in Italy, however, and after the bomb of Douglas' diabetes had been defused, Margaret eagerly resumed work with both the 'loyal grousers' and the new Bureau. E. A. (Teddy) Radice, who was for a while general secretary to both bodies, recalled her as their 'general organising factotum . . . who did not contribute greatly to policy formation'. Margaret was consciously playing second fiddle to Douglas, but was 'admirable in getting hold of, or in knowing, people who could be useful in speaking on this, or in doing that'.[14]

As the records show, Margaret was an assiduous attender at committees, occasionally deputising for Douglas, and conscientiously fulfilling her different commitments. She served on the NFRB Political and Research Commitee, on the Publications Committee, and, with Professor Tawney and Beatrice Webb's niece Barbara Drake, on the Education Group. Margaret, like Beatrice

Webb, always welcomed able young graduates into the Fabian fold, especially if they happened to be good-looking, and would encourage them subsequently to seize political or academic opportunity. John Cripps — son of Sir Stafford Cripps and long-time editor of *The Countryman* — (Sir) William (Bill) Nield later a distinguished civil servant, John Parker and H. D. (Billy) Hughes were among the staff who won approval for their 'intelligence and capacity for hard work'. Not surprisingly, employment with the Fabian Society became, and long remained, a recognised path to political preferment.

Meetings were sometimes held at the Cole house over weekends when Douglas was home from Oxford, and from them interesting ideas would often emerge. Plans for the *NFRB Quarterly*, for example, were brought to fruition by Douglas, Dick Mitchison, Colin Clark and John Parker, the Bureau's new general secretary, with Margaret as editorial functionary. The journal, created to provide 'facts and statistics on Trade, business trends and wages', was packed with information, and subsequently acquired the dubious distinction of being mentioned during a debate on the King's speech when Sir John Simon designated it 'this very interesting publication' and Sir Archibald Sinclair dismissed it disparagingly in Shakespearian terms: 'Away thou rag, thou quantity, thou remnant.'[15]

Visiting the USSR

The NFRB also had an investigative function, and early in the thirties, at Douglas' suggestion, arranged a visit to the USSR. No collective attitude was to be formulated by the party, which included Ray Postgate, Dick and Naomi Mitchison, Kingsley Martin, Dorothy Woodman, Hugh Dalton, D. N. Pritt, H. L. Beales and Margaret — Douglas was prevented from going by illness — but each member had to investigate a specific facet of Russian life. Margaret dealt with women and children, and included in her report only matters told to her or seen personally, but where information differed she 'noted the differences and tried to arrive at the correct answer'. She wrote approvingly of how the Soviet Plan utilised the energy and ability of the women on equal terms with men, and postulated the need 'to rethink our methods of continued education or re-education whereby women after bringing up children should not be barred from useful work in and for the community' — significant in the light of her later work for London education.

The individual contributions were edited by Margaret into *Twelve Studies in Soviet Russia* (1933) which, as one of the earliest appraisals after the introduction of the first Five Year Plan, was enthusiastically received. The book, original and interesting, contained an essay on Soviet agriculture by John Morgan, which Margaret and others thought particularly good. A farmer who later became an MP, Morgan travelled over the Ukraine and other provinces, was appalled by the standard of cultivation he then saw, and said so. Margaret herself long retained recollections of Soviet inefficiency, but, though mildly critical, was generally understanding. 'Their way of doing things', she recalled, 'was almost as inefficient as Peter the Great found it centuries before . . . but this was nothing to do with Marxist, Leninist or Stalinist Communism; it is simply Russian.'[16] Nevertheless, re-reading the book years later, she considered that her colleagues, 'neither fools nor untrained investigators, had been surprisingly objective'. More humorous reactions to the trip bubble through her own lively letters to Douglas. Undated, and hitherto unpublished, they were written during July and August 1932,[17] and well illustrate her powers of witty observation:

(At sea) (July) . . . Dick decided yesterday that he was quite incompetent to investigate anything and that the expedition was useless . . . Ray developed a brooding fit at the same time, and I felt as if I'd got two enormous dogs that wanted exercise . . . I do miss you and keep wanting to turn and talk to you . . . though I don't exactly wish you were here . . . you wouldn't like garlic sausage and I think you'd get fidgety . . .

(Still on board) . . . Dick, Ray and I learn Russian every morning (in a lifeboat!) I'm beginning to get the hang of the beastly language . . . though I shouldn't work if it weren't for their keeping me up to the mark . . . It's curious how one doesn't like to be bottom boy even in that . . .

(Leningrad) . . . the most astonishing thing is how clean people are — far cleaner than the English working class. I keep noticing it because I don't think anyone has mentioned it so far . . . they

clean the streets ferociously with a hose . . . and cleaned me in
the process, though I don't think I needed it . . . Dick went
factory chasing and apparently got a lot of stuff about wages
which I must pick off him . . . He's very critical and persistent
and goes on trying to get the information he wants.

(Moscow) . . . much more Russian than Leningrad . . . It's a
staggering city. I do not want exactly to live here, but I feel I
could . . . whatever the criticisms or faults, and there are plenty
. . . it is like a dream coming true. To meet and talk to civil servants and heads in large hospitals — and they talk like The
Movement — one keeps forgetting to be surprised because (and it
comes so natural) . . . one has come home. And all the thinking
[is] topsy turvy; education first, children first, workers first. I
sound excited but I'm not really as much as I thought, because
it's as simple as becoming a Socialist. I'm not half as excited as
Pritt, who has fallen in love and gets really cross if anybody com-
plains of anything . . . I do miss you . . . I keep wanting to say
what do you think about this . . .

(Moscow, Saturday) These people are extraordinarily un-alien
. . . I feel as I never felt about French or Italians . . . that if one
could only master their bloody language there wouldn't be any
difficulty . . . I think I might feel that more than you, because
the slightly happy-go-lucky-ism, the casualness, the 'here's a
good idea let's do it now' and the extreme friendliness appeal to
me . . . and the women . . . you see, Russian women have always
worked and been alongside their men . . . When I think of all the
dead weight of getting Englishwomen out of their homes . . . and
putting them to work, I'm appalled . . . The Russians had their
women with them from the start; ours we've deliberately cast out
and left uneducated . . .
    I do feel at present that if anything happened to you I would
take a chance and come here. I could get quite a decent job; the
children would get paid for and educated — if I came to a town.
And if we went a bit short nobody would die of that . . .
    (homeward via Vienna) . . . it will be nice to see you . . .
Russia's settling into impressions . . . I shall probably babble
incoherently for a while . . . I love you my Dear, my Dear.

Unlike the Webbs, Margaret never fell overwhelmingly in love with the Soviet Union, but her qualified enthusiasm long persisted. She admired, for example, the co-operative element in Russian life, whereby 'everyone lent a hand to a neighbour in difficulty, yet recognised the overriding importance of loyalty to a collective', she accepted that this 'wholly Russian approach' was totally alien to the political traditions of north-western Europe, and conceded that 'anyone who has non-conformity and habeas corpus . . . in his very bones . . . finds it extremely hard to appreciate, except intermittently, the Russian sense of the supreme value of the community transcending . . . any individual human rights'.[18]

Over the years Margaret modified her views, but because she had not returned to Russia to see for herself, would only criticise matters of which she was certain. What she did find 'fundamentally shocking' was their deliberate falsification of history and denigration of those who fought to create the Soviet Union, yet she remained sure that 'for the masses of Russians the revolution had brought improved conditions, enlightenment and above all hope, enthusiasm and a chance of life'.[19]

Margaret would always listen to the doubters, and present facts in perspective. She could, for example, fully understand the sceptics who questioned why so many intellectuals had supported the Soviet Union between the wars in spite of the 'long story of almost maniacal oppression followed by the stupid tyranny of faceless bureaucracy'. What they could not in her view appreciate were 'the high hopes that so many had had of the revolution', and that what

the makers of that revolution in the thirties were in part achieving, compared with the dead hoplessness of bread lines and the dole, was more than enough to dispel any beginnings of doubt . . . Many of us saw in Soviet Russia the negation of the immoralities of industrial capitalism and the system of private profit, and were eager to follow the gleam without seeking to imitate it in detail.[20]

The thirties had indeed, for some, been days of hope.

Fabianism Revitalised

Margaret's major political commitment during this decade was to the NFRB and to Fabianism. Like others of conscience, in the face of rampaging unemployment at home, fascist persecution abroad and the flow of refugees accelerated by the Spanish Civil War, she found it impossible to remain politically aloof or inactive. So, as the Labour Party struggled to clarify its attitude to foreign policy, Margaret gradually was redefining her own beliefs.

Her conversion from pacifism began in 1932 with the crushing of the Austrian socialists. She had seen and loved 'Red' Vienna and was deeply saddened by the murder of Viennese comrades. The invasion of Abyssinia by Mussolini brought her a step further, although, like the official Labour Party which so harshly rejected George Lansbury for his pacifism, she was ambivalent over rearmament.

> We were willing to accept rearmament if it meant saving Europe and ourselves from fascism, but there was widespread distrust of giving arms into the control of Baldwin and Chamberlain, lest when zero hour arrived the guns should be found pointing the wrong way.[21]

For her, the Spanish war was the deciding factor.

> On the rights and wrongs of non-resistance we had not a moment's hesitation . . . for the first time in a generation young men volunteered like Rupert Brooke [in the First World War] to save the world for a high ideal. Public opinion polls showed great majorities favouring the Republicans: and the instructed pointed out that Fascist powers were using Spain to stage a dress rehearsal for a greater war.[22]

Opinion within the Labour Party gradually hardened. Late in 1936 the PLP formally rejected non-intervention, influenced by the blatant disregard for international agreements shown by Italy and Germany, and the following year the Party Conference recognised the need — in spite of far Left doubts — for some rearmament. Belatedly a Spanish Campaign Committee to aid refugees was set up. The Spanish Civil War may have completed Margaret's conversion, but it was not until Munich that the Labour Party as a whole agreed to support a policy of total rearmament.

Indecisiveness did not, however, characterise the NFRB, and through Margaret's and Douglas' initiative the organisation developed into a small but effective intellectual force within the Labour Movement. If Douglas as chairman was the *éminence grise* of the Bureau, Margaret, who succeeded him as honorary secretary (with Dick Mitchison as treasurer), assumed a major administrative role helping John Parker, the general secretary, with routine work and policy planning.

The atmosphere of the day was conducive to the Bureau's success, for within the Labour Movement there was an 'awakening to the need for constructive thinking'. With Herbert Morrison winning control for Labour of the LCC, the return to the House in 1935 of several experienced Labour members, and an alert administration at Transport House, the need was recognised for shaping a realistic Labour programme. To that end the Bureau contributed both in practical and in intellectual terms. As Margaret pointed out in *The Story of Fabian Socialism*, it was an admirable arrangement that the Labour Party's Policy Committee co-operated with uncommitted Fabian specialists and used the Bureau as a supporting body for policy kite-flying. Moreover, because the Bureau published for study and criticism suggestions for socialist policies which carried 'no built-in commitment to Transport House thinking; fresh ideas could be examined and rejected without creating ill-feeling'.[23]

By 1938 the NFRB had published over forty solid pamphlets which received wide press coverage. They tackled such subjects as *Public Finance and Taxation Policy* (Colin Clark and Evan Durbin), *A Living Wage*, nutrition policy, marketing boards, *The City, Justice* (contributed by the Haldane Society in which Dick Mitchison was active), education, *Workers Control* (Cole and Mellor), *Local Government Reform*, specific aspects of nationalisation, the socialisation of iron, steel and electricity supplies, and *Planned Socialism* (G. D. H. Cole).

The International Section (which later became the Fabian International Bureau), under Leonard Woolf, studied India and colonial problems. The NFRB also published several important books, including *Public Enterprise*, edited by (Professor) W. A. Robson — the first full-length study of industries and services brought under public control — and *Studies in Capital and Investment*, edited by Cole. The proposals made in an important work on *Parliamentary Reform* by (Sir) Ivor Jennings were accepted by the Labour Party, and the greater part put into effect in 1945. 'Had that not been done', Margaret commented, 'the legislation of the session 1945/50 could scarcely have got through.'[24]

The Bureau also introduced the *Quarterly Journal*, which later became the *Fabian Quarterly*, and organised specialist conferences embracing international socialist planning, industrial legislation and foreign policy. Of one conference in particular, Margaret wrote to John Parker:

> I agree a Conference on Spain having suggested it . . . [although] I should have preferred that more time be given to the underlying conditions that led to the war . . . The first session should be directed to that entirely . . . and Brailsford or someone who has been there recently should be invited to speak.[25]

Virtually the last investigative project undertaken by NFRB was sending a team to Sweden to study the apparent success of its Social Democratic Government in defeating economic depression. The visitors — academics, civil servants and Bureau members including both Douglas and Margaret — were granted every facility to meet the Prime Minister and top experts, and their specialist reports, which Margaret and Charles Smith edited into *Democratic Sweden* (1938), excited considerable interest.

The work of the NFRB was noticeably overlapping with that of the elderly Fabian Society. This was partly because long-term research, by mutual agreement, had become the Bureau's responsibility, but mainly because, in spite of the Society's loyal and sizeable membership, it had grown moribund under a disastrous general secretary, F. W. Galton, 'a man whose amiability was matched by his obstinacy, and who had no views whatsoever on socialist policy'.[26]

Inevitably the question of 'fusion' between the parent body and the NFRB was mooted. Emil Davies, an LCC Alderman and treasurer of the Fabian Society, was a strong advocate; others were less enthusiastic, and Margaret wrote cautiously to John Parker:

> We don't want a political affiliation to the Fabian Society and we certainly don't want Galton . . . My feeling is that the bulk of what we could get by any sort of amalgamation — summer school, lecturing and the bookshop — will fall into our laps if we wait.[27]

The idea, of course, had to be fully examined and Douglas as

Bureau chairman took a hand. Memoranda were drafted, joint discussions initiated, and after much heart-searching and with the
wholehearted approval of the Webbs, amalgamation of the two
bodies was agreed late in 1938.

The rules of the 'new' Fabian Society were clarified and
redrafted by Douglas, who considered it 'an error of tactics to start
negotiating on the basis of existing rules'. The original 'vague and
verbose' (but historically significant) *Fabian Basis* of 1887 therefore disappeared for ever and familiar personalities reappeared.
Douglas became chairman of the reinvigorated Society, John
Parker general secretary, Margaret the honorary secretary, and
Emil Davies treasurer. Beatrice Webb signified her and Sidney's
approval by becoming the Society's first president.

The 'aims and activities' of the phoenix-like Society, which
largely reflected Margaret's personal views, were clearly spelt out
and stand firm today:

> The Society consists of Socialists. It therefore aims at the estab-
> lishment of a society in which equality of opportunity will be
> assured, and the economic power and privilege of individuals
> and classes abolished through the collective ownership and
> democratic control of the economic resources of the community,

ends which were to be achieved 'by the methods of political
democracy'.

The Society, 'believing in equal citizenship', would be affiliated
to the Labour Party, and

> its activities shall be the furtherance of socialism and the educa-
> tion of the public on socialist lines by . . . meetings . . . lectures
> . . . conferences . . . summer schools, the promotion of research
> into political, economic and social problems, national and inter-
> national, and the publication of books and pamphlets.

An innovation of which Margaret strongly approved was the
'self-denying ordinance', unique among socialist societies. This
stipulated that the society would have no collective policy beyond
that already spelt out and that its research was to be free and
objective in its methods. Thus 'no resolution of a political
character expressing an opinion or calling for action, other than in
relation to the running of the Society itself, shall be put forward

. . . [and] delegates to the Labour Party . . . shall be appointed without mandate'.

Accordingly, all publications would represent the personal view of individual contributors, and there was to be no 'collective opinion' of the Fabian Society. Margaret was at one with Beatrice, who in her first presidential 'message' stressed that

> research and active propaganda of immediate proposals are uncongenial companions: the one insists on an open mind, the other a closed one. If Fabians want to influence the immediate policy of the Parliamentary Labour Party they can fall back on their local Labour party or their trade union.[28]

The amalgamated Society thus deliberately debarred itself from the formulation or promotion of any policies in opposition to the Labour Party, and so evaded the trap of excommunication into which the Socialist League had fallen. It chose rather 'to pursue the policy of pulling its political weight not by passing resolutions . . . but by making its individual members trustworthy . . . so getting their opinions invited and listened to'.[29]

These aims have been spelt out partly because Margaret fully supported them, partly because the Fabian objectives of integrity and detachment in research indicate qualities she exemplified in her own scholarship. Margaret once observed of a Fabian Cabinet Minister who had been a student of Douglas', that although Douglas hated his ideas he respected his intellect,[30] and this epitomised her own attitude.

Influences on Socialist Ideas

The new and the old Fabian structures merged and thrived. In the opinion of Hugh Gaitskell, 'The NFRB would never have existed had it not been for Margaret and Douglas who founded and cherished it through the thirties and made it into a force whose influence was felt in post-war years.'[31] Even so, the dissemination of socialist ideas was no Fabian monopoly. From the early thirties Victor Gollancz, whom the Coles had persuaded to publish various Fabian pamphlets, was establishing himself as an 'encyclopaedic publisher of the Left'. This trend, which began with Douglas' *Intelligent Man's Guide through World Chaos* (1932), was followed by other *Guides*, all highly popular, and culminated in Gollancz's founding the unprecedentedly influential Left Book Club. Its flow of exciting and usually original left-wing publications, which included G. E. Gedye's *Fallen Bastions*, Simon Haxey's *Tory MP* and Strachey's *Theory and Practice of Socialism*, made immense impact, and together with other Left Book Club activities helped to educate and canalise the progressive opinions which triumphed in 1945. During the war, ABCA arranged lectures and provided reading material on contemporary issues for service men and women. These provoked much discussion and controversy and alerted 'students' to the need for change in the post-war period.

While the Left Book Club gathered momentum and Fabian amalgamation was in train, Ray and Margaret were launching *Fact*, a thoughtful, albeit short-lived, publishing venture. This was a series of monthly investigative booklets devoted mainly to a single subject, studied in depth and written with authority. Ray was the editor, Francis Meynell the designer and Margaret, Stephen Spender (the poet), Joseph Needham and (Professor) Lancelot Hogben (the mathematician) contributing editors. For the first issue, in April 1937, Margaret wrote a long analysis of communist and fascist economic policies, 'The New Economic Revolution', and subsequently produced book reviews and short articles. Generally the quality was high, but the second issue fell foul of authority over a satirical (and anonymous) exposure of the experiences of a private on military service: 'I Joined The Army'; this 'the printers refused to print, the distributors to distribute, and Smith's refused to stock. It's so nice having a free press, isn't it', Margaret wrote to Lawrence Hammond.[32]

After some two years *Fact* foundered on financial rocks. Margaret, however, had greatly enjoyed her association with the paper and was philosophic about its failure. It was just one more of the journalistic enterprises high in socialist principle but low in profit with which over the years she was so often associated!

Notes

1. M. I. Cole, *Makers of the Labour Movement* (Longmans Green, London, 1948), p. 266.

2. G. D. H. Cole and R. Postgate, *The Common People (1746–1938)* (Methuen, London, 1938), p. 574.

3. M. I. Cole, *Growing Up into Revolution* (Longmans Green, London, 1949), p. 156.

4. Ibid., p. 138.

5. M. I. Cole, *The Story of Fabian Socialism* (Heinemann, London, 1961), p. 222.

6. Papers of Kingsley Martin, Sussex University.

7. *Beatrice Webb's Diaries (1924–32)*, vol. 2, 7 April 1924, ed. M. I. Cole (Longmans Green, London, 1956), pp. 21–2.

8. Cole, *Growing Up*, pp. 145–7.

9. *Beatrice Webb's Diaries*, pp. 21–2.

10. Cole, *Growing Up*, p. 149.

11. Cole, *The Story*, p. 225.

12. Cole, *Growing Up*, p. 150.

13. Beatrice Webb to G. D. H. Cole, 26 March 1931 (CFP).

14. E. A. Radice, interview.

15. Fabian Society Papers, Nuffield College, J7/J8.

16. Cole, *Growing Up*, p. 160.

17. July and August 1932 (CFP).

18. Cole, *Growing Up*, p. 162.

19. Ibid., pp. 160–6.

20. M. I. Cole, *Life of G. D. H. Cole* (Macmillan, London, 1971), p. 190.

21. Cole, *Growing Up*, pp. 170–3.

22. Ibid., p. 182.

23. Cole, *The Story*, pp. 238–9.

24. Ibid., p. 236.

25. Fabian Society Papers, 18 June 1937, J11/1.

26. Cole, *The Story*, p. 192.

27. Fabian Society Papers, 9 May 1938, J11/1.

28. *Fabian News* (February 1939).

29. Cole, *The Story*, pp. 248.

30. M. I. Cole to the author.

31. Hugh Gaitskell in Asa Briggs and John Saville (eds.), *Essays in Labour History* (Macmillan, London, 1960).

32. M. I. Cole to Lawrence Hammond, 25 May 1937, Hammond MSS, Bodleian Library, 26, fo. 200.

PART THREE:

MRS MARGARET COLE

THE FABIAN SOCIETY

War Work

'You make the Fabian Society your main war work, and I will help you all I can,' Douglas said to Margaret in September 1939. And this she did, with the result that 'most of the day-to-day war-time expansion of the Society did fall on me'.[1] So alongside John Parker, Margaret worked voluntarily, consistently and hard as honorary secretary; she did not relinquish the position until 1953.

The Cole family had returned from holidaying in Ireland on the day evacuation began in London. Margaret, busy making arrangements for the protection of her own children, dealing with the blackout and other necessary domestic demands, still managed to assure Beatrice Webb that 'we have arranged to carry on [the Society]'; and later wrote to her:

I think it is extremely important to retain a centre of independent thinking and discussion (and publications) . . . We are continuing the lectures . . . arranging a conference . . . Douglas has written a tract. I have drawn up a series of headings for work on the Home Front . . . and as soon as Leonard [Woolf] gets back to town we shall be getting together some sort of War Aims or Peace Possibilities work . . . I feel it is important because Transport House has gone to Nuneaton, and apart from Greenwood's speeches the Labour Party is doing nothing.[2]

By the summer of 1940, Churchill had become Prime Minister, with Attlee as his deputy, and several Fabians had been appointed to seats of power. Beatrice recorded with obvious satisfaction 'the inner circle of the Fabian Society is today in close contact with Fabians in Cabinet; Attlee, Morrison and even Bevin come to them for information. They no longer have to go through the bottleneck of Transport House.'[3]

The political truce at national level during the war proved a stimulus to Fabian activities. Since socialists generally had few opportunities to meet together and plan for the future the Fabian summer schools, lectures and lunch meetings which Margaret helped to organise became extremely popular. Moreover, stirring appeals made by Victor Gollancz and others at the 1941 summer school, after the USSR had entered the war, for grass-roots activity greatly encouraged the growth of local Fabian societies.

Margaret, unlike Beatrice Webb, thoroughly approved of summer schools. When nearly eighty she recalled early gatherings which had been memorable for the friction between the Webbs and the 'rebellious Guild Socialists' who to Beatrice's intense annoyance had insisted on singing the Red Flag outside Keswick Town Hall, where a convention of Nonconformist ministers was in progress. However, by the time Margaret first attended a school, soon after her marriage, 'a truce had been called, and we had a lively time', although she would chuckle gleefully over memories of Douglas' inciting the ranks to insurrection.

Fabian summer schools 'came again into their days of glory' during the Second World War and were held at Frensham Heights, Surrey, or Dartington Hall, Devon. To the latter, Christopher Martin, a delightful man who died far too young, 'brought in the Ballet Joos and many friends'. The schools were packed, attracting future MPs in and out of uniform and refugee socialists from Occupied Europe. Amid sunbathing and swimming, serious discussion and satiric entertainment, the schools maintained their tradition of freedom. Even Professor C. E. M. Joad, previously expelled for 'excessive wenching', was allowed back into the fold!

Behind the holiday spirit, however, much serious thought was given to Labour policy, and the schools in Margaret's view exerted a contributory influence on Labour's programme. 'If therefore you feel like cursing the 1945 Labour Government, I would say that we take some responsibility, though not for everything that happened,' she told a Fabian school long afterwards.[4]

Margaret took a direct hand in meticulously planning lectures. For example, to every contributor in a wartime series on 'Socialism and the Future of Britain', at which Professor Harold Laski was the first speaker, she explained:

This series is meant to form . . . a consistent whole, in order to give a definite lead to socialists . . . Each lecturer will, of course, have the last word in what to say . . . [but] there should be consultation in advance between the lecturers . . . Each is therefore asked to prepare a reasonably full syllabus of what he means to say.

She then set down suggestions 'to give lecturers an idea of the ground they were expected to cover . . . but are not meant to adhere to, too rigidly'.[5]

This was typical of her tactics. Nothing devious, consultation with all, but clear-minded as to the best approach for implementing a purpose of which she and Douglas were jointly convinced — in this case the necessity to spell out a plain, definite socialist programme to which the political climate was becoming favourable.

Local Societies

Margaret was also anxious to foster local Fabian societies and, with leading colleagues Jim Griffiths, Ellen Wilkinson and Billy Hughes among many, she travelled across Britain, often under gruelling conditions, to address meetings. She went from Llandudno, where Jim Callaghan had formed a society with civil servants in Colwyn Bay, to Exeter, where the landlady of brother Richmond, then with the RAF in West Africa, informed her (to her great amusement) that he was 'not in at the moment, and she couldn't say exactly when he would be'.[6]

Local societies grew rapidly during the war and peaked to over 130 in 1947. As the young canalised their political enthusiasm into working for the Fabian Society, development was helped by new MPs, notably Arthur Skeffington, James Johnson, Arthur Blenkinsop and (Lady) Irene White. After the war, Margaret as sometime chairman of the Local Societies Committee, became a regular attender at local and regional conferences and was a helpful guide with Mary Stewart over local society research projects. From the acorn of this research little oak trees really did grow. One unscientific investigation into local museums, for example, produced material on which Margaret based two articles for the then *Manchester Guardian*.[7] These prompted correspondence from and activity by experts and subsequently stimulated ideas, then largely innovatory, for promoting the use of museums by schools. Such ideas bore fruit, notably in the Horniman and Geffrye Museums, for which through the LCC Education Committee Margaret became responsible and had for the latter a special affection.

She genuinely valued the active participation of Fabians living in the provinces. 'I think it is important that we (and our work) should not be confined to London, and that those members not

centralised should be helped to get together to do what they can,'
she wrote to Dorothy Fox, who for 25 years was the organising
secretary and 'mama' of all local societies.[8]

Mrs Fox found Margaret 'a marvellous chairman, always writing
at length or phoning up after a difficult meeting . . . really
bothering about people',[9] as later general secretaries Bill Rodgers
and Shirley Williams also found. Indeed, Margaret's explanatory
or hortatory postcards became almost as famous as those of
Bernard Shaw, although she never emulated his alleged achievement of writing one that contained 200 words![10]

Margaret's kindnesses to Fabian colleagues and staff were
legion; matters of concern to them were never lightly rejected. She
was also wise in handling personal problems. John Parker recalled
that 'I always brought Margaret in whenever I had difficulties with
female staff, and they did sometimes act as prima donnas!'[11] On
one occasion, to Dorothy Fox, who was tired and depressed about
her work, she wrote:

> I think it is not only your bit of the Society that can seem futile
> . . . The whole affair is rather small, and being plucky is apt to
> take on more that it can do . . . Also the confused political situa-
> tion makes it easy for the clever Cassandras to make convincing
> noises, Douglas does it continuously . . . they prove a bit too
> much . . . I think the tiny membership of the Fabian Society does
> really do a good deal, even if not always in the directest way one
> would have chosen . . . I think you should get away for a bit . . .
> even if your departure produces some consternation as no doubt
> it will.[12]

Kindness did not, however, diminish the attention she directed to
administrative detail. Writing to Beatrice Webb about a pending
article on the Society for *Picture Post*, Margaret begged her to
cajole Shaw into having his photo taken. 'Could you bully him into
doing this for the sake of his old Society?' she asked, 'nobody but
you is likely to have sufficient influence on him.'[13] She was equally
alert to internal tangles. When Billy Hughes' successor had to be
sacked she wrote to Richmond, 'The shake-up forced everyone to
look into organisation and may have been something of a blessing
in rather heavy disguise . . . we have appointed Oliver Gollancz, so
that's a better hope.'[14]

Margaret also made another important, if intangible, contribution in looking to the future. As both Professor Brian Abel-Smith, a long-time member (and officer) of the Fabian Executive, and (Lord) Tom Ponsonby, general secretary (1964–76), recalled, she thought about 'the Fabian succession' and looked ahead to find new leaders. She was thus quick to identify men and women with research and/or administrative potential. She could indeed see skill beneath the skin. Her general accounts of Fabian happenings were often spiced with lively comment in her letters to Richmond: 'John Parker has got into the Labour Party Executive . . . I hope he likes it . . . It's the horridest body I know, but you can't bypass the Labour Party by just saying you don't like its face.'[15]

The White Paper on education, she commented, was

> all right as far as it goes . . . and no one could expect Butler to go much further . . . Harold Clay [NEC spokesman on education] said that no child at present in school would benefit by it . . . We have such a horrible leeway to make up. The Fabian Society continues, as they say, to work on the subject . . . It has recently been abandoned by Joan Clarke who has pulled out to run a one-man show pushing Social Security [helping Sir William Beveridge]. I think she will be happier there. God did not make her a good collaborator with equals.[16]

It was with great pleasure she reported John Parker's election to the Front Bench: 'I think he thoroughly deserves it . . . on more than one occasion he has stuck by his principles when he could have had some career advancement if he'd been more flexible.'[17]

All aspects of Fabian activity held Margaret's interest. Soon after amalgamation she helped reorganise the Women's Group, of which Agnes Murray, a close friend and later a Home Office Inspector, became Secretary. It investigated feminist and allied matters, instigated enquiries into issues such as the family and the state, and contributed material to several pamphlets — *The Evacuation Survey, War Time Billeting,* and *The Rate for the Job* — written or edited by Margaret. A lively membership included Molly Bolton (a future chairman of the LCC), Mary Sutherland (the Labour Party's Chief Woman Officer), Beryl Hughes and Leah L'Estrange Malone (an LCC councillor) and invited speakers ranged from Jenny Lee to Harriet Cohen, the distinguished pianist. Again, Margaret was loyally supportive, and when in 1947 she was ill, the secretary, Elizabeth Thomas, wrote acknowledging 'how much the group owe you for your continued interest in its work and your consistent attendance at meetings'.

The International and Colonial Bureaux

Margaret also encouraged the Fabian International and the Colonial (later Commonwealth) Bureaux. The former, actively promoting international socialism, attracted experts such as (Lord) Phillip Noel-Baker and Leonard Woolf, its chairman for a decade. Woolf and Margaret often crossed swords, but more on literary than on political issues. They were firm allies in preserving harmony within the Society, and when, after the war, it was in financial disarray owing to the misjudgement of Bosworth Monck, then general secretary — 'his plans were well-intentioned but came near to ruining the organisation' — Margaret wrote entreating Leonard to delay his proposed resignation from the Bureau.

> Harold [Laski] is not unnaturally worried, coming home [from America] as Chairman of a Society that looks as though it might fly to bits . . . I very much hope that temporarily you will consent to being Imperial Caesar, stopping the hole against the wind,[18]

and he did. Not for the first time, Margaret played the role of a successful mediator. Monck, who resigned, was tactfully co-opted on to the Executive Committee, and wrote, gratefully appreciative of her efforts at 'easing tension'.[19]

Although she never sat on the committee of the Fabian Colonial Bureau (formed in 1940), which Rita Hinden guided and galvanised, Margaret was proud of its impact. After a Fabian conference on international affairs, Rita had suggested to John Parker the idea of setting up a Colonial Bureau. It aimed to formulate in practical terms the liberation of (mainly) British dependencies into self-governing states, and to that end directed its research, propaganda and information, often strengthened by political pressure. Members highly knowledgeable in colonial matters were attracted — Lord Faringdon, James Griffiths, (Lady) Hilda Selwyn Clarke, Frank Horrabin, Marjorie Nicholson — and also overseas students, many of whom became active in the politics of their own emergent states.

The Bureau's first chairman was Arthur Creech Jones. He became an Under-Secretary of State for the Colonial Office in the 1945 Labour Government, subsequently the Minister, and was succeeded by James Griffiths. Four members were also appointed to the Colonial Development Council. The Bureau might prove an irritant to officialdom, but its expertise could not be ignored.

Behind the scenes there were of course conflicts. Margaret had a warm regard for Rita's energy and devotion to principle, but she was not uncritical of the Bureau, and Marjorie Nicholson, who succeeded Rita as secretary, recalled that as a member of the Executive Committee 'Margaret could be very difficult', for whereas she envisaged the Bureau as devising long-term socialist policies such as ten-year plans for individual colonies, Rita and Marjorie wanted policies to be more short-term, conceived and applied piecemeal in the light of local needs and aspirations. Margaret became, for example, 'highly critical of our concentration on Central African Federation', Marjorie recalled, but

> having listened endlessly to the views of Africans from Rhodesia and Nyasaland, Rita and I used to point out that we had not got ten years, and that if we didn't act we'd get a white-ruled Central Africa when independence came.[20]

There were indeed clashes of policy and personalities, yet in her *Story of Fabian Socialism* Margaret acknowledged warmly the role played by the Bureau in making suggestions and in formulating policy that was actually 'taken up in whole or in part' by virtue of the close relationship of its officers and members with those running the Colonial Office in the Labour government'.[21]

When, after ten years, Rita resigned from the Bureau to become editor of the new Socialist Commentary, she and Margaret drew much closer together. Rita came to rely a great deal on her ideas for the paper's policy, and although she did not always accept Margaret's comments, she rarely ignored them. For her part, Margaret wrote regularly for the journal, and her pungent, thoughtful *Notes by the Way* were widely considered among its best contributions.[22]

1945 Onwards

By promoting ideas and discussion about socialist policies, the

Fabian Society had contributed positively to Labour's 1945 election triumph. Margaret, one of jubilant thousands, calculated that nearly two-thirds of the 394 Labour MPs were Fabians, among whom were two former officers of the Society, H. D. Hughes, later Principal of Ruskin College, Oxford, and John Parker, who was to become a Father of the House. Zena Parker's remark on visiting the House that 'it looked just like an enormous Fabian school' was indeed fair comment![23]

After the Labour Party had gained power, the Fabian Society, which had worked so hard to that end, lost one of its roles, and those many Fabians in government had of course less time to spare for active Fabian work.[24] There was, however, widespread goodwill towards the Society, and on this Margaret did not hesitate to capitalise. As Harold Wilson recalled:

> she always had the right of access to Labour Prime Ministers, and would press her ideas hard, be they in Fabian or in LCC interests . . . [later] she would nobble me too for publicity purposes . . . although she didn't come all that often.[25]

Margaret continued as honorary secretary to the Society until 1953, when she resigned soon after she had finished working with Dick Crossman on *New Fabian Essays*. This had been Douglas' brain-child, and initially he had chaired a group of Fabian specialists which included Members of Parliament Anthony Crosland, Denis Healey, Roy Jenkins and Ian Mikardo. During the gestation period Douglas resigned in passionate disagreement over Labour's foreign policy, particularly its attitude over the Korean War. Subsequently Douglas played little active part in Fabian Society politics, but he did not break with Fabianism. Indeed, he became President in 1952, and remained so until his death.

The essayists met regularly at Gavin Faringdon's home, Buscot Park, Berkshire, and Margaret often attended with her friend Rosamund Broadley, one of Douglas' secretaries who had become particularly indispensable to him and who acted as amanuensis.[26] It is noticeable from reading annotated drafts of early discussion papers how defensively Margaret would take issue with critics of Douglas' ideas. The essays were an attempt to fill 'the dangerous hiatus of thought and action' which had yawned since the election of the Labour Government and the completion of the Fabian programme. As the editors explained in the Introduction, 'they sought a new analysis of the political, economic and social scene as a basis for reformulating Socialist principles'.[27]

Margaret contributed a chapter on 'Education and Social Democracy' in an attempt to bridge 'the most glaring gap' in the Labour Party programme — a gap which had certainly handicapped Ellen Wilkinson and other Labour Ministers of Education. Assuming that socialists aimed at an egalitarian society, she outlined some of the major impediments to achieving that aim, of which the existence of private schools was one major factor. In this context she analysed the little understood implications of the 'common or multilateral' school, as comprehensives were then called (and of which she became the Labour Party's most lucid exponent), and concluded by urging one of her essential beliefs — the need to inject a humane attitude into administration: 'Anyone who has worked in education must know the harm that can be done by a single act of apparent injustice . . . and how much confidence can be generated by vigilant humanism on the part of the [local] authority.'[28] When published, the book was widely discussed and well received, although the editors recognised it could not hope to make the impact of the original *Fabian Essays* of 1889, which made socialism a best seller!

> We cannot write today without a much soberer consciousness of history, and a much more acute scepticism about the particular interpretation we give it . . . We do not claim either finality or comprehensiveness . . . but if the *Essays* ask some of the new, pertinent questions, their authors will be content.[29]

It also prompted two leading feature articles in *The Times*, which, although ignoring Margaret's specific contribution, concluded that the book 'had cleared away a lot of undergrowth which had long obscured socialist thinking'.

In 1961 her extremely readable *Story of Fabian Socialism* appeared, which supplemented and continued the earlier history by Edward Pease, the Society's first secretary. This graphic account of the fluctuating fortunes of the Society is enlivened by anecdotes of great Fabian figures. Certain hurried passages in the book caused Leonard Woolf to review it ungenerously in the *Political Quarterly* for wordy overwriting. And indeed although the offending passages are few, he had some justification. But his allegations that Margaret had deliberately underplayed the contribution of the

Webbs to Fabian development in order to enhance Douglas' reputation were both unfounded and unfair, and distressed her greatly.
Indeed the high regard and affection in which she held both
Beatrice and Sidney are patent in her many relevant writings. Only
rarely did Margaret commit errors of style, but it should be remembered that while working on this particular book she had been
under great personal stress. Douglas' health was visibly deteriorat-
ing, she was heavily committed on the LCC, and had been ill herself intermittently. Although she firmly believed in the axiom that
private anxieties should not intrude into public commitment, there
were limits to its fulfilment. Inevitably an extended correspondence
ensued, for Margaret had understandably been hurt by the seeming
disloyalty of a long-standing colleague as well as the unfairness of
his attack. She must, however, have been somewhat mollified by
Woolf admitting to her privately that probably 'I ought not to have
reviewed the book.' The reason he did so was that 'I wanted to read
it, but being a publisher I never buy books and am apt to review a
book if I want to read it.'[30]

If Margaret's work for the Society changed after Douglas' death
to being advisory rather than administrative, she remained watch-
fully available. When in 1962 she stood down from the Executive
'to make way for younger people', the chairman, Tony Crosland,
wrote expressing

> the extreme regret and deep gratitude from all members of the
> Executive . . . not just for the number of years' service you have
> given . . . but quite simply for the fact that you have done more
> for the Society than any living person. The Executive will not be
> the same without you . . . You are not only our foremost
> historian, but also our Patron and friend.[31]

Past and present general secretaries wrote in similar vein, not
least Shirley Williams, expressing gratitude for Margaret's
'forbearance':

> I have learnt a lot about the Fabian tradition from you . . . and I
> am glad that this was so. It seemed singularly appropriate, since I
> also learnt a great deal from your husband at meetings of the
> Cole Group when I was up at Oxford.[32]

In recognition of Margaret's yeoman service to the Society, she was elected President in 1962, and after a celebratory dinner wrote appreciatively to the general secretary:

> I shall not forget it easily, not the kind things that were said . . . I did almost feel that Asa [Lord Briggs] had given me a handsome obituary, but I assure you that I shall still be available for any help you want.[33]

And so she was, always ready to advise upon any matter of Fabian import and ever insistent that standards must be maintained. In a small Society, she told Dr Brian Harrison, the way to be influential 'is not by passing resolutions, but by getting down to work',[34] and quoted her favourite precept of Sidney Webb: 'The Fabian Society is a society of individuals'.

Above all, it was in recounting to research workers and others details of the Society's history with wit and perfect recall that Margaret excelled. Nothing angered her more than being interviewed by those who had not delved into Fabiana carefully, and she was especially scornful of the investigator who 'takes no account of the previous work of real scholars, and who doesn't want to trouble to know enough about environmental conditions to evaluate his interview'. To the genuine scholar/researcher, however, Margaret would patiently relay facts and experiences, spiced with wit, and offer pertinent guidance over sources. She had one strong reservation about history written for research degrees. 'In our time', she wrote to Robin Page Arnot, 'historians, if they wanted to be published, had to learn to write English. Now they don't, and the result is not a book, but a bed of crackly thorns, often full of mistakes!'[35]

Until her mid-eighties, Margaret assiduously attended Fabian functions and annual general meetings, at which — from the front row — she would make audible, often sharp, asides or mumbled criticisms of misjudged policies. As she became increasingly deaf her articulation, never of the best, did become difficult to follow, but that mumbling invariably contained gems of wisdom. If impatient younger Fabians found her an irritant, as half a century earlier she and Douglas had the Webbs, one long-standing member, Sybil Jeger, sagely observed that although Margaret on occasion could be excessively annoying, she was widely respected for her practical approach and 'contributions of earthy commonsense'.[36] The summation came from Margaret herself. 'When one is old, and one wants to keep in touch,' she wrote to Jane a few years before she died, 'one must be prepared to do some work.' And this she always was.

Notes

1. M. I. Cole, *Life of G. D. H. Cole* (Macmillan, London, 1971), p. 227.
2. M. I. Cole to Beatrice Webb, October–November 1939, Fabian Society Papers, Nuffield College, L/42.
3. Diaries of Beatrice Webb, 29 June 1940, British Library, vol. 54, fo. 6914.
4. M. I. Cole, Lecture, Fabian Easter School, 1972.
5. Fabian Society Papers (probably spring 1944), C62/2.
6. M. I. Cole to Richmond Postgate (CFP).
7. Fabian Society Papers, F58/3.
8. M. I. Cole to Dorothy Fox, 7 May 1943 (in the possession of Dorothy Fox).
9. Dorothy Fox, interview.
10. Fenner Brockway, Fabian Lecture, June 1984.
11. John Parker, letter to author, 21 February 1985.
12. M. I. Cole to Dorothy Fox, 7 May 1943 (in the possession of Dorothy Fox).
13. Fabian Society Papers, 18 July 1940, A56, fos. 1–12.
14. M. I. Cole to Richmond Postgate, 20 December 1942 (CFP).
15. M. I. Cole to Richmond Postgate, 16 June 1943 (CFP).
16. M. I. Cole to Richmond Postgate, 26 July 1943 (CFP).
17. M. I. Cole to Richmond Postgate, 17 November 1943 (CFP).
18. M. I. Cole to Leonard Woolf, 2 November 1946, Leonard Woolf Papers, Sussex University.
19. Fabian Society Papers, 31 January 1947, A11/1.
20. Marjorie Nicholson, letter to author, 2 February 1982.
21. M. I. Cole, *The Story of Fabian Socialism* (Heinemann, London, 1961), p. 333.
22. Sir Harold Shearman and others.
23. Cole, *The Story*, p. 301.
24. Sir Leo Pliatzky, letter to author, 18 March 1983.
25. Sir Harold (Lord) Wilson, interview.
26. Mrs Broadley was not only a first-class secretary, she was also remarkably perceptive. When secretary to the great and controversial educationist Sir Michael Sadler (1886–1943), she unerringly selected Douglas' application form from the many submitted for the Readership in Economics at Oxford. And in this she was at one with Sadler! Cole, *Life*, p. 141.
27. R. S. Crossman (ed.), *New Fabian Essays* (Turnstile Press, London, 1952).
28. *New Fabian Essays*, p. 20.
29. *New Fabian Essays*, Introduction.
30. Leonard Woolf to M. I. Cole, 5 July 1962, Leonard Woolf Papers.
31. Anthony Crosland to M. I. Cole, 24 September 1962 (CFP).
32. Shirley Williams to M. I. Cole, 7 October 1962 (CFP).
33. M. I. Cole, 6 March 1963, Fabian Society Papers, G67/115.
34. M. I. Cole to Dr Brian Harrison, 31 July 1975 (CFP).
35. M. I. Cole to Robin Page Arnot, 4 June 1975 (CFP).
36. Sybil Jeger, interview.

9 THE WEBBS AND THE COLES

An Incomparable Partnership

The influence of Beatrice and Sidney Webb upon Margaret and
Douglas, initially through the Fabian Society, was pervasive and
long-standing. It dated from the anti-collectivist Guild Socialist
days of the FRD, after which 'rollicking opposition' matured into
deep admiration and friendship, and on Beatrice's death in 1943
Margaret could write to Sidney, 'both Douglas and I owe more to
her — and to you, too — than we can ever say', to which Douglas
added, 'You have been an incomparable partnership and have
meant a great deal to us who have tried to follow in your footsteps.'[1]

Margaret assessed the Webbs' inseparable contribution to the
Labour Movement — and by implication to her own understanding
— in terms of research, propaganda, social institutions and policy
formulation. The Webbian approach to research insisted upon the
importance of searching for facts and in formulating proposals
accordingly, 'even when those facts turned out to be not what they
expected to find'.[2]

The towering range of the Webbs' research produced, among
their many books, the seminal *History of Trade Unionism*,
Industrial Democracy and the monumental series on *English Local
Government* which, as Margaret observed, 'has been supplemented
but will never be superceded'. Indeed, their collaboration was so
complete that Bernard Shaw declared, 'I cannot lay my hand on a
single sentence and say this is Sidney or that is Beatrice.'[3]

The Webbs' propaganda technique, based on the objective study
of facts, was effected largely by way of Fabian permeation: by their
advising and influencing those who wielded power. As for example
in Beatrice's Minority Report to the Poor Law Commission, which
Sidney drafted: for although its ideas failed to sway the government of the day they became a main plank in building the welfare
state. It was because the Labour Party accepted the Minority
Report and supported the Webbs' National Committee for the
Prevention of Destitution that Sidney and Beatrice became

members, and exerted a strong Fabian influence therein. Sidney drafted, with Arthur Henderson, the Party's 1918 Constitution, and a major policy statement, *Labour and the New Social Order*. This was before his distinguished work on the Sankey Commission on the Coal Mines, his election to Parliament, and his becoming a (not notably successful) Cabinet Minister. Tangible evidence of the Webbs' achievements lay in the social institutions they created: namely the London education system (devised in conjunction with Dr William Garnett, Education Adviser to the LCC), in the re-planned University of London, the founding of the *New Statesman*, and in the London School of Economics, which they established.

Arguably their most indestructible bequest to posterity was Beatrice's diaries. They were written by her alone, and were begun long before her marriage, but without 'the Other One' as she called Sidney, their joint deliberations and their joint experiences, the contents — like her life — would have been incomplete. As a record of politicians and policy making, of social conditions and change viewed from the inside wherein the Webbs operated, the diaries are unsurpassed.

The excellence of the Webbs' work was not in the forefront of Margaret's mind when she first encountered Beatrice. She merely thought her 'infinitely frail and old-looking . . . and when one is twenty, a thirty year gap seems enormous . . . Then we were all Guild Socialists, brash and rude, but as the war boom died away so did the uppishness which went with it.'[4] With her sensitive appreciation of sheer quality, however, Margaret came to realise that Beatrice was unique.

The Webbs, for their part, benignly tolerant and wholly without rancour, readily identified ability in the young, and in the mid-twenties invited Margaret and Douglas to Passfield Corner, their much-loved Hampshire home. After the first of their many visits Beatrice noted in her diary:

> GDH Cole and his wife — always attractive because they are at one disinterested and brilliantly intellectual and, be it added, agreeable to look at — stayed with us — middle age [Margaret was 33!] finds them saner and more charitable in their outlook . . . Cole still dismisses this man or that with 'I hate him', but this is the remnant of a mannerism . . . [and] he is disillusioned about Workers' Control.

She concluded, with a sharp flash of insight, 'despite a desire to be
rebels against all conventions, the Coles are the last of the Puritans.
GDH will end, I think, by being a scholarly historian; certainly his
Life of Cobbett is his best bit of work.'[5] A mellowing Margaret
wrote appreciatively to her hostess,

> It is a long time since we have spent so pleasant and comfortable
> a weekend . . . it is a real privilege to meet and to know better
> two people . . . who have done, I think, more for the Labour
> Movement and the cause of knowledge than anyone else living —
> unless we (don't) except Shaw![6]

Admiration seemed mutual, for two years later Beatrice commented, 'Cole and his wife . . . are perfectly harmonised partners
at work . . . altogether model citizens as well as exceptionally
attractive friends . . . among the most distinguished I have met in
mental make-up.'[7]

Later she tempered regard with criticism, disapproving of the
Coles' 'unremitting brain work with no open air exercise, daily
doses of whiskey and continuous smoking'. Since these remarks
were written only months after the diagnosis of Douglas' illness,
their mode of work was defensible, and indeed Beatrice concluded,
'I like them both . . . they are honest and disinterested, dutiful and
loyal to causes and friends, and personally attractive.'[8]

'A Kind of Umbrella'

By the mid-thirties Beatrice regarded the Coles as 'old friends and
associates' even though for a long while Margaret felt that
'Douglas was, in her eyes, the important person, and I a kind of
umbrella he was allowed to bring with him!'[9] Indeed, although
Beatrice placed Margaret and Douglas among 'the most active and
respected intellectuals of the Labour Party . . . turning out count-
less books, articles and detective stories with amazing industry and
skill', and quoted with relish Douglas' dictum that 'if you are in
active life it was useless to be a pessimistic fatalist; you have to fight
back for the right side for all you are worth' (she noted with
approval that 'he and she do it'),[10] it is significant that until the
Second World War Beatrice rarely, if ever, referred to Margaret's
activities independently of Douglas. 'For both the Coles I have a

respect,' she wrote, gratified by the Fabian revival, adding that

> the Fabian Society dominated by the Coles is rapidly increasing
> its membership and developing branches throughout the country
> . . . [and] altogether is the centre of life and learning in the
> Labour Party . . . They are carrying out Fabian policy of tolera-
> tion for all types of socialistic thought.[11]

Yet although aware of Douglas' involvement with the Nuffield
Survey at Oxford and with Beveridge in London, Beatrice seemed
wholly to underestimate Margaret's personal commitment to the
Society at Dartmouth Street during the war. One can only conclude
that she identified the Coles' partnership as being similar to that of
her own, and therefore regarded the work of Margaret and Douglas
as inseparable.

A warm relationship had, however, developed between the two
women, and Beatrice was increasingly pleased when Margaret
visited Passfield Corner with or without Douglas, sometimes from
Fabian schools at nearby Frensham, and occasionally taking her
'enigmatic but significant small boy' with her. Both women
enjoyed political gossip enormously, and Margaret was adept at its
relaying. During the latter months of her life, Beatrice noted that
Margaret was 'very affectionate to the aged Webbs, and pleased at
the prospect of being one of our executors'.[12] Earlier she had
recorded: 'Barbara Drake and I discussed the disposal of the Webb
property as Sidney and I are adding a codicil to our will, appointing
two Trustees in place of the two no longer desirable.' At this time
the Trustees were Barbara Drake, Professor Sir Alexander Carr-
Saunders, Professor Harold Laski, C. M. Lloyd and Herbert
Morrison. Lloyd, however, was dying and Morrison had become
'reactionary and anti Soviet', and was therefore unacceptable, so
they appointed at Barbara Drake's suggestion John Parker MP and
Margaret Cole. In Beatrice's opinion, 'she will represent GDH Cole
and herself . . . They practically share our views.' Near the concluding pages of her diary Beatrice wrote, almost complacently:

> The Fabian Society under leadership of the Coles, Laski,
> Kingsley Martin and John Parker remains the most influential of
> political propaganda organisations for the socialist reconstruc-
> tion of the world, whether at home or abroad . . . Margaret Cole
> asked me if I would help to organise the Diamond celebration

of its foundation. 'If I am still alive,' I answered.[13]

Beatrice, then suffering from cystitis and a paralysed colon, was enduring severe pain. The penultimate entry in her diary reads: 'I find living a painful experience . . . but it is clear that so long as Sidney is alive I could not leave him. When he is dead I shall at once disappear gladly, and by my own act.'[14] Eleven days later she died peacefully, not by her own hand.

Eulogies over Beatrice's achievements were world-wide. Margaret paid her personal tribute in a deeply affectionate biography, written with Sidney's blessing, *Beatrice Webb* (1945). It was not intended to be a definitive Life, but, she wrote, 'a brief account for this generation of the life and times of the greatest woman I have ever known, set down by one who had the privilege of being her friend and fellow worker within the Fabian Society'.[15]

The book pleased Sidney ('I am glad that you think the book good. Of course I could not expect you to agree altogether with my evaluations,' Margaret wrote to him) and many friends. Bernard Shaw commented that the book, 'extraordinarily well-informed, did not contain a superfluous or thoughtless word'; it was beyond criticism, because 'No critic, with the possible exception of myself, knows half as much about the Webbs, or understands that knowledge, as Mrs Cole.'[16]

While she was working on this book, Sidney granted Margaret access to the voluminous diaries which Beatrice had kept for over seventy years. He had always said that Beatrice's illegible scrawl was sufficient to keep them secret.[17] (Indeed Beatrice could not always read her own handwriting: 'You had to guess, occasionally . . . one would ask on a postcard "What did you say on this?" And she would reply, "I don't know"!') Margaret, immensely excited, was not easily defeated. 'I was the first person who ever read the Diaries; even Sidney hadn't seen them,' she told C. H. Rolph.

They were stacked in brown paper parcels at Passfield Corner and I went down with Barbara Drake and sat up till four in the morning reading . . . by which time I really could not see them! I had to go down twice again to read the rest.[18]

The next record about the Webbs was published in 1948, the year after Sidney's death. Margaret, with Barbara Drake, edited *Our Partnership (1892–1911)* which Beatrice had planned as a sequel to

My Apprenticeship, and for which Margaret compiled an exhaustive biographical index. This book she considered 'was much more than a personal record: it was a slice of English social history'.

LSE and the Webbs' Biography

The following year Margaret edited *The Webbs and their Work*, which, contrary to Professor Harold Laski's spiteful assessment as being 'quite an unimportant book', is probing and perceptive. It depicted different facets of the Webbs' activities, in chapters contributed by friends and colleagues when memories were still green. Margaret wrote a vivid and precise account of labour research.

While working on this book, and in her capacity as a Trustee to a foundation set up to facilitate research from funds of the Webbs' estate (the Passfield Trust) Margaret became entangled in a curious controversy over an abortive biography of Sidney. Some 18 months after Sidney's death Professor Carr-Saunders, Director of the LSE, on behalf of the Trust invited Professor Tawney to write a life of Sidney. Tawney refused, partly because of pressure of work, but primarily because 'Mrs Cole was doing the *Webbs and their Work*, and also editing Beatrice Webb's *Diaries*'. Carr-Saunders, prepared to wait, wrote:

> Yes, I know about Mrs Cole's book. It is an odd performance that one of the Trustees should jump in in this fashion. It cannot but be awkward for the author of a (projected) biography — but you know what Mrs Cole is, and will realise that we cannot stop her,[19]

a comment not distinguished for generosity of thought.

Later Margaret wrote to Tawney expressing pleasure that he was to undertake the biography, and explaining that at the suggestion of Barbara Drake the Trustees had asked her to prepare for publication a volume of Beatrice's diaries (from 1912 to 1924): 'I hope you will not think it conflicts with what you may do . . . It will be published well before you start to write.'[20] Tawney was noncommittal and Margaret wrote again saying:

> Douglas and I will be glad to help in any way. This volume of

the Diaries will be well away before you need them at all . . . I have edited a book on the *Webbs and their Work* which comes out this summer which you may find of interest . . . The essays range from Shaw to Pease to Kingsley Martin. This is why . . . it is coming out in a hurry — before the contemporaries die![21]

Tawney finally declined to write the Life, but admitted that 'in all fairness . . . Mrs Cole . . . appeared to be unconscious that she had done anything to which exception could be taken'. Indeed, Margaret was oblivious to the various undercurrents until June, when writing from Carradale, she explained to Tawney:

> I was horrified to learn from Carr-Saunders yesterday that you took so serious a view of my book of Essays . . . if I had the remotest idea of your reactions I should not have mentioned it to you in that casual way in a letter . . . I was asked to make this collection not as a Trustee, but as an old friend of the Webbs shortly after Sidney's death, and before there was any considera-tion of an official Life . . . the other Trustees were informed about eighteen months ago and none raised any doubts . . . It did not occur to anyone that a book of Essays upon two figures, whose interests for historians and sociologists must be perennial, could in any way interfere with an official and scholarly biography . . . [My] book is essentially ephemeral.

Apologising for 'any discourtesy', she continued:

> considering the length of our acquaintance I feel you might have written me direct when you got my letter, rather than leave me with a blast of which I had no warning, though you it seems had spoken personally both to Carr-Saunders and to Laski . . . I don't think it quite fair to pillory me before the Trustees as one who had wantonly prevented the best person available from writing Sidney's Life, do you? I am sorry, to quote Sidney, 'for having been betrayed into a little heat', but I do feel rather ill-used.[22]

Laski, writing to Tawney, exercised no generosity:

> I had no idea, nor I think had Carr-Saunders, that Mrs Cole, apart from the Diary, had embarked on these ambitious projects

and I do feel very strongly . . . that this has been a grave breach
of her responsibility as a Trustee . . . I have as you know a deep
affection for the Webbs, and I feel as though Mrs Cole had taken
over their legacy as a permanent source of income[23]

to which Tawney replied, 'Even if Mrs Cole's present work could
be withdrawn, which obviously it cannot be, differences arising
from her position as a Trustee . . . with a taste for bookmaking on
the Webbs, would still remain.'[24]

In one final attempt to persuade Tawney to reconsider, Laski
wrote later conveying the 'reborn eagerness of the Trustees' and
suggesting that it was reasonably possible to safeguard him 'against
the interference of that not too divine lady . . . As to the *Webbs
and their Work*, apart from the contribution of GBS I thought
most of it a mixture of the ungenial and the fatuous.'[25] Tawney's
petulance and Laski's spite seemed indefensible in view of
Margaret's genuine eagerness for a biography to be written. What,
however, makes the hostility towards her appear so unjust is that
she told the Trustees of her commitment, made at the behest of
Barbara Drake, long before the Life had been contemplated. The
whole affair smacks of academic and personal rancour.

A Second Attempt

Two decades after the dust of the Tawney fracas had settled, the
Trustees tried again. In 1967 they authorised Dr Royden Harrison
(later Professor), then at Sheffield University, to write the official
Life of the Webbs and their times and made generous grants to that
end. Margaret, who had a warm opinion of Harrison, agreed with
her colleagues that no censorship should be exercised over the
work, and the following year Harrison wrote to Margaret:

I am delighted that you look forward to my book. I am as keen
that it should make an early appearance as you are . . . but I do
want it to be as definitive in character as can properly be
expected.[26]

Earlier he had told Professor Robson, then the Trustees' chairman,
that he hoped to have 100,000 words in typescript by that
October.[27] The final manuscript had to be submitted by autumn
1971, and 'I believe I will meet that date.'[28]

1. Margaret Isabel Postgate, c. 1899

2. Margaret Isabel Postgate at university

3. Margaret Cole, *c.* 1922

4. Sidney and Beatrice Webb. Early days of The Partnership, 1894 (Courtesy of the British Library of Political and Economic Science)

5. Sidney and Beatrice Webb. Later days at Passfield Corner, *c.* 1940 (Courtesy of The British Library of Political and Economic Science)

10. Raymond Postgate (with Mr White of J. Lyons), *c.* 1956

11. Chairman, Further Education Committee, LCC (*c.* 1958)

12. Dame Margaret with Michael Foot, MP, at the University of Sussex, April 1976 (Courtesy of the *Evening Argus*)

13. Margaret and G.D.H. Cole at Freeland. *The Bystander*, 20 April 1938 (photograph by Howard Coster)

The time factor, however, had been greatly underestimated. Several years later Harrison was explaining to John Parker that 'the Life had forced itself into two volumes'[29] and later still Professor Robson, testily seeking a progress report, wrote:

I believe that you have been working on the Life for six or seven years, and although I am sure you are a perfectionist that does seem a very long time. I understand that Nelson are no longer going to publish.[30]

Margaret, anxious only for a good book to be produced, had written several critically helpful letters to Harrison. On one occasion she gently admonished him for being ungenerous about a *Life of Beatrice Webb* by Kitty Muggeridge, her niece, and Ruth Adam:

I don't think it as negligible as you . . . though it is certainly weak on the public side . . . I think the general conclusion is wrong . . . but it is an interpretation made by someone who knew Beatrice personally over quite a long period, and as such has to be taken into consideration.[31]

The Trustees, now chaired by John Parker, were 'becoming heartily tired', since they could only insist that 'the book should be published in a dignified manner suitable to the importance of such a biography', and since legally the Passfield Trust should have been wound up ten years previously, Robson agreed with Parker that 'There is no use waiting any longer for the biography before terminating the Trust.'[32] And this they did.

It was indicative of Margaret's high opinion of Harrison that she had offered to stand as guarantor if Trust funds did not cover the total cost of his research.[33] In the event the Trustees had resources enough, but no biography emerged. As Robson had surmised, Harrison was too great a perfectionist.

Margaret's hopes for a definitive biography of the Webbs were not, then, to be realised, and by the time this had become obvious, she was not well enough to undertake the project herself. The pity was that the Trustees had lacked both the vision and the generosity of spirit to commission her after Tawney had finally withdrawn. Posterity has been the poorer.

Ironically it was not until the Fabian Society centenary that a scholarly biography of the Webbs by Dr Lisanne Radice did in fact appear. This, together with the outstanding publication of Beatrice's complete *Diaries*, edited in four volumes by Professor Norman and Jeanne MacKenzie, would have surely satisfied Margaret's exacting standards.

Beatrice's Diaries

The diaries, some thirty-odd volumes, were never intended for publication, but merely as a 'source and record' written in the early hours, during Beatrice's frequent bouts of insomnia. Partly because she disregarded Sidney's exhortation of 'no personalities please', partly because Beatrice never attempted to justify herself in the eyes of contemporaries or posterity, the sheer quality of content make the diaries (as Margaret wrote) 'a most remarkable quarry for historians'.

Margaret did in fact edit two volumes of the diaries herself, after *Our Partnership*. They covered the periods 1912–24 and 1924–32 and were published in 1952 and 1956 respectively. Much material had then to be omitted, partly to avoid excessive length, partly because there were personal passages (concerning Joseph Chamberlain) 'some of which Beatrice had clearly typed herself and . . . I concluded that she never would have published them.' It is certainly apparent in the Appendix to volume 2 on 'Beatrice and Chamberlain' that Margaret (presumably out of affection for Beatrice) greatly underplayed the intensity of Beatrice's feelings for Chamberlain. However, with the passing of time, this the MacKenzies were able fully to reveal in their recent edition of the *Diaries*. Margaret also excised passages 'which appeared either libellous or likely to give pain to those mentioned'.[34]

The Passfield Trust did consider publishing a third volume and twice asked Margaret to read and report; but she did so unfavourably. As the Webbs were virtually in retirement from 1933, much of what Beatrice wrote after that year, Margaret pointed out, was hearsay or ephemeral — such as the long conversations she had with Ivan Maisky, the Soviet ambassador, much of which was already in *Soviet Communism* — so the material would neither be 'of great public value nor enhance the Webbs' reputations'.

Soviet Communism

Margaret was not unsympathetic to their last massive book, *Soviet Communism — A New Civilisation?* She recognised that it was a most remarkable feat for two septuagenarians to have the energy and intellectual curiosity even to want to visit, let alone write about, the Soviet Union; but it was a country with which the Webbs had fallen 'hopelessly in love'. Margaret, however, explained, even if she did not wholly defend, their volte-face from profound scepticism about Russia's central planning and workers' control to their devoted enthusiasm over planned production for community consumption. The sudden change in their allegiance, she conceded, did take some people by surprise. 'No prominent right-wing socialists had eaten their own printed words so wholeheartedly . . . people might have guessed. Douglas and I did not have to, we had heard them talking.' The reasons she gave for this change were

> chagrin at their failure in the 1929 government, of which Sidney [as well as Beatrice] was quite aware, and which bit deep, because it was as an administrator — at which he ought to have been good — that he made such a mess . . . and (secondly) they thought they had found a perfect, or perfectible, administration with no sentimental nonsense about the triumph of the underdog about it.[35]

The Webbs were sometimes criticised for making up their minds about what they would find before they had looked at the facts on the spot, 'thus doing exactly the opposite of what Beatrice had so praised in the case of Charles Booth in his great London Survey'. This criticism, Margaret considered, was well founded, for paradoxically 'They did regard with the gravest suspicion any fact which did not fit into the picture they were evolving, and young volunteer investigators were sometimes told to go away and find a more amenable one.' Further, 'although . . . in *Soviet Communism* they paid attention to features of the regime which they saw and did not like, they were very resistant to facts reported by other writers which tended to conflict with their own conclusions'.[36] Nevertheless, putting into context the book which is too often summarily dismissed, Margaret considered that it was

less of a blinkered encomium than some of those who have never bothered to read it through would believe. It is true that the Webbs in parts of that book are dealing with subjects, such as agriculture, about which they did not know nearly enough, and that they were too ready to accept official answers to their questions; nevertheless, they did ask many questions, and it must always be remembered that in 1932, the year of their visit, Soviet Russia seemed to many more eyes than theirs to be the hope of the world.[37]

Probably the neatest epithet on the Webbs' Soviet venture came from Margaret in her tribute on Beatrice's eightieth birthday:

> Anyone who knows the Webbs will agree that at eighty years old Mrs Webb shows more eagerness to understand and welcome new developments than most people half her age. There will not, I fear, be another book like *Soviet Communism*: but if there were ever a case for the fulfilment of Shaw's *Back to Methuselah* prophecies it is here.[38]

Another Mr and Mrs Webb?

Occasionally Margaret and Douglas have been described as 'another Mr and Mrs Webb', but this, though flattering, is untenable. Indeed, as Margaret insisted, they were 'emphatically not complementary to one another in the same way as that unique partnership', adding:

> We are in fact pretty different . . . the comparison is only true insofar as that politically we have pursued broadly the same end — Socialism — by broadly the same means — writing, organisation and propaganda — and that we have worked pretty hard for it.[39]

There were indeed marked contrasts between the couples. The Webbs were curiously elitist ('I know they were elitist,' Margaret wrote to Norman MacKenzie), well aware of the power and privilege that emanated from wealth, and interested in the concept of a new ruling aristocracy based on popular consent. And Beatrice, not Sidney, was acutely conscious of belonging to a class which habitually gave orders but seldom executed the orders of others.[40]

They are often seen as authoritarian in wanting to impose democracy from above, and 'were certainly not prepared to go as far as Cole in giving democratic rights to the workers'. For whereas the Coles believed in the participation of the many in the tasks of democratic self-government, with Sidney there was implicit caution. 'The masses', he wrote, 'will always be found apathetic, dense, and unreceptive to any unfamiliar idea.'[41]

The Coles were essentially disseminators and popularisers of information. Not only was Douglas a pioneer of social history, believing its function was 'to arm the worker with a sense of his own past which would create a confidence to make his own future',[42] but also both he and Margaret firmly believed that knowledge must not be esoteric. 'The specialist, in the interests of scientific precision,' they argued, 'has to write in the terminology of his own technique,' which shut him off from popular appeal, and this was where the social historian came in. In their view

it is his business to express the analyses and the conclusions of the specialist in terms which can be understood by any intelligent person prepared to take a little trouble. If the social historian takes proper care this process of popularisation need not distort the conclusions of the specialists. Most things which it is important for ordinary people to know . . . can be stated in untechnical language . . . [and] our motive has been to promote knowledge not for its own sake but with a view to action.[43]

The Webbs would have approved; but this was not wholly their method.

Graham Wallas once said that the Webbs were interested in town councils whereas he (like the Coles) was concerned with councillors. Indeed Margaret and Douglas underestimated neither the frailties nor the illogicalities of human nature, but the Webbs 'were such a completely contented unit in themselves that they just could not comprehend irrational emotionalism'.[44] Leonard Woolf went further: in his opinion, as a close friend, they were just not concerned with individuals. 'They were both . . . exceptionally humane and civilised people seeking to produce a civilised society . . . [but] they were doctrinaire, and their doctrine led them to concentrate almost exclusively upon the structure and function of government and institutions'[45] — that could never have been said of Margaret or Douglas.

This single-mindedness partly explains the Webbs' arid, almost philistine attitude towards the arts. Whereas Douglas collected beautiful glass, and Margaret was no mean critic of paintings, the theatre and music, the Webbs 'would scarcely have mourned the disappearance of all the art and literature in the world'. As a friend remarked:

> if they had been writing a book on Elizabethan England they would have lumped Shakespeare and all the poets, songwriters, and painters into one chapter along with the sanitary conditions in towns, and called the whole thing Amenities in the Elizabethan Age![46]

The Webbs' achievements merged so indefinably into the 'end product' that the contribution of either was indistinguishable. Only Beatrice's diaries are positively attributable, yet they would have been infinitely diminished without Sidney's ubiquitous presence. Margaret and Douglas, in contrast, worked both together and independently: perhaps the most personal significance of their partnership was the way Margaret grew from being consciously 'Douglas' Wife' (as Kingsley Martin saw her) into being Margaret Cole, distinguished in herself. For, as her friend Bernice Hamilton wrote after Douglas' death, 'You are so very much a person in your own right, and were never swallowed up in Douglas, as some wives are.'[47]

Certainly Margaret could never have said of Douglas as Beatrice did of Sidney, 'I tremble to think how utterly dependent I am on him both on his love and on his unrivalled capacity for putting things through.'[48] Nor would she have felt, as again Beatrice did after Sidney had had his first stroke, that 'we shall never march together again in work and recreation. I cannot march alone.'[49] For this is exactly what Margaret continued to do after she had come to terms with Douglas' death.

Notes

1. Passfield Papers, 1 May 1943, British Library, N/50, and 2 May 1943, N/101.
2. See M. I. Cole in Introduction to *Index to the Diaries of Beatrice Webb (1873–1943)* (Chadwick-Healey, Cambridge, in association with the London School of Economics and Political Science, 1978).
3. George Bernard Shaw, Introduction to Beatrice Webb, *My Apprenticeship*

(Penguin Books, London, 1938).

4. M. I. Cole, *The Webbs and their Work* (Frederick Muller, London, 1949), p. 160.

5. Diaries of Beatrice Webb, 5 September 1926, British Library, vol. 41, fos. 4381−4.

6. Passfield Papers, 7 September 1926, H/69.

7. Diaries of Beatrice Webb, 2 September 1928, vol. 42, fos. 4650−4.

8. Ibid., 10 December 1931, vol. 45, fos. 5220−2.

9. M. I. Cole, *Growing Up into Revolution* (Longmans Green, London, 1949), p. 135.

10. Diaries of Beatrice Webb, 11 September 1937, vol. 51, fos. 6380−1.

11. Ibid., 5 April 1942, vol. 56, fos. 7299−300.

12. Ibid., 25 September 1942, vol. 57, fo. 7400.

13. Ibid., 20 February 1943, vol. 57, fos. 7476−7.

14. Ibid., 19 April 1943, vol. 57, fo. 7513.

15. M. I. Cole, Preface to *Beatrice Webb* (Longmans Green, London, 1945), p. 5.

16. *Times Literary Supplement*, 20 October 1945.

17. S. K. Ratcliffe to M. I. Cole, 25 August 1954 (CFP).

18. M. I. Cole to C. H. Rolph, interview, 10 May 1971.

19. Tawney Papers, 20 December 1948, British Library, Box 24/1−5 (110); notes 20−25 taken from same source.

20. Ibid., 15 March 1949.

21. Ibid., 22 March 1949.

22. Ibid., 2 June 1949.

23. Ibid., 24 May 1949.

24. Ibid., 30 May 1949.

25. Ibid., 23 September 1949.

26. Professor Royden Harrison to M. I. Cole, 25 June 1968 (CFP).

27. Professor Royden Harrison to M. I. Cole, 4 June 1968 (CFP).

28. Professor Royden Harrison to M. I. Cole, 22 October 1969 (CFP).

29. Professor Royden Harrison to M. I. Cole, 8 September 1973 (CFP).

30. Professor W. A. Robson to M. I. Cole, 28 October 1975 (CFP).

31. M. I. Cole to Professor Royden Harrison, 26 May 1972 (CFP).

32. Professor W. A. Robson to John Parker MP, May 1976 (CFP).

33. John Parker, letter to author, 6 October 1982.

34. M. I. Cole to Patrick Davis, Publications Officer, LSE (British Library), 7 June 1970 (CFP).

35. M. I. Cole to Professor Royden Harrison, (probably June) 1972 (CFP).

36. M. I. Cole to Professor Royden Harrison, June 1972 and to Robin Page Arnot, 26 April 1972 (CFP and Hull University Archives, DAR/1/14).

37. Cole, Introduction to *Index*.

38. M. I. Cole, *New Statesman*, 22 January 1938.

39. Cole, *Growing Up*, pp. 77−8.

40. Kingsley Martin in *The Webbs and their Work*, p. 293.

41. A. W. Wright, *G. D. H. Cole and Social Democracy* (Clarendon Press, Oxford, 1979), p. 56.

42. Ibid., p. 147.

43. G. D. H. and M. I. Cole, *The Condition of Britain* (Gollancz, London, 1937), p. 20.

44. Cole, Introduction to *Index*.

45. Leonard Woolf in *The Webbs and their Work*, p. 261.

46. M. I. Cole (ed.), *Women of Today*, 1946 edition (Nelson, London, 1938), p. 272.

47. Bernice Hamilton to M. I. Cole, 24 February 1959 (CFP).

48. Lisanne Radice, *Beatrice and Sidney Webb*, (Macmillan, London 1984), p. 166 (16 February 1907).

49. Ibid., p. 310 (5 January 1938).

10 PUBLIC LIFE

Servant of the County

Margaret's deep admiration for Sidney Webb — 'the Napoleon of the Technical Education Board' — and London's network of secondary, technical and further education, coupled with her own long-standing commitment to adult education, explain her intense satisfaction at being co-opted on to the LCC Education Committee during the war. Joining such friends as Helen Bentwich, her brother Hugh Franklin, Barbara Drake and (Lady) Eleanor Nathan, she later was elected an Alderman and, with a brief break after Douglas' death, served until the demise of the LCC. Subsequently she sat on the Inner London Education Authority (ILEA) for two years, but stood down in 1967 to make way for a younger member.

In September 1941, at Herbert Morrison's suggestion, Margaret had become, in her own words, 'a Servant of the County', and assumed obligations independent of any work she might undertake with Douglas. Indeed he was not even remotely interested in the LCC, regarded it as a bureaucratic colossus and tended to deride Margaret's role. For her part, Margaret loved London, which she saw as a city grown from a clutch of villages, and was proud to be associated with the administration and development of Sidney Webb's heritage. Above all, she regarded the expansion of, and widening accessibility to, education at every level as essential for a strong democratic society. 'As the soldiers of Cromwell's army claimed three hundred years ago,' she wrote, '"the poorest He that is in England hath as much a life to live as the greatest He", and without education he cannot really live his life.'[1]

Comprehensive Schools

Throughout the war, London's County Council and councils of other great cities worked under intense pressure. In the sand-bagged cellars of County Hall the LCC Education Committee debated matters concerning the evacuation of schoolchildren, damaged buildings, the depletion of teaching staff, and above all plans for post-war secondary education.

The virtue of multilateral or common schools, as comprehensives were then known, became a burning educational issue — so much so that experienced cynics said it was the first time in years that the Education Committee had really discussed education.[2] The 1944 Education Act made secondary education free, and envisaged that provision for each and every child should be of equal concern to the nation. Soon after the Bill became law the LCC Education Committee embodied their wartime discussions in a report arguing the case for 'Comprehensive High Schools' which was accepted by Council. For although the Tory opposition did not subscribe to the comprehensive idea in general, it was willing then to see it tried out. Knowing this, the Minister in 1947 approved the London School Plan for developing secondary education, with 67 projected comprehensives.

Since building programmes for new schools could not be started immediately, the Committee, as an experiment, combined certain schools into quasi-comprehensives working in more than one building. Several such schools, notably Walworth (which was mixed), Peckham Boys' and Peckham Girls' — all in south-east London — were remarkably successful in spite of great physical difficulties. When, however, the building of new comprehensives was translated into planning reality the Tories went back on their agreement, tore the relevant building programmes to shreds and fought comprehensive development 'at large and in detail':

> They stage debate after debate in Committee and in Council; they fill the press with angry cries; they endeavour . . . by means of engineered propaganda among teachers, parents and even children . . . to ensure that each new school shall start life in an atmosphere of strife and prejudice . . . they want them to be failures,[3]

Margaret wrote, expressing her party's general exasperation.

The Education Committee, which had had notable educationalists such as Professor Tawney in its ranks, and in 1944 had drawn in (Sir) Harold Shearman, was indeed a 'powerful brainbox'. Yet it was Margaret who became the foremost publicist for comprehensive schools. Long before any relevant research studies were practicable, she explained their significance, countering bitter criticisms in numerous articles and pamphlets of outstanding lucidity, notably *What is a Comprehensive School?* and 'Comprehensives in London'.

A firm but undogmatic protagonist, she presented in the former pamphlet one of the clearest and most succinct expositions, stressing the flexibility essential in planning and organising comprehensive schools. She demolished the theory that there were only three types of children, Grammar, Technical and Modern, of which the grammar child was 'the best', and each type should be educated separately. This categorising, she argued, was a nonsense, for as with adults, so with children, there were not three but many types, and education should be suitably varied.

> We believe strongly that in a modern democratic community it is important, both socially and educationally, that children of all types shall learn to live with one another in youth; we believe that the advocates of 'segregated education' who would separate . . . five per cent of the nation's cleverest children at eleven years old and educate them apart from their fellows to become 'leaders' are making a great educational mistake . . . There is no process known which can reliably separate out the clever children so young . . . If they were so separated out and separately taught . . . they would never come across the important fact that everyone (including themselves) is a duffer at something; [so] . . . the most likely end-product would not be great leaders but small boffins.[4]

It was not, however, only a belief in social justice that made Margaret so keen an advocate. She added substance to theory from life at Roedean, and from her first-hand experience of secondary reorganisation acquired as a governor of schools, including Holloway School in north London, where she succeeded Lance Beales as chairman. She helped the school through the trauma of its becoming a comprehensive establishment, and in so doing showed herself infinitely understanding of both mundane administrative detail and human anxieties engendered by the uncertainty of change.

Meredith Brown, headmaster of Holloway during this crucial period, and later an LCC Senior Inspector, assessed Margaret's contribution warmly. When he was appointed, Holloway had three years to run as a grammar school: but the comprehensive idea was anathema to most of the staff (some of whom had been there for over forty years) and to the flourishing Old Boys' Association.

> I needed all the support and guidance I could get . . . and Margaret was remarkable . . . for although committed to the comprehensive idea, she was never so doctrinaire that she could not understand, and allow for, the feelings of others who did not share her views. This was very evident in her relationship with the staff, most of whom disagreed with her about the future plans for the school, but without exception had confidence in her . . . because she had experienced, and knew, the teachers' point of view . . . The staff knew, as events proved, that she would do her utmost to safeguard their interests and status. She even won over the Old Boys, and was guest of honour at their annual dinner! I am sure that in large measure the successful reorganisation was due to her wisdom, clarity and judgement.[5]

In spite of firm convictions Margaret almost always tolerated reasoned criticism, although she never lost sight of her objectives. As she wrote to her friend Agnes Murray when hostile public discussion was at boiling point:

> Certainly I don't mind your criticising comprehensive schools; if I gave that impression it was unintentional, though one gets a little prickly when so many people open remarks with 'your dreadful comprehensive schools' . . . I think at the start that Heads will organise the way they can best do it with the staff they have . . . They have a Conference of themselves which meets regularly and we hope for cross-fertilisation of ideas that way . . . but I dislike the party's 'comprehensive panacea propaganda' only less than I do that of the other side. One good result is that we are getting something done at last for Modern schools in areas where there ain't going to be no comprehensives. Some of my dyed-in-the-wool friends regret this, as taking the edge off the demand for comprehensives where it exists, but I think this is an irresponsible sacrifice of a generation.[6]

Margaret was also a governor of Camden Girls' School, linked under the Frances Mary Buss Foundation with North London Collegiate School, and with which through her mother she had a personal association. Doris Burchell, the head of Camden for over twenty years (1947–68) won her warm regard. Margaret as a governor supported her during gruelling years of discussion about the school's voluntary-aided status, its new site, post-war building programme and reorganisation. Her insight is shown in a shrewd account — again to Agnes Murray — of one ordinary governors' meeting:

There was a very complicated row between the Foundation and the Council officers about the price to be paid for the old Camden School. An old solicitor, Treasurer to the Foundation, behaved abominably and insulted the officers so that Houghton [London's Chief Education Officer, later Sir William] lost his temper, and wished to break off all negotiations . . . Miss Burchell was much depressed, well knowing that human nature being what it is, it is not good for an aided school to get the Council's officers feeling cross and injured![7]

The row was settled, but only after a lot of time had been spent in mollifying the irate participants. The chairman of governors, Canon Edward Carpenter (subsequently Dean of Westminister), fully appreciated Margaret's contributions to the well-being of both schools, and on her retirement wrote warmly that 'Your wide experience . . . your deep concern to enlarge opportunity in the educational field and the conscientious way you have attended meetings have added considerably to our deliberations.'[8] And later he remembered how Margaret

always sat in the same seat for our meetings, so if (and it was rare) she was not there, it seemed as if something significant was missing. She . . . had a low gruff voice, was never voluble, but when she spoke it was always to the point and with authority. People certainly listened to her, and took account of her suggestions. Her general mien was somewhat forbidding, and her known intellectual high quality could be off-putting, but everyone who knew her well realised that hers was a very warm heart . . . and that she had the interests of the girls at heart. Particularly as she was concerned with the less privileged: I felt that in her heart she was for the maintained system, though at the same time she was equally anxious to promote excellence and would seek to marry the two together . . . Her visions of a juster, more egalitarian and humane society remained with her throughout her life.[9]

This was a shrewd assessment: Margaret's heart lay indeed with improving the maintained system. Professor Lionel Elvin, a former Director of the London University Institute of Education, recalled arguing with her that the direct grant schools might be made the local authorities' answer to Winchester and Eton. This could be effected by LEAs increasing their grants and by insisting, in return, on 100 per cent public places. The existence of a number of such schools, he believed, 'would really pull up the educational level of the public sector'. With this Margaret strongly disagreed. She considered that direct grant schools were bastions of local snobbery, and that the basic solution was either for direct grant schools to go properly independent, or for them to come into the public system under the LEA. 'She came, of course,' Professor Elvin concluded, 'from an exceptionally good local education authority!'[10]

Further Education Sub-Committee

Although Margaret observed the progress of comprehensive schools carefully and critically, secondary education was not her prime interest. Her particular realm of responsibility was London's further education and its swiftly growing ramifications, and she served on its committee from 1948 until 1965. She was chairman from 1950 to 1960 and again from 1961 to 1965, and then when the Inner London Education Authority came into being, she was briefly vice chairman to Sir Harold Shearman on the newly created Further and Higher Education Committee. The range of responsibilities was vast, embracing student awards and a network of evening and recreational (now adult education) institutes, and specialist technical and teacher training colleges, each with their manifold problems of staffing, accomodation and maintenance. Yet she tackled everything with probing interest.

For the seventy-odd evening institutes providing non-vocational classes for over 150,000 men and women, Margaret had a wry affection. She saw the variety of classes as helping the many for whom there was no statutory education after their 'early leaving' to tackle the 'difficult and unnatural task of living in a big city'.[11] Whether it was cooking for newly weds, studying music, drama, ballet, acquiring skills, developing hobbies (live demonstrations of bee keeping or chicken rearing were not unusual at certain institutes) or learning karate or costume making, they were all, she wrote, 'thoroughly civilising in the proper meaning of the word'. She considered that all such classes fully justified the ratepayers' outlay, and resolutely guided her committee into keeping fees as low as practical. What was more, Margaret often visited institutes, and was always well briefed over their individual specialisms, which greatly pleased the principals. She well appreciated that to be the head of any sizeable educational body is a lonely operation. When Margaret temporarily relinquished the chairmanship of her committee after Douglas' death, the Association of LCC Principals and London Continuation Teachers wrote deeply regretting her absence, for they 'greatly valued her constant surveillance of their work and her support for their activities'.[12]

The London Youth Committee, which represented youth organisations of the London boroughs, was another responsibility. It reported regularly to the Further Education Committee but was a constant worry, because the flow of stable, dedicated leaders tended to wax and wane. Involved with their staffing problems, Margaret enjoyed visiting clubs to see what was happening and to meet youth leaders, so forging personal contacts which were excellent for staff morale. A former LCC Youth Officer in Paddington recalled one such visit over which, as a newcomer, he had been unduly apprehensive.

Colleagues had informed me that Mrs Cole could be very direct in asking questions and in expressing opinions. However, I found her pleasant, humorous and very knowledgeable . . . even after twenty years I can still remember the happy atmosphere she created.[13]

(Lord) Michael Stewart once commented in a speech to Fabians that acquiring higher education in England was made as difficult as possible by authority. Margaret, well aware of this, was keen to open up academic opportunities. She sought therefore to operate the Council's scheme for major awards and grants (for university courses, professional training, and some vocational studies) as generously and fairly as possible within the official framework. Under her chairmanship scales of assistance were upgraded and anomalies or obsolescent rulings adjusted, but with meticulous care, for she recognised the need to avoid errors of omission. In disposing of the obsolete, she warned:

Be careful that you do not inadvertently introduce fresh anomalies, with the possible result of depriving some student of a scholarship he or she ought to have had. You are playing with people's lives, and their chance of a career, not simply with legal tidiness.[14]

No one was more pleased than Margaret when as the scale and scope of eligibility for awards in further and higher education broadened, the numbers of London and overseas recipients rose dramatically.[15]

In the fifties the Council maintained nearly thirty prestigious institutions, technical colleges, art schools and colleges of commerce, for which Margaret's committee was also responsible. Many have now been vastly expanded, regrouped or assimilated, but even then several were nationally distinguished. There was, for example, the Central School of Arts and Design Crafts whose students played a big part in designing the Festival of Britain, and for which the LCC built the adjacent Jeanetta Cochrane Theatre; the London School (now College) of Printing; the Brixton School of Building, now part of the Polytechnic of the South Bank; and Westminster Technical College, with its Hotel School which provided memorable banquets on special occasions.

There were also 18 'non-provided' colleges, partly endowed by foundations or trusts, but mainly relying on the Council's substantial funding. This category ranged from all the big polytechnics to Toynbee Hall (a community centre if ever there was one — associated with reformers and socialist politicians), King Edward VII Nautical College in Poplar, and Morley College for adult education, whose music department was made famous by Gustav Holst and (Sir) Michael Tippett.

For Morley Margaret had special affection, partly because of her admiration for Principal Eva Hubback, but mainly because of the immense cultural variety and liveliness of its courses. The college had suffered badly in the Blitz, and Margaret did her utmost to get it into an early building programme. Mary (later Baroness) Stocks has recorded approvingly how Margaret continued Morley's 'guerilla tactics' by making spirited sallies on its behalf. During 1953 Margaret wrote to the Prime Minister, Winston Churchill, putting the matter fully before him, and conferred with the Minister of Education, Florence Horsburgh. She, however, merely reaffirmed her Department's previous refusal on the grounds that priority must go to the needs of schoolchildren and vocational education. Sir Harold Nicolson, diplomat and author, who was then Morley's president, wrote somewhat sourly of this overture:

> I go with Mrs G. D. H. Cole to see Florence Horsburgh. She has that sulky bewildered manner that I have noticed before in Fabians. Florence is ministerial and firm. We were asking that a licence be granted to rebuild Morley College. She replied that she cannot allocate material and labour without cutting down on primary and secondary school work, and they must have priority. Mrs Cole mumbles and grumbles that this is all nonsense — how can she prove it in steel and cement? I fear that I am always impressed when reasonable people meet my requests with reasonable denials . . . I can see that Mrs Cole regards me as a weak and useless brother.[16]

Sadly, it was many moons before Morley was rebuilt and its extension completed.

Through her committee Margaret was responsible for the appointment of entire governing bodies for, or individual nominees to, various institutions. These included London's seven Day Colleges (from which she had hoped in vain that the County Colleges proposed in the 1944 Act would evolve), five colleges of education, London University and various national bodies.[17] All this necessitated her securing political balance among lay nominees (usually by agreement with the minority party) and also finding knowledgeable, interested academics to serve on specialist institutions. Devising this was no sinecure. Ill-judged appointments could create a disproportionate amount of trouble, and Margaret took infinite care, through consultation with professional organisations and others, to find reliable nominees.

In order to circumvent rumblings of discontent, and also because she really was curious both to understand the inner workings of specialist institutions and to get to know staff individually, Margaret served herself on many governing bodies. When in May 1960 she was reappointed chairman of Further Education she wrote to Agnes Murray:

> I have been made chairman again . . . I'm not sure I want to go on for long, the ancillary commitments are so heavy . . . and I might want to be a bit looser . . . but I won't duck out now. I'm

on about fifteen bodies of one sort or another, apart from other things.[18]

In addition to secondary schools, these governing bodies included the Geffrye Museum, where as chairman for many years Margaret was remembered by her successor Hugo Bell as being 'decisive, concise, to the point',[19] Westminster Hotel and Technical School, the London School (College) of Printing, Chelsea Polytechnic, Camberwell School of Arts and Crafts, and Regent Street Polytechnic (later part of the Polytechnic of Central London), founded by Quintin Hogg, Lord Hailsham's grandfather.

She also represented the LCC (and later ILEA) on the council of Bedford College, London University. There she attended informal college gatherings, and during the mid-sixties was active on various sub-committees when the college was facing up to change. For the first time men were to be admitted, and in college government a more participatory style was emerging. Kathleen Spears, then secretary to the council, remembers that 'although Dame Margaret did not speak a lot, when she did it was to make a contribution penetrating and effective'. When the GLC did not renominate her, Dame Mary Smieton, the chairman of Council, recalled: 'we were sorry . . . it was suggested that Dame Margaret should be appointed an individual member, but although greatly touched, this she did not wish'.[20]

The Training of Teachers

After the war teacher training became a major educational issue. The baby bulge, the rebuilding of bombed schools and the raising of the school leaving age accentuated demand for qualified teachers which even the excellent results of the Emergency Training Scheme could not satisfy. When in 1957 training courses were expanded from two to three years, the equating of supply with demand became a matter of national concern. At this time the LCC, through the Further Education Committee, administered several training colleges: Avery Hill, Furzedown, Philippa Fawcett, Shoreditch, Garnett (for technical teachers) and Battersea. Later it assumed responsibility for Rachel MacMillan in Deptford and for Dartford College of Physical Education in Kent. Needs of the time, and government policy, urged expansion, and to this the LCC

Education Committee made substantial contribution. Not only were existing colleges such as Philippa Fawcett and Battersea College remodelled and expanded, but also new colleges, Manresa and Sidney Webb, were created.

Margaret was a governor of Battersea College of Domestic Science and Sidney Webb College of Education. She became chairman of both, and there is no doubt that of all her educational interests, training colleges in general and Sidney Webb in particular — which she had helped to create — were closest to her heart, not least because of the opportunities they offered to older women.

Battersea, under its distinguished Principal, Frances Laidler, had acquired a national reputation for training excellent teachers of home economics. After its elegant, if highly inconvenient, Georgian premises on Clapham Common had been extended and officially reopened by Dame Edith Evans, and after a London hotel (Cadogan Court) had been acquired, adapted and staffed as a hostel for Battersea students by the Further Education Committee, yet another project was started. Manresa House, a beautiful eighteenth-century Jesuit seminary at Roehampton, one of several great Palladian houses designed by Chambers, was purchased by the Council and adapted for training primary and secondary teachers. Here for the first time mature students, men as well as women, were recruited alongside school leavers. When the college opened in 1963 such was the cheerfully mixed intake that new students were endearingly dubbed 'Laidler's All-sorts'.

Administratively Manresa was joined with Battersea, under one governing body, and Margaret, who succeeded Dorothy Elliott (a distinguished trade union organiser who had nurtured the short-lived Institute of Houseworkers) as chairman, helped to effect its transformation. Like her co-governors Margaret admired the eighteenth-century buildings with beautiful ceilings, stone flagged passages, inner courtyard and curved wrought iron stair rails. When, prior to the Council's purchasing the property she had tried to visit with officers to inspect the premises, Margaret had been intensely amused at being denied access. For even though chairman of the responsible committee, as a woman she was prohibited at this stage from entering an all-male religious sanctum! Sadly, Battersea, Manresa and Cadogan Court have now been redesignated for other purposes, mainly to feed the maw of the South Bank Polytechnic and Garnett College. Needs change with the times.

In its day Manresa contributed handsomely by training keen and able teachers and over its development Margaret exercised a watchfulness and wisdom that was deeply appreciated. Frances Laidler, who never meted out praise without justification, wrote gratefully at the time of her own retirement:

> Throughout all the growth that had taken place you have been our main prop and stay . . . you are established as a person of authority and integrity . . . I realise I have made great demands upon you, but . . . (right from the beginning) I have known that it was you who fought for us and you who succeeded in obtaining all manner of advancement for us . . . It has been a great experience to have you as a chairman . . . There are not many people of your character and erudition.[21]

While the transformation of Manresa was in train, Margaret was also involved with the creation of Sidney Webb Training College for mature men and women teachers. She chaired the Advisory Committee which brought the College into existence (housed first in the Post Office buildings at Victoria and then in the centre of London, in Barrett Street), and was the prime mover in persuading the Education Committee to adopt the name Sidney Webb — sadly, an all too ephemeral tribute.

Apart from her ability to plan ahead, to cut through red tape, and to encourage her officers to get on with the job, Margaret's great strength lay in her excellent judgement: particularly in the interviewing and selection of staff. Rosemary Beresford, a former LCC District Inspector, highly regarded for her intellect and irreverent sense of humour, who was appointed Principal of Sidney Webb in autumn 1960 and subsquently became a close friend, graphically recalled her first encounter with Margaret.

> After two interviews and two and a half hours wait, I was summoned back to be offered the post. Margaret explained that the Advisory Committee wondered whether I had had adequate experience of institutional experience and life . . . however she explained they had decided that my experience with the LCC compensated for any shortfall . . . Through regular interviewing with Margaret during the next fourteen years I learnt that this was the type of speech she would make to a candidate whose appointment had been under dispute. A speech which invariably

indicated a principal source of criticism of the candidate, and counterbalanced this with an asset. It waved a warning flag to the appointee not to let his or her deficiency justify the doubters.

Margaret's technique of interviewing, Miss Beresford considered, was helpful, because it set the candidate on his mettle and also acted as a record of the queries that had been expressed. Even more importantly, it revealed Margaret's style of professional relationships:

These relationships were characterised by frankness — the more she regarded the colleague as a peer the franker she became — by impartiality, close attention to evidence and to its weight, and by a positive stance, the unobtrusive communication of an expectation that colleagues would justify the confidence reposed in them.[22]

This was the style she also brought to bear in her various political and administrative roles.

It was a personal tribute to Margaret that, although during her chairmanship the Tories won control of ILEA for a spell, she was re-elected to the chair of Sidney Webb, unopposed. Interestingly enough, had this been pushed to a vote, the staff governors (the Principal ascertained) would have unhesitatingly voted for Margaret 'by reason of their complete confidence' in her chairmanship. They were convinced that impartiality always dictated her judgements.

Margaret was chairman of Sidney Webb for ten years, after which she stood down, but remained a governor supporting it as hitherto through all the traumatic complexities of amalgamation with the Polytechnic of Central London. When in her late seventies Margaret relinquished the chair it was not only the Academic Board who wrote regretting her decision. The Student Union sent her a student scarf and badge 'as a token of our esteem and thanks, but with great sadness, for you are truly one of us', and added:

In many colleges a wide gulf exists between the Governors and students which has led to discontent . . . not so here. We know that in you we have had a good friend and guide, who has done so much to make the college a real community.[23]

No tribute could have pleased her more.

Margaret's 'acuteness of judgement', which Rosemary Beresford rightly assessed highly, although some might occasionally dub it 'acidulated comment', was often and wittily applied to the analysis and identification of specific problems. On one occasion when governors of Regent Street Polytechnic, long before amalgamation, were debating whether the institute should become more selective in the level of entrants accepted and in the range of courses offered, Margaret observed magisterially that 'the Polytechnic is in danger of becoming an intellectual Woolworths'. This summed the matter up, and a decision was taken to restrict the range and raise the level.[24]

Sidney Webb, Battersea and other smaller training colleges were soon to lose their identities. The pattern of need for teachers had changed dramatically during the sixties from a steep upward trend of demand to an abrupt decline in the early seventies. This was accelerated by married women, already trained, returning to teaching and by a falling birth rate. So, alongside this sharp reversal, the role of the small monotechnic came under close scrutiny and a policy of amalgamation and closure was evolved by the DES.

Margaret was one of the first to recognise that the days of Sidney Webb as an independent entity were numbered, a development that generally caused heart-searching, argument and sadness. After the Polytechnic of Central London had been created, and Sidney Webb absorbed as the nucleus of its Education School, the life of that School was short. A year later the DES decided that it must be phased out, which it was, within five years. Rosemary Beresford, who by virtue of Margaret's insistence as well as her own ability, became a Pro Proctor at the Polytechnic, was convinced that without Margaret's active intervention the life of the college would have been even briefer, and less productive. During the 19 years of its total existence some 1,000 teachers, full- and part-time, had been trained there. Sidney's shade must have glowed with satisfaction.

A Manager of People

Ensuring the actual inclusion of Sidney Webb as a small component in a relatively new polytechnic formed from Regent Street Polytechnic and Holborn College of Law, Languages and

Commerce was not easy. It involved consultation and planning between personalities among whom, as Margaret well knew, relationships were not always harmonious. While she herself unreservedly supported Tony Crosland, when Minister, in his policy of trying to raise the status of the polytechnics to equate with universities (her academic standards were always of the highest), she clashed head on over this with the Principal, Colin Anderson, who maintained, as an electrical engineer, that polytechnics should be technological universities, and was fearful of the arts side dominating. Margaret, however, gave practical assistance to amalgamation. According to Hector Jelf, then secretary to the Polytechnic, she influenced building expansion by 'getting the needs of the Polytechnic recognised by its inclusion in a building programme'. Further, she helped to 'pull the Polytechnic towards Education'. She was indeed a 'manager of people' at all levels.[25]

At her peak Margaret had been a splendid chairman both at County Hall and on governing bodies. Fair, patient and well informed, she was always willing to listen before she attempted to reconcile conflicting opinions, although she once admitted that she disliked going into committee without knowing what she thought was the solution to a problem. This, however, never precluded her from attentively weighing criticism before guiding her committee to its decision. She always attended well briefed, for she studied the implications of agenda items, and would visit with her officers any institutions likely to come up for discussion. She had good, trusting relationships with her chief officers: particularly with George Mavor, whom she considered 'an excellent officer' and later with Eric Walker, his successor. This relationship was strengthened by Margaret's real appreciation of the work undertaken:

I wish those who perpetuate the image of local councillors and officials as a collection of reactionary Bumbles . . . could see the enormous amount of sheer time which those in the service of a large authority, paid and unpaid, spend in consultation, meetings and discussions at all levels of interest, as well as with central government

she wrote.[26] For their part, officers respected her 'erudition, wit and administrative flair', and one senior official considered her 'the best chairman under whom I have ever served'.[27] Sir William Houghton, the Chief Education Officer, did however inject a pungently critical aside. 'Being driven home by Mrs Cole', he once remarked with deep feeling, 'is like having electric shock treatment!' An irrelevant comment, but one which all who knew Margaret would endorse.

In *Servant of the County* Margaret's analysis of a chairman's role is interesting both for its sharp delineation of responsibilities and for her appreciation of the human element. The official function of a chairman might seem to be, she wrote,

> to read, understand and explain the agenda for Committee, having ensured that accompanying documents are written in clear understandable English, and to preside at the meeting and get through business with the minimum amount of friction, delay and frustration . . . But the job does not end there . . . The Chairman . . . is the representative of the Council to the outside world, the world of complaints, petitions and bright ideas. In the last resort he (or she) with his (her) Committee is responsible and cannot shelter behind the officers whose advice may or may not have been taken . . . he/she must therefore be prepared to answer letters, to receive deputations, to attend to grouses by other members and to take action, make decisions, or start enquiries according to his/her best judgement . . . a complex of little things that make up the inner texture of the public service in the welfare state.[28]

Margaret was noted for her unfailing consideration towards staff and friends. Whether to a headmaster with family anxieties, a committee clerk who had won promotion, or a bereaved colleague, she always found time to pen personal notes of condolence or congratulation, and was loved for this generosity of spirit. Consideration for people extended into a watchfulness for misrepresentation or inaccuracy over any organisation or body for which she cared. When, for example, the *New Statesman* alleged that 'caucus ridden techniques' were prevailing at London's County Hall, and that 'the LCC has always provided one of the worse advertisements for the seamy side of Labour politics',[29] Margaret's wrath was visited upon the head of the editor, John Freeman.

'As one of the many insulted by this comprehensive smear,' she wrote, 'may I be permitted to ask for chapter and verse, with emphasis on the word "seamy"?'[30] The editor's mollifying remarks concerning the 'excellent work done by the Labour-controlled LCC through the devoted efforts of such public spirited men and women as Mrs Cole' did not assuage Margaret's anger. As the debate continued, it was marked by a generous contribution to the paper from John Connell Robertson, a Conservative journalist who for nine years had been a co-opted member of the Education Committee:

> The phrase, 'seamier side', was unfortunate and inaccurate . . . the caucus did exist, but . . . in the Education Committee there was a group of Labour men and women who were obviously good in their devoted, arduous and unselfish service to the children for whose education they were responsible. In that committee one learned pretty quickly who cared for their own political careers and who were interested in education. Service, quite regardless of Party consideration, of the quality which . . . London's schools have had from these volunteers is not easy to come by.[31]

Such a tribute from a political opponent warmed Margaret's heart, and she sent an appreciative note of thanks to which he replied:

> I had come to respect the majority party . . . and it was rude and inaccurate to call you disreputable. I thought of people like yourself, Lady Nathan, Dr. [Leonard] Browne, [Harold] Shearman and others, and I remembered that you combined courtesy and tolerance of the opposition with sincere conviction and firmness of purpose, and with a great deal of unselfish, unpublicised hard work.[32]

This did not, however, end the matter. John Freeman in further correspondence admitted 'in all sincerity' that the remark about the seamy side of Labour politics obviously 'caused deeper offence than we intended, and I regret it'. He had genuinely intended the criticism to refer only to the 'methods of the Labour Party's democracy, and not to the achievements of the LCC'. Nevertheless, 'I strongly deprecate some of its rules, its work would be even better if it were more libertarian.'[33]

Margaret persisted, and Freeman wrote again:

> I am exceedingly surprised by your belief that the *New Statesman*

seems to be informed by such hostility to the LCC generally . . .
It is simply not true, and I will try to ensure that in the future
there are no grounds on which anyone could believe we are.[34]

Postgate tenacity had won another battle.

There is no doubt that in later years, after the demise of the
LCC, something of the former Miss Postgate's long-suppressed
wilfulness, hauteur even, began to surface. Margaret would behave
imperiously, erratically, and even on occasion with a sharpness that
could be disconcerting. Dr D. M. Leggett, Vice Chancellor of
Surrey University, recalled sitting with her at a selection interview
when he was Principal of Battersea Polytechnic: 'the candidate was
less than scintillating . . . Mrs Cole said to me in what was meant to
be an aside, but which I am sure was audible to the candidate, "a
damned bore, this chap".' Dr Leggett added, 'trivial, but typical'.[35]

She also tended in her late seventies to be somewhat autocratic at
governors' meetings. She would arrive late, shuffle papers, and
loudly request that not only the dates of future meetings be altered
to suit her convenience, but also the sequence of items on the
agenda. At the Polytechnic of Central London with which, as
Regent Street Polytechnic, she had had some thirty years' association, Margaret almost always sat next to Lord Hailsham, both of
whom, a fellow governor recalled, would make forceful and often
idiosyncratic contributions in between their private conversations.[36]
Lord Hailsham remembered Margaret as

> an admirable colleague with a constant fund of common sense
> almost always on the side of moderation and immensely know-
> ledgeable about the workings of local government . . . The only
> time she ever got cross with me was when I failed to mention the
> Webbs when opening the new Polytechnic building in Mary-
> lebone Road![37]

With age, Margaret's speech, never of the clearest, became
increasingly difficult to follow, for her voice had acquired a deep
gruffness from excessive smoking, and one colleague on the Education Committee remembered her 'speaking so badly and swallow-
ing her words that I rarely understood what she was saying'.[38] It
was certainly necessary always to concentrate hard when talking to
her, but there is no doubt that this tendency to mumble was aggravated by increasing deafness. Margaret did admit that her deafness

handicapped her in public life, although once when asked how she managed to hear candidates in interviews she observed shrewdly that 'taking facial expression into account and several other clues' she could deduce what any adult said. 'It's only children who say the unexpected.'[39]

If there was nothing cosy in Margaret's public or private attitudes, there was indeed everything that was stimulating in her interventions and her caustic wit. Louis Bondy, a fellow governor of Chelsea Polytechnic, antiquarian bookseller and later chairman of ILEA, summed this up: 'In her old age she interrupted whenever she wished; at times her behaviour was uncontrollable, but in her clarity of mind and her ability to get to the heart of the matter she outshone everyone else.'[40]

In spite of her latter-day quiddities and truculence, Margaret made outstanding contributions to the development of London's education and had indisputably helped 'to make a more humane and compassionate society'.[41] Yet it is virtually impossible to quantify her specific achievements for so much council and public work, as she often stressed, is done out of committee behind the scenes.

Human relationships were to her all-important. Work in local government is composed of an infinity of detail. She wrote to Francis Meynell, '"He who would do good to another must do it in minute particulars," and this still seems to me a pretty correct statement for public service.'[42]

In the context of her public commitments, Margaret was extremely modest and denied making any special contribution to the education service. Yet she was as interested and knowledgeable about building programmes and ideas as she was concerned for people and, because she liked the young so much, she thoroughly enjoyed her work at County Hall. She possessed, however, more profound qualities than a mere knowledge of how London education functioned. She was deeply sensitive to the susceptibilities of those who made it work, and understood how personal worries, lack of recognition or mere professional loneliness could clog the smooth running of any establishment, humble or high. As she wrote in her autobiography:

I claim no particular credit for my educational services. What I do claim is that trying in even the most inadequate way to get a public service into tolerable order gives one an insight into the problems . . . and thoughts of those working in it . . . in a way which no reading of books or Parliamentary debates . . . can possibly do. As G. K. Chesterton says . . . 'There are some things which a sixth rate organist knows which a first-rate judge of music does not know.' In politics I would urge that there are some things which a humble administrator or committee member knows which the greatest philosophers do not . . . It is exactly those things which traditional schools of politics at universities have tended to ignore: but they are among the things which the modern world must learn or perish.[43]

As a skilful administrator Margaret never forgot that the human factor in government was as important, if not more so, than those 'minute particulars' of William Blake.

Notes

1. M. I. Cole, *What is a Comprehensive School?* (Pamphlet, London Labour Party, 1953).
2. M. I. Cole, *Servant of the County* (Dobson, London, 1956), p. 19.
3. Cole, *What is . . .*, p. 4.
4. Ibid, p. 8.
5. Meredith Brown, interview and letter to author.
6. M. I. Cole to Agnes Murray, 22 October 1955 (in the possession of Beryl Hughes).
7. M. I. Cole to Agnes Murray, 15 March 1957 (in the possession of Beryl Hughes).
8. Canon Edward Carpenter, 24 November 1967 (CFP).
9. Canon Edward Carpenter, letter to author 28 March 1983.
10. Professor Lionel Elvin, letter to author 24 April 1982.
11. Cole, *Servant*, p. 76.
12. LCC Principals to M. I. Cole, 24 May 1960 (CFP).
13. R. W. Hewstone, letter to author, 14 May 1982.
14. Cole, *Servant*, p. 88.
15. Some major statistics of post-war expansion in London's further and higher education during Margaret's regime are significant.

	1946	1954	1964
Major scholarships and exhibitions			
(1) University	660	1,266	3,718
(2) Non-university	360	589	3,418
Grants for supplementary expenses for training college students	316	639	1,910

Sources: *London Education Statistics*, vol. 1 (1945–54) and vol. 2 (1955–64) (LCC and GLC, London).

16. Harold Nicolson, *Diaries* (Collins, London, 1968), vol. 3, p. 241 (28 May 1953).

17. The actual appointments submitted via the Education Committee were, of course, approved formally by Council, but, in the main, responsibility for nomination and selection lay with Margaret as chairman, in conjunction with the Chief Whip.

18. M. I. Cole to Agnes Murray, probably May 1960 (in the possession of Beryl Hughes).

19. Hugo Bell, letter to author, 7 March 1983.

20. Dame Mary Smieton, letter to author, 5 July 1982.

21. Frances Laidler to M. I. Cole, 23 March 1964 (CFP).

22. Rosemary Beresford, November 1981, correspondence and interview.

23. John Kensell, Student President, to M. I. Cole, 1 November 1971 (CFP).

24. Rosemary Beresford and others.

25. Hector Jelf, interview.

26. M. I. Cole, *Socialist Commentary* (November 1966).

27. Naomi Mitchison, *Guardian*, 8 May 1980.

28. Cole, *Servant*, pp. 84–5.

29. *New Statesman*, 15 December 1961.

30. M. I. Cole, *New Statesman*, 22 December 1961.

31. John Connell [Robertson], *New Statesman*, 19 January 1961.

32. John Connell [Robertson] to M. I. Cole, 24 January 1961 (CFP).

33. John Freeman to Margaret Cole, 31 January 1961 (CFP).

34. John Freeman to Margaret Cole, 13 February 1961 (CFP).

35. Dr D. M. Leggett, letter to author, 19 June 1982.

36. Charles Griffiths, letter to author, 4 May 1982.

37. Lord Hailsham, letter to author, 17 November 1981.

38. Amy Bush, letter to author, 2 June 1982.

39. Rosemary Beresford, letter to author, November 1981.

40. Louis Bondy, telephone interview, 10 June 1984.

41. Sir Toby Weaver to M. I. Cole, 17 June 1970 (CFP).

42. M. I. Cole to Francis Meynell, 17 May 1973 (Lady Meynell's Papers, privately held).

43. M. I. Cole, *Growing Up into Revolution* (Longmans Green, London, 1949), p. 215.

11 THE FAMILY IN WARTIME — AND AFTER

Family Matters

Although Margaret and Douglas were truly 'humane politicals', Margaret rarely permitted outside obligations to take precedence over family affairs. She practised what she preached in separating, wherever practical, public from private commitments. 'Any woman working at both motherhood and a job must keep several lines of thought going simultaneously without getting them confused,' she wrote, 'and move from one field of attention to another, without being conscious of any great sense of strain.' She herself was certainly compartment-minded, able to avoid fuss and taking problems from the office home with her.[1]

Jane and Anne, both of whom attended St Paul's Girls' School, and subsequently achieved professional qualifications (Jane as a housing manager, Anne as a doctor), grew up well aware of the high standards that their busy and distinguished parents expected of them. Certainly Jane always felt that any major decision in her life needed her mother's approval before it could be the right one. If in childhood there was any curtain of awe between them it was drawn back in later years, when she and her mother grew very close indeed. Anne, according to Nanny Cole, always tended to be 'Piggy in the Middle', but 'the sun always shone from Humphrey's eyes'.

Margaret was intensely interested in all the doings of her children, and felt greatly bereft when both her daughters left England — Jane with her husband to live, as it transpired, in several of the world's major trouble spots, and Anne later to practise as a paediatrician in Canada. It was certainly not Margaret's fault that communication with Anne became so intermittent, and with Jane she sustained a rich correspondence until her death. 'No one else wrote like she did,' Jane recalled. 'Her letters held the family together.'[2]

Wartime letters inevitably embody much personal detail, and those Margaret wrote to Richmond when overseas in the RAF provided lively progress reports about all the family, and emphasised a special solicitude for her mother. Anne, training to be a doctor,

146

was 'full of medical excitement and her conversation is apt to be professional', Margaret reported.

> I think it is the right job for her if she can overcome the obstacles of examinations . . . After getting through her second MB she acted as an unqualified House Surgeon . . . and was also allowed to do a good deal of helping in the theatre. This responsibility and the sense of getting on with patients and nurses should be good for her.

Humphrey's progress earned ongoing comment. 'Just home from Winchester, he brought an unexpected maths prize for the best junior mathematician,' she wrote proudly, although he was

> a perfectly lousy member of the JTC . . . and a cynical critic of the Great Men who came to address them . . . Montgomery, Mountbatten, Waverley et al . . . his description of the proceedings reminded me of the MP who addressed the lads in *Stalky and Co!*[3]

On another occasion she told Richmond that Humphrey had 'an enormous mouth . . . an awful lot of curly black hair . . . and one of your suits fits him nicely (though he only uses it occasionally!)' and that Winchester thought highly of him. 'His report says that he is a "tower of strength in our agricultural work" — a kind of silo?' she wrote mischieviously, and when he won 'only' an Exhibition to Oxford University, she reported that 'the school was rather comically plaintive about the Philistine failure of Trinity to recognise the beauty of their own. Anyhow, Douglas only got an Exhibition to Balliol, so maybe it is peculiarly hereditary.'[4]

Margaret showed considerable sensitivity towards her daughters' problems, especially over Jane's engagement. In August 1944 she told Richmond that Jane, now a qualified Housing Manager, 'full of dampness, dry rot and the law of Landlord and Tenant', had become engaged to Will Abraham, an American corporal in the US Army, 'a statistical economist by trade . . . a nice gentle lad, very solemn and responsible about his duty to take care of Jane'.[5] For his part, Will well remembered Margaret asking 'particularly since I was Jewish, how my mother would feel about my marrying a gentile. I distinctly recall her saying, "sometimes these things cut deep."'[6]

There was an unusual background to Jane's marriage, for, unlike most husbands, Will met his mother-in-law before he ever set eyes on his wife, when attending a course at Morley College, London. 'The Instructor was none other than Margaret . . . I was tremendously taken with her . . . her brilliance . . . her style . . . her looks,' he wrote.[7] It was only later that he met Jane.

Margaret for her part liked Will enormously. 'Apart from the 3,000 miles of sea, I think it [the marriage] is for the best,' she told her brother. 'Will is firm and steady . . . and Jane needs firmness. It would be hopeless for her to have married a sloppy person . . . He has endeared himself to Anne and Ray and behaved with consideration in a difficult situation.' Predictably Douglas disliked the marriage initially, just because 'Will is an American and all Americans are wicked to him . . . but he behaved reasonably in fact.'[8]

Tactfully Margaret had entreated Will to get Douglas' formal consent, which he did, vividly describing

> Douglas rising from his desk in the book-lined room, a desk with two sides, one of which was Margaret's, and pouring out drinks. I imagine I needed one to face this most patrician of socialists! Margaret must have softened him up, for his main concern was that I would not leave Jane with child while I was in the army and the war was raging in the Pacific.[9]

'Thoroughly well pleased,' Margaret reiterated to Richmond the high opinion she held of her son-in-law, adding, 'Jane is too pretty and too anxious to be obliging to be left around just engaged. She will be happier wearing a collar and being a good steady wife!'[10] An excellent rapport with Will was maintained, and after the war, when Margaret was lecturing in the States, he would occasionally accompany her. Will recalled one such visit to Princeton University. 'The lecture was held in a building to which normally women were not admitted; Margaret wound up her lecture by doing an animated jig, and the Princeton staff loved it!'[11]

Margaret appears to have been less willing to share Humphrey with his wife, Hilda. Although she was sincerely sympathetic over Hilda's family anxieties, one suspects that, like Mrs P, she could not readily accept that much-loved sons do get married. Remarking to Richmond when he was still single how badly Mrs P treated her own daughters-in-law ('what she'd do about *your* wife I can't imagine!'), Margaret concluded that probably this was 'the normal tendency between mothers and daughters-in-law, particularly when the mother so definitely interests herself chiefly in her sons'.[12]

Mrs P — and Others

Affection for the younger generation did not obviate Margaret's concern for the older. She was, for example, insistent that both Ormond and Richmond should secure appointments worthy of their abilities when they returned to England. To that end she persistently prodded friends on their behalf. It was, however, her mother who absorbed most attention.

Since 1939 Mrs P had been living with Ormond and his wife Pat in Egypt and then in Jerusalem, but, nearing eighty, she elected to return home at the height of hostilities. 'I remember her telling me that she thought she would die at fifty!' Margaret wrote to Richmond, opposing the whole project.

She was thoroughly apprehensive about the effect of the home front conditions upon 'the Old Lady . . . particularly the risk of air raids and the noisy, frightening air defence' and the 'absolute, practical impossibility of finding her anything to do of the kind she has been accustomed. I see no likelihood of her being anything but miserable.'[13] For once Margaret had made a demonstrably wrong assessment by totally underestimating her mother's capacity for enjoyment. Mrs P wanted to return home, and return home she did.

Accepting that she had been outmanoeuvred, Margaret conferred with her sister Ethel, who was running a market garden in Beaconsfield, as to whether their mother might live there. 'I think this is the best possible idea,' she told Richmond,

She'll be able to potter around and Ethel can take her in the car with the cabbages . . . you do, I hope, realise that I am not trying to shirk having her here, but I think she'd be very bored and unhappy . . . and Beaconsfield is just out of range of the London raids.[14]

Mrs P finally arrived in mid-November and Margaret reported the hilarious event in detail.

A telegram was received saying Arrive Euston 2.20 hope you can take me in, Mother. I was at the Fabian Office; Douglas was broadcasting; Daisy in bed with lumbago, and Ray unobtainable . . . I jumped into a taxi and fled to Euston; in time to receive the Old Lady in an absolutely incredible hat . . . with circumvalent yellow scarf perched on top of blue scarf and further on top of grey hair ('I must push a piece of grey forward so that people know that I am old!') Humping baggage all alone at Liverpool she had had two minutes before the train's time of departure and had got herself, baggage and all, into the guard's van . . . Goodness knows what would have happened if I hadn't found her . . . However I did and took her home . . . Ray [then nearing fifty] came round that evening in Home Guard uniform, and she said, 'My dear, how you've grown!'

This was on Monday. On Friday I took her down to Ethel's, having dealt with the local police, had her medically inspected, bought her a new earpiece, collected rations, and taken broken glasses and watch to be mended . . . I have cut God knows what . . . had to dash off to take meetings in Leeds and Sheffield, but I think all is well.

. . . I have suggested to Ethel that she gets the [family] 'vocabulary' back from Mondie [Esmond] and encourages reminiscence-writing when the trunks turn up.[15]

A few days later Mrs P wrote saying she thought she could be very happy, and had packed some tomatoes. 'As long as she stays fit . . . it seems as good a pattern as one could hope for . . . I could not provide her with pottering jobs here,' Margaret told Richmond, 'nor could I amuse her without upsetting my arrangement of life entirely . . . It was a good job that Dick [who stayed at Freeland during much of the war] was away when she came, Nou [Naomi] being in town.'[16]

Early the following year Margaret was laid low with pneumonia. It was a prolonged bout which prevented her having Mrs P to stay, and made her 'feel guilty at not relieving Ethel', but she felt 'very half cock, fed on tonic, glucose, luminol and damn all, with a left arm that won't work properly'.[17] Margaret was pleased that the English spring delighted their mother, 'for I had feared she would be comparing it with the flowers on the Mount of Olives, to its disadvantage!'

That summer Freeland suffered in the Blitz. A single 'bugger' doodle bug caused an immense amount of material damage, but after Margaret had dealt with the first agonising round of disruption, she fulfilled her promise to Ethel of taking their mother away. The family had a revivifying holiday at Wast Water in Cumberland, where 'You could see all the screes and Gable and Scafell looking down on you, which delighted Mrs P.'

Margaret was still finding it difficult to walk, she told Richmond, although she was far better than in April when it took 'ten puffing minutes to go round the block at Hendon'. Mrs P, however, was

a wonder. She walked eight miles in one day and we got her up 1,000 feet with help in getting down . . . On the whole she was very good and enjoyed herself . . . I found a new flower and she sent it to Gilbert Carter, Curator of Cambridge's Botanical Gardens.[18]

The long and lively wartime correspondence with Richmond ended on a happy note. Shortly before the 1945 election Margaret reported taking her mother with Jane to Cambridge, where the three generations of graduates, Mrs Postgate, Mrs Cole and Mrs Abraham, took tea with the Mistress of Girton. It was a memory cherished by all.

It was typical of her generation that Mrs P, like Susan Lawrence and others, learnt Braille. This she undertook in order to be able to help the blind to read — which she did — and admirably. Mrs P died ripe in years in 1952, still living with Ethel, whose market garden was then at Burghfield, Reading. She told Richmond that 'she wanted to go, but not before the raspberries were picked'. And that was how it was.[19]

With Richmond's release from the RAF imminent, Margaret arranged a family holiday in north Devon. 'I shall be deeply enraged if you can't come,' she wrote to him from Freeland. 'But remember this is your home for as long as you have need . . . what's the Next of Kin for?'[20]

That August Richmond did return to England, and to a job 'over which you and Roger Armfelt are still awfully cagey', his sister wrote, somewhat reproachfully — probably because she felt so protective towards her youngest brother, to whom she had long been virtually a deputy Mum.[21]

In contrast, Margaret's relationship with Raymond, the brother who had opened up the world of politics to her, was equally close, but one of equals. They had so much in common: interest in classical literature (over which they corresponded at length), in the history of radical socialism, in good food and in journalism. Ray had written a number of political books and several novels, edited various left-wing journals, and created *The Good Food Guide*.

Margaret was also fond of Ray's wife, Daisy, and there are amusing tales of their supervising together Ray's and Douglas' collaboration in writing their immensely popular book *The Common People (1746–1938)*. The authors disagreed consistently over form and content, argued incessantly, and insisted on communicating only in writing, even though they lived barely half a mile apart!

> Since neither could bear to wait before firing off an instant reply to any letter received . . . the two wives felt like harassed officials of the League of Nations until we decided that the High Contesting Parties must be brought face to face. Once we had got them into one room, the sound and fury began to dissipate.[22]

There is a pleasing footnote to these family anecdotes. Margaret sent her mother a copy of her own autobiography, which delighted Mrs P. She considered the book 'a really wonderful performance,' and told Margaret that she was 'a wonderful woman'.[23]

If during the war safeguarding Mrs P's well-being was Margaret's frequent concern, anxiety over meeting Douglas' needs was ever present. His diabetes was a permanent backdrop to all their activities, although watchfulness and careful dietary planning long kept serious effects at bay. The outstanding fact, Margaret found in retrospect, was 'that he was able to do so much and to keep going with a strict regime and a delicately balanced physique, without giving to the wide world the semblance of an invalid'.[24] This would not have been the case without her unobtrusive vigilance. Margaret never fussed overtly, as Douglas would have resented direct interference,[25] but she did cosset him. She made sure that punctual meals conformed with dietary regulations, and arranged occasional holidays. All of this necessitated reliable domestic staff at Freeland and able secretarial help in both Oxford and London, which Margaret always found.

Although Margaret provided for Douglas' practical needs and always gave interested, if sometimes critical, support to his work, she did not automatically fall in with all his personal requests.

Early in the war she firmly resisted his urging her to join him at Oxford; but was greatly torn. 'Douglas is ill as a result of air raids and sleepless nights and must leave London,' she wrote to Naomi,

> he's going to Oxford and it's very worrying to know what to do. He doesn't want to be without me and I can't go until I've dealt with Jane and Anne. Also I don't want to quit. I've work here at the Fabian Society which I'm expecting people in worse conditions to go on with, and I'm not as frightened as that yet. Of course I may be by tomorrow.[26]

Nevertheless she missed Douglas badly. 'He has removed himself and all his belongings to Oxford, at least three rooms full of books, which is the bulk of his personality,' she told Naomi.

> One feels so lost and quiet, he does so want me to live at his scratch home at Banbury Road . . . and I don't want to . . . I would have nothing to do in Oxford and if the Fabian Society and *Tribune* are any use (*if* of course) I'm really needed there and I don't like running away.[27]

She was in fact based at Freeland throughout the war; but she visited Oxford whenever she could, generally sustained the family and, when the doodle bug came, coped admirably with the extensive damage it caused. Not surprisingly, she abhorred the break-up of families.

> Men don't mind, Douglas doesn't, and though Dick is more paternal than Douglas, he doesn't either. But I do, and my children aren't young. I think to separate mothers and children forcibly is a biological wickedness, and I have never wondered at the refusal of the East-Enders to go[28]

she wrote to Naomi.

The Nuffield Survey

Margaret was always loyally defensive of Douglas' interests; and nowhere is evidence of this more apparent than in her account of the disputes about the Nuffield Survey.

During the phoney war period, Douglas had produced for Sir William Beveridge at the Ministry of Labour a countrywide survey into manpower and war material production, using volunteers (often Fabians) as investigators. When Nuffield College was created it was administered by the University through the Hebdomadal Council and was not, like other colleges, independent. In 1940 Douglas suggested to the Nuffield College Committee that he should try to organise a Social Reconstruction Survey using the existing Manpower Survey machinery, an idea which received enthusiastic support, notably from Arthur Greenwood in the wartime Reconstruction Department. The National Survey Reconstruction Committee was created, and Douglas was eventually appointed its first Director. It produced a vast amount of material, covering such problems as reconstruction, the relocation of industry and the transition from war to peacetime conditions. Douglas initiated private conferences between academia, industry and the civil service which Margaret often attended with Lydia Grier, then Principal at Lady Margaret Hall, to discuss major policy matters. One distinguished participant, Samuel Courtauld, commented admiringly how leading industrialists at these conferences 'marvelled at the skill with which Douglas produced a sentence embodying a common measure of agreement amid a crossfire of suggestions. His perfect firmness and suppression of any personal views were equally remarkable.'[29]

All, however, was not well. By the autumn of 1942 structural weaknesses, Margaret explained, had become apparent, arising from the divided responsibilities inherent in the original scheme, and politically motivated criticisms were undermining the efficacy of the survey. There was a growing impression that 'its Director was running away with the College . . . might even be turning it into an institution of Social Studies . . . with Fellows set to work out planned schemes . . . and the Director was a Socialist!'[30] Moreover, Lord Nuffield disliked Douglas' criticising the conduct of the war, and expressed 'perturbation' about the survey. Douglas, heavily overworked, was never told of his Lordship's complaints. Yet, Margaret remembered saying to him 'when he was complaining angrily about obstruction by civil servants and lack of understanding among fellow academics, "You seem to have too many enemies" . . . but he did not realise how serious the opposition was becoming.'[31] In the spring of 1943, a memorandum drawn up by Sir David Ross, Vice Chancellor, and others was sent to the

Hebdomadal Council. It referred to current rumours, Lord Nuffield's concern, questioned the quality and impartiality of material the survey was providing, and insisted that future enquiries should come under civil service control.

This communication, not unexpectedly, produced 'an explosive reaction' from Douglas, who was indignant at the general slur cast upon his colleagues, many of whom were of high academic standard, but his chief anger

was roused by the phrase 'Lord Nuffield's concern' which he took to mean that very senior members of the University were prepared to accept from a wealthy donor dictation of a kind which had been an open scandal in the United States — and this without a word to the man in charge.[32]

The fat, as Margaret drily observed, was properly in the fire.

Many people in high places defended the survey, notably Professor (Lord) A. D. Lindsay, chairman of the wartime Research Committee, and an academic committee of enquiry also exonerated its work. At the time, however, Douglas was so visibly ill and overworked that Margaret, with the help of his physician, Dr Batten, induced him to take a lengthy break. He resigned from office, but returned in the autumn to supervise the winding up of the survey. When, however, the Hebdomadal Council introduced a modified constitution which still left the college on the Council's leading strings, Douglas walked out of Nuffield and refused to return. He considered the Council's conduct a disgrace to the academic reputation of the University. This was a deplorable ending to a brave project and, as Margaret remarked, no one would ever know what part the Nuffield Reconstruction Survey, had it continued, might have played at the end of the war.

This account, in Margaret's *Life* of Douglas, written in 1971, is recorded without rancour, but that was certainly not how she felt at the time. For in May 1943 she wrote to Gilbert Murray concerning 'this scandalous business about Nuffield which would not have happened if the wicked had not thought they could get away with it'.[33] Later that year Margaret was less critical, telling Richmond:

Douglas went back to Oxford a few days ago, very partially recovered . . . I think he has been badly treated by some people, though not by so many as he imagines . . . I'm really rather worried about him and can't see what he is going to do next. It's impossible to discuss things — almost anything — because immediately one strikes a patch of almost hysterical hatred which neither helps him, nor makes for peace in the home . . . I dare say something will happen to solve things; at present it's too like the early diabetic atmosphere of 1931 for my liking.[34]

The following spring, while recovering from the severe attack of pneumonia which had left her with most painful arthritis, she wrote again to her brother:

Douglas has pretty certainly severed all connections with Nuffield. He was doing too much, but I'm sorry it ended like this. Of course I don't want to suggest he was right all along — who is, after all — and you know he is difficult to criticise. All the same, do people in the RAF get so incredibly petty and spiteful?

adding

Douglas has finally left Nuffield and is now Research Fellow of University College . . . He won't try for a Professorship . . . which involves possibilities of intrigue by those who don't like him . . . We are surprised and rather disheartened as to human nature by the amount of spite, obstruction and honest-to-God silliness that goes on in organisations, and . . . I don't mean Oxford only.[35]

Douglas' anger was not long sustained, and in 1944 he was elected to the newly established Chichele Chair of Political and Social Theory, which carried a Fellowship at All Souls. He was also appointed a Professorial Fellow to Nuffield and later elected to a Research Fellowship. Peace was made, and Nuffield under its new Warden (Sir) Henry Clay, 'proceeded calmly to self government'. Margaret, clearly relieved, wrote almost happily to their old friend Lawrence Hammond:

It's nice about Douglas, isn't it? Even though he's not sure whether he is pleased or not! After all those quarrels and recriminations I'm glad the University have done the right thing and also glad he won't have to leave — for I am sure he would be unhappy severed from Oxford: he's too much of a natural conservative![36]

Douglas himself, in one of his rare family letters, provided Richmond with an almost contented postscript:

You will have heard of my translation to All Souls . . . in spite of which I go on for the present living here in University, as All Souls have no rooms that will take my books . . . I'm really rather glad to get away from theoretical economics and back to my first love, Social Theory; and I seem to myself to be lecturing quite well, although there isn't much of an audience to lecture to in these days.[37]

The most tangible evidence of reconciliation was Douglas' conveying his unique library to Nuffield, which the family has continued to augment. It was over the alleged neglect of Douglas' papers, which she presented to the college after his death, that Margaret had one of her few explosions with authority there. She was deeply incensed by delay over their indexing and classification and made no secret of this to the then Warden, D. N. Chester, but it was a breach healed with time.

The Nuffield saga has been told in some detail, for it indicates that in spite of the personal distress Margaret must have experienced at the time she could relate the long unhappy chain of events with singular detachment. And more than this: the whole story underlines how closely on basic issues such as academic freedom, forward thinking and administrative independence she and Douglas were, and remained, at one.

War Reactions

Throughout the war Margaret made Freeland a welcoming haven for family and friends. With Douglas to cosset at Oxford or in London, the Fabian Society to organise, recently acquired LCC commitments to fulfil, and a family to supervise, her days were full even before their home was blitzed.

Although Freeland did not sustain direct attack until late in the war, damage generally was widespread in the Hendon area.

Land mines got Ray out of bed [as Home Guard] at two in the morning . . . The guns make a fearful row . . . As the bomb comes down you wait for it to burst . . . When it's quieter you hear the drone of a plane coming over — wonder how many seconds it will be before the guns find it, and whether the bombs or the guns will come first . . . go out and see if there are fires and think how stupid it all is,

she wrote to Naomi, adding

We had a handful of incendiaries, some flaming away in the cellar — Dick appeared saying, 'where is the sand?' and we put them out very quickly . . . they fell both sides of the house, but not on it . . . I didn't sleep much that night partly because I had been reading of Coventry after doing a dockland tour with Ray to see for ourselves.[38]

Dick, who stayed at Hendon through much of the war, acted promptly and allayed any panic. Naomi, who would visit as often as she could, remembered how they would all listen to Douglas' great brown horn gramophone playing Bach during air raids, and its soothing effect.

Margaret considered the wanton destruction utterly shocking, 'because of its senselessness . . . it's absolutely unnatural to build things deliberately and then smash them up quite aimlessly,' she wrote again to Naomi.[39] And always there was the

underlying physical worry which weakens one (in a war which won't stay put) and prevents one doing even what one could in the way of forward thinking. I don't think I'm more frightened than most people, but I'm not immune from the sudden thought, 'well, that was a smasher all right: it might be you next time!', or from thinking while doing a memorandum, 'how can anything liberal survive a destruction of values and property, which a continuation of this means?' One is enfiladed on both flanks, as it were, one physical and one anxiety-neurosis.[40]

War strain, anxiety over family and general pressure took their toll and by 1944 Margaret was at a really low ebb. After a long bout of pneumonia which kept her in Oxford, she wrote Dorothy Fox an uncharacteristic 'wail': 'I am all right so long as I sit or mooch and do nothing,' but nobody could suggest what was really the matter with her.

> I am simply despairing. I can make no plans . . . for I can't move beyond the limit of my invisible string which tightens in a sudden stranglehold if I do . . . A wry consolation is that the Fabian Society will at least have learnt to do without me by the time someone has found out what's the matter! Douglas is not used to this sort of thing. I've always looked after him and the brats . . . end of howl.[41]

After several weeks she returned home, gradually convalescing, 'A very slow snail . . . It seemed I ought to write a letter to the papers like Churchill [because] on 9th January I was a pretty doubtful case!' she told Dorothy Fox, but hope and activities revived alongside her health. With Richmond returning there was a holiday in Cumberland to plan, more visits to Carradale and — a great reason for satisfaction — Douglas was re-established academically in Oxford. Additionally there were Fabian schools, holiday breaks, the excitement of Jane's marriage, and electioneering.

As a Fabian delegate, Margaret had attended the 'impressively exciting' Labour Party Conference at Blackpool in spring 1945, chaired by the weary but dynamic Ellen Wilkinson. Margaret wholly approved the decision for Labour to 'get out of its wartime shackles and fight an election by itself on its own programme, against all the prestige of the Man Who Won the War'.

'There is,' she told Richmond,

> a pendulum swinging. But how far and how fast? Douglas standing for Oxford University is filled with fear he may get it! Prophesy? Not me. What with the register in such a mess, and radio speeches, whose effect nobody knows, and the numbers who have never voted before . . . it's rather a Tar Baby election. So many ain't saying nuffin . . . I have been speaking most nights to varied audiences in varied parts, but still don't feel I can say anything effective . . . However at least I have kept fit and so has Douglas . . . The Oxford Group called today. D told them he was an atheist; but they said all their members were being advised to vote for him, because he was much nicer than A. P. Herbert. This I thought was funny.[42]

Douglas did not win his seat, but the Party triumphed, and Margaret shared the elation with Fabian friends and colleagues at the Labour landslide during that blazing, exhilarating July in 1945.

Her analysis of the reasons for victory is penetrating. Once the wartime danger had passed, she suggested, the adult community, particularly those in the Forces, no longer felt the need for a great paternal figure as leader. It was not, they remembered, Churchill who had won the war, but *they*, the ordinary people who had worked and fought and stood up to the bombing. As Margaret saw it, they rejected the patronising implication of the wartime poster, '*Your* Courage, *Your* Cheerfulness, *Your* Resolution, will bring *us* victory.'

Secondly, the electorate had grown up. Whatever the gratitude and affection they felt for Churchill, they felt neither for the political allies he had chosen and were well able to distinguish between the man and his party. Among the many complex factors and the different organisations which contributed to these changing attitudes the Fabian Society and its allied political coteries had played a small but not insignificant role in the electoral eruption.[43]

There was one other important factor: the quality of the Labour Party's policy statement, *Let us Face the Future*. Its clarity and sincerity were patent, because, as Margaret remarked, it made no effort to become an 'encyclopaedia of good intentions'. Sidney Webb had left his imprint.

American Tours

As a practical assertion of independence, as well as a desire to visit Jane in New York, Margaret undertook her first overseas lecture tour to America and Canada in 1947, and repeated her visit in 1949. Neither the popularity of her lectures nor the favourable publicity she received distracted her from thoughts of home. 'Please ask Lotte to start now making Christmas puddings,' she instructed Douglas, but remained far more concerned with his personal feelings.

> I was so glad to hear from Rosamund that you told my mother you had had a lovely life . . . of course you shall be loved, you silly chump, but restrain your feelings about Ernie [Bevin] for a while after meeting me![44]

When later the publication of her autobiography received glowing reports, she deliberately underplayed this, writing to Douglas:

Please don't mind if [the book] turns out successful — you sound as if I were putting your nose out of joint. I haven't had an awful lot of writing success; and anyway, the things I write about don't last like a lot of yours. I love you Lamb, don't be despondent.[45]

Usually, concern for his susceptibilities took precedence, but in a rare, self-centred outburst, Margaret did comment upon her own ill health and how a 'top' American doctor had diagnosed 'mental worry'.

It's psychosomatic . . . whether I stay better or not depends on my state of mind . . . I think the diagnosis is correct and that the cause has been strain about my family — the future of it and me, and particularly political differences with you and the way your disappointment with the world and others has fallen on me. This isn't said as a complaint, but as a fact that cannot be got away from.[46]

Both lecture tours did much to 'burnish up my ego' but did not prevent her from missing Douglas. 'I felt very dismal to leave you . . . much sadder than two years ago,' she wrote,[47] as the second tour went well:

I lectured in Washington to about 120 on Devaluation, a bit alarmed on that subject . . . with people from the State Department listening . . . but thanks partly to your admirable *Herald* notes I got through, was hugely thanked . . . and given a large inconvenient box of flowers . . . I'm sorry if this sounds self-laudatory, but I do feel I'm doing much better than when here last.[48]

A little later, after participating in a very dull radio forum in Los Angeles and delivering six crowded-out lectures in Boston, she could still write encouragingly to Douglas, 'it sounds as if you handled the Fabian AGM brilliantly'.[49]

Her letters were packed with humour, sharp observation on the American way of political life, gossip and facts. She likened the famous Manhattan skyline to 'a lot of irregular teeth of an aged mastadon',[50] derived immense amusement from being described by the *Saturday Review* (in a foreword to an article she had written on Sidney Webb) as 'one of the original Fabians' — a gaffe she gently repudiated, but often related — and gleefully reported to Douglas a mystery she had unearthed in the library of Stanford University.

> They have Fabian stuff in the catalogues contributed by E. W. Darling [an assistant secretary to the Fabian Society 1933–5] . . . it includes Caustin's *Gas Report*, the *Flour Mill* pamphlet which was suppressed, and a great deal of other stuff. I was so astonished that I began to make enquiries . . . It will be interesting at least to discover how much Darling was paid for pinching Fabian pamphlets![51]

Travelling from coast to coast, Margaret gave interviews, wrote articles, broadcast and lectured with such *élan* that one organiser from Minneapolis assured her, 'you have made new friends for your country and strengthened those of us who were your old friends'.[52] Paul Fox, an academic friend at Carlton College, Ottawa, added his own flattering postscript: 'I don't know how you weathered your "grand tour" as well as you did. I'd have been flat on my back with a schedule such as you had . . . People are still talking about it.'[53] Margaret was indeed firmly recognised as her 'own woman'.

'A Worsening State of Things'

Douglas held the Chair at All Souls until 1957, and in spite of black patches of ill health, filled his academic roles with distinction, and continued with his writing. From the early fifties until his death he was working on a monumental work, *The History of Socialist Thought*, the fifth volume of which was published posthumously. He still had many commitments outside the University, was a regular contributor to the *New Statesman*, of which he became Board Chairman shortly before his death, and was the original inspiration behind the group which formulated and published *New Fabian Essays*.

From 1952 Douglas was gradually, but perceptibly, going downhill, although he worked as hard as ever. He and Margaret did have several holidays abroad, and as late as 1958 he accepted an invitation to become the first Visiting Professor at Roosevelt University in Chicago, 'largely for my sake', Margaret stressed, 'so that we could visit our daughters together'. This proved an exhausting but triumphant trip. Douglas kept up a 'continuing hymn of hate against America, though it's something that everyone petted him good and plenty'.[54]

After the Chichele Professorship ended (in 1957) Freeland had to be sold. This was traumatic for them both, but for Margaret in particular, because the burden of disposal and home hunting fell wholly upon her. 'We go back tomorrow', she wrote Agnes Murray from Carradale, 'to resume the awful business of trying to sell and to find a flat. I've been to thirty agents and written to more.'[55]

Sell they eventually did and moved to a dark Victorian flat in Oakwood Court, Kensington, which they both loathed. It was, however, reasonably spacious, and even though 'Douglas is in a state of suicidal rage because it will take only half the amount of shelving for the books that he has here,' Margaret found that it offered 'an awful lot more room than I expected'. She organised the move with great stoicism, but not without some justifiable exasperation, for in protest over the move Douglas took to turning giddy, and to saying

> that he only wishes to be dead, before he is reduced to living in squalor . . . Also that anything to do with Richard [their grandson] makes him sick, because all sex, suckling and children are disgusting . . . It really *is* naughty. He has a huge flat, is keeping his own rooms at Oxford, and has a continuing job there . . . It's like trying to shove an enormous stone up a hill, which keeps coming back and hitting you.[56]

Rarely, and never in public, did Margaret criticise Douglas, but later that year, 'partly because I have no daughters' and partly because she was feeling depressed over the deaths of several close friends, she sent Agnes a real *cri de coeur*. Douglas' general disgruntlement was nothing new, she explained.

> It's been increasing and increasing until it is almost continuous. Of course, I know all you say about feeling ill and frail, and I don't want you to think I don't recognise and sympathise. But if one got any thanks or anything of the sort, rather than being

whipped for the sins of the world as well as one's own, it would be a great deal easier. I have been half a sicknurse for many years now; but I am not good at being a mental nurse as well . . . I don't think there's any point in maundering on. I only wanted to say that I hadn't suddenly lost my temper, though I had rather lost hope.[57]

This had all 'been growing steadily for some years, as Humphrey knows', she reiterated a few days later, 'but although I can cope with crises, I am not so hot at coping with a continuous and worsening state of things'.[58]

Self-pity, however, rarely persisted and, practical as ever, as Douglas was 'visibly going downhill', Margaret suggested to Kingsley Martin that some friends from the *New Statesman* might visit him.

His doctor who has known him for over thirty years says 'don't let him retreat from living' . . . so if you or John [Freeman] or anyone could say occasionally, 'I'd like to come . . . to talk about the paper, policy or what not' it would I am certain do good . . . to cope with the problem of decline is not really easy and I would appreciate some small (repeat, small) help from those who feel they have reason to be grateful to him.[59]

Douglas' Death

Douglas died in harness, 'as he would have wished', on 14 January 1959, after chairing a meeting at the *New Statesman* office, where he went without Margaret's knowledge. Frank Horrabin, an old friend from The Movement, tenderly summed up the loss in *Socialist Commentary*: 'GDH is dead: a light has indeed gone out in the world.'[60]

Tributes to Douglas — the Secular Saint, as Kingsley Martin called him, or the Radical Patrician, in Professor Hugh Clegg's words — were international. Modestly Margaret published but few tributes in the biography she subsequently wrote, because she 'hated adulation'. The many letters she did preserve, however, reveal the genuinely high estimation in which Douglas was held: from Professor Richard Titmuss, who recognised his qualities 'of integrity, distinction of mind and steadfastness', to Rajani Palme

Dutt, who regarded Douglas as 'a brilliant and genuine Socialist, good to everyone and in the simplest sense, a Good Person'.[61] The warmest all-round assessment came from Lord Chorley. Douglas, he assured Margaret, 'played a unique part in the political education of my generation, not in simply what he wrote, but by what he was . . . Anyone who knew him must have felt his immense integrity and have realised that this gave a moral force and fire to his convictions, and by extension, to much in the Labour Movement.'[62]

Significantly, many friends paid tribute to them both. Mary Adams, then of the BBC, remembered the Coles as 'catalysts to us all in the old Tutors' Association'. Lady Elizabeth Longford, the historian, told Margaret 'how we have always been inspired by you and Douglas as a most wonderful pair', and Lady Simon of Wythenshawe sagely observed, 'we know how much of his work was shared by you, and that even those books which bore only his name were joint in the deepest sense'.[63]

Margaret produced the definitive record some years later in the *Life of G. D. H. Cole* (1971), which in its 'scrupulous objectivity' was considered a model biography. Yet the book was written under heavy physical and emotional pressures. She was already in her mid-seventies, suffering from painful arthritis, had no research assistance at all, and constantly had to relive times of stress and sadness.

Reviews, nevertheless, were laudatory. Professor A. J. P. Taylor, the historian, observing that 'wives rarely make good biographers of their husbands', conceded that Margaret

> was an exception. Although occasionally she slipped . . . too much from biography into general history and sometimes exaggerated the importance of what were really coterie affairs, broadly she held the balance right . . . frank as a wife should be, devoted yet without illusions.[64]

It was, however, Michael Foot's 'intelligently kind' piece in the *Evening Standard*, praising 'the story of an old fashioned socialist saint . . . which must be read to see how a biography should be written'[65] that pleased Margaret above all. She wrote him appreciatively:

> I don't think any body ever received a more generous review . . .

I was very hesitant about writing the book at all — and when it was finished and I had killed Douglas all over again, I was really quite uncertain whether or not I had done a decent job.[66]

With his conclusion that 'Margaret Cole has produced a volume which is moving, instructive and beautiful to read', all doubts must finally have been dispelled.

Notes

1. Margaret Cole (ed.), *Roads to Success* (Methuen, London, 1936), chapter on 'Doing Two Jobs'.

2. Jane Abraham, letter to author.

3. M. I. Cole to Richmond Postgate (all letters to Richmond Postgate cited are in his possession).

4. M. I. Cole to Richmond Postgate, 7 April 1945.

5. M. I. Cole to Richmond Postgate, August 1944.

6. Will Abraham, letter to author, spring 1982.

7. Ibid.

8. M. I. Cole to Richmond Postgate, 31 April 1944.

9. Will Abraham, letter to author, spring 1982.

10. M. I. Cole to Richmond Postgate, 15 June 1944.

11. Will Abraham, letter to author spring 1982.

12. M. I. Cole to Richmond Postgate, 17 November 1943.

13. M. I. Cole to Richmond Postgate, 9 May 1943.

14. M. I. Cole to Richmond Postgate, 8 July 1943.

15. M. I. Cole to Richmond Postgate, 15 November 1943.

16. M. I. Cole to Richmond Postgate, 17 November 1943.

17. M. I. Cole to Richmond Postgate, 18 April 1944.

18. M. I. Cole to Richmond Postgate, 1 October 1944.

19. Richmond Postgate, letter to author, 11 July 1983.

20. M. I. Cole to Richmond Postgate, 11 May 1945.

21. Richmond Postgate, letter to author, 11 July 1983.

22. M. I. Cole, *Life of G. D. H. Cole* (Macmillan, London, 1971), pp. 218–19.

23. Mrs Postgate to M. I. Cole, 15 November 1949 (CFP).

24. Cole, *Life*, p. 188.

25. Lady Chorley, interview.

26. M. I. Cole to Naomi Mitchison, September/October 1940 (all letters to Naomi Mitchison cited are in her possession).

27. M. I. Cole to Naomi Mitchison, October/November 1940.

28. M. I. Cole to Naomi Mitchison, September/October 1940.

29. Cole, *Life*, p. 243.

30. Ibid., p. 245.

31. Ibid.,. p. 246.

32. Ibid., p. 248.

33. M. I. Cole to Gilbert Murray, Gilbert Murray Papers, Bodleian Library Box 95, fos. 89–91.

34. M. I. Cole to Richmond Postgate, 7 September 1943.

35. M. I. Cole to Richmond Postgate, 26 March 1944.

36. M. I. Cole to J. L. Hammond, 7 July 1944, Hammond Papers, Bodleian Library, MS 26, fo. 200.

37. G. D. H. Cole to Richmond Postgate, 25 January 1945.

38. M. I. Cole to Naomi Mitchison, 26 September 1940.

39. M. I. Cole to Naomi Mitchison, October/November 1940.

40. M. I. Cole to Naomi Mitchison, November 1940.

41. M. I. Cole to Dorothy Fox, January 1944 (in possession of Dorothy Fox).

42. M. I. Cole to Richmond Postgate, 30 June 1945.

43. M. I. Cole, *Growing Up into Revolution* (Longmans Green, London, 1949), pp. 201–2.

44. M. I. Cole to G. D. H. Cole, November 1947 (CFP).

45. M. I. Cole to G. D. H. Cole (San Francisco), 15 November 1949 (CFP).

46. M. I. Cole to G. D. H. Cole, November 1947 (CFP).

47. M. I. Cole to G. D. H. Cole, 2 October 1949 (CFP).

48. M. I. Cole to G. D. H. Cole, October 1949 (CFP).

49. M. I. Cole to G. D. H. Cole, November 1949 (CFP).

50. M. I. Cole to G. D. H. Cole, 2 November 1947 (CFP).

51. M. I. Cole to G. D. H. Cole, November 1949 (CFP).

52. Mrs M. Horsley to M. I. Cole, 4 November 1949 (CFP).

53. Paul Fox to M. I. Cole, 8 January 1950 (CFP).

54. M. I. Cole to Agnes Murray, 9 May 1957 (all letters to Agnes Murray cited are in possession of Beryl Hughes).

55. M. I. Cole to Agnes Murray, 24 May 1957.

56. M. I. Cole to Agnes Murray, 22 July 1957.

57. M. I. Cole to Agnes Murray, 17 December 1957.

58. M. I. Cole to Agnes Murray, 23 December 1957.

59. M. I. Cole to Kingsley Martin, 17 July 1958 (CFP).

60. Cole, *Life*, p. 288.

61. Professor Richard Titmuss, 12 January 1959; Rajani Palme Dutt, 14 January 1959 (CFP).

62. Lord Chorley, 28 January 1959 (CFP).

63. Lady Simon of Wythenshawe, 15 January 1959 (CFP).

64. Professor A. J. P. Taylor, *New Statesman*, 1 October 1971.

65. Michael Foot, *Evening Standard*, 5 October 1971.

66. M. I. Cole to Michael Foot, 8 October 1971 (CFP).

12 A LITERARY AND PRACTICAL SOCIALIST

Author and Journalist

Margaret was a writer through and through. Although a first-class administrator and a provocative teacher, it is as an historian of the Labour Movement that she will best be remembered. There was rarely a period in her life when she was not editing a socialist journal or preparing a book or an article for publication. A redoubtable research worker, Margaret was a 'scribbler' with a shrewd sense of socialist purpose and an ability to set events in perspective. The sensitivity to words woven into her prose, and arguably attributable to the teaching of her pedantic father, was as acute as her sensitivity to colour. She once admitted that clashing colours really hurt her susceptibilities; similarly, the unfeeling use of the English language could genuinely distress her.

Her shrewd and witty literary style, as Naomi Mitchison said, was 'beautifully clear and lucid', and although Margaret never wrote with Douglas' fluency, fully covered foolscap pages could flow from her pen, virtually without correction. The quality of her prose, pithy and vivid, was infinitely superior to that of her husband's. In later years she found that 'cardiac laziness' made writing more burdensome, yet the discipline of long practice was such that in her late seventies she could still produce to order 'two essays of 7,000 words each, plus a 5,000 words contribution for the *Political Quarterly*', although 'they take so long and need so much rewriting'.[1]

Apart from the poetry of her youth, one of Margaret's early literary ventures was a highly derivative piece of science fiction (a genre she always enjoyed reading), *The Last Man from England*, which was published in *Time and Tide*: vegetation is killing man, and trees march on parliament. The story unashamedly plagiarised H. G. Wells, and the experiment was not repeated.[2] She did, however, write tales for children and produced a charmingly illustrated small, happy book, *The Story of Santa Claus for Little People*.

Among her later writing, in the thirties, was an obscure little monograph, *Books and the People*. In it Margaret expressed herself 'much in favour of any media that extends the availability of books to a wider readership', notably through paperbacks and book clubs, which at the time were relatively new to England. Such innovations, she argued, turned books and book reading 'from the privilege of a class into a possession of all'. Even though not all new ideas were necessarily good, the fatal thing was 'to shut oneself up in a box and assume, as the book trade is all to ready to do . . . that any change from the conditions prevailing at the beginning of the century is bound to be bad'.[3] When that was written, the great publisher, Allen Lane, had only just begun his pioneering trek into Penguin territory!

The writing output of Douglas and Margaret was prolific. Douglas' was immense and included some works of assured permanence, particularly *The Common People (1746–1938)*, written with Raymond Postgate, and his five-volume *History of Socialist Thought*. These will live as certainly as his works on Cobbett, and there is also a reviving interest in Guild Socialism. However, because so much of what he wrote was intended for immediate impact, it has inevitably been superseded. In contrast, Margaret's more restricted output stands the test of time well. Her books on *Marriage* (1938) and *Women of Today* (1937) reflected not only feminist achievements and attitudes, but also revealed some of Margaret's personal opinions. It was, however, her vivid *Makers of the Labour Movement* (1948), and later, in greater detail, *Robert Owen of New Lanark* (1953), which confirmed her as a first-class historian of the Labour Movement.

She intentionally counters the tendency of historians to write history books mostly from the point of view of diplomacy and military matters[4] and therefore in *Makers of the Labour Movement* selects those men (curiously there are no women included at all) 'who fought and died for freedom, social justice and the rights of the common people'. She sets their activities and beliefs in a political/economic framework, but does it with a lightness of literary touch and erudition that make the book a joy to read. Those men, illustrating different phases and facets in the battle for democracy, range from Cobbett, Tom Paine and Francis Place to William Morris, Keir Hardie and H. G. Wells.[5] Much later she rewrote and amplified several of the vignettes for inclusion in the *Dictionary of Labour Biography*.

Growing Up into Revolution (1949), to which this book owes much, is Margaret's essentially happy, hopeful record, written for

Jane, then in New York. Initially Margaret had had reservations, and just before its publication she wrote to Gilbert Murray:

> I have just finished a book of reminiscences which the publishers say they like very much, so I hope somebody will. It feels rather presumptuous, especially after editing *Our Partnership*, but I have seen something of life and have something to tell which may be fun . . . and I wanted to get it down before I started forgetting. As it was Chris Hollis in a review of my last book began 'Mrs Cole is an *enviable relic* of a happier age' — my italics![6]

Margaret need not have been apprehensive, for the autobiography was a triumph. Friends and critics found it delightfully evocative, and twenty years later Francis Meynell, after re-reading it 'with such pleasure and admiration', wrote to her: 'You have supplied so many memories that I had lost or waylaid and now resume through your skill and wisdom and wit.'

The lovingly detached *Life of G. D. H. Cole* (1971) was in large part an autobiographical sequel. To both, *Servant of the County*, although written earlier, gives an added if less lively dimension. It was an excellent exposition of the workings of a great council, but with justification the *Times* reviewer regretted that any details of the political life and personalities of those concerned with the LCC were missing. Naomi Mitchison found the *Life of Douglas* deeply evocative. Soon after its publication she wrote to Margaret:

> the book does give one a real picture. I keep recalling odd moments . . . a poem about you, of which I only remember 'April evenings in Bramerton Street' . . . but I do remember how full of outsize furniture it was, and Douglas leaning against a vast amount of books . . . how remote it all is — another world.[7]

It is, however, for Margaret's pioneering and editorial work about Sidney and Beatrice Webb, and for the *Story of Fabian Socialism* (1961), 'the book she found [to date] the hardest of all to write', that Margaret the Labour historian will be best remembered. For her various books on the Webbs and the Diaries, scrupulously researched and cross-checked, are stylishly written or edited with an affectionately personal insight which in their day blazed a trail.

After the Second World War, Margaret became widely recognised as an excellent journalist, not least by Michael Foot and Malcolm Muggeridge. She could have become a top political correspondent, but chose rather to channel her literary skills into mostly impecunious, mainly socialist, journals. She wrote for various papers, including the *Political Quarterly*, the *Contemporary Review*, the *New Statesman*; reviewed intermittently for *The Listener* and regularly for *Tribune*. In 1940 she produced for the latter a bitter series of forceful, factual articles on current conditions, which exposed Britain's Two Nations by tearing apart on the grounds of maldistribution of income and capital any claims to equality between classes. She analysed 'Murder by Poverty' whereby the 'poor have housing but the rich possess houses', used Boyd Orr's statistics to analyse the impact of limited expenditure upon food consumption and health, and concluded with a searing attack upon under-provision of education. It was a powerful onslaught.

For some thirteen years Margaret sustained a monthly column, 'Notes by the Way', in *Socialist Commentary*. A chatty precursor to this had been her column, 'The World of Labour', in the *New Standard*, the journal of workers' control, which she and Douglas had edited briefly in the early twenties. *Socialist Commentary*, edited by Rita Hinden and, after her tragically early death, by Peter Stephenson, regrettably folded in 1977, but until then Margaret had had a totally free hand over her contributions and thoroughly enjoyed her commission. 'I spread myself freely on anything I find interesting to write about,' she told Robin Page Arnot.[8]

Rita relied heavily on Margaret's advice and opinions, and they used to have long phone conversations about the paper's policy and the content of leading articles. Margaret could upset the editor by her sometimes caustic remarks, but although Rita by no means always accepted her criticisms, she rarely failed to respect them. Margaret would help constructively by finding new writers for *Socialist Commentary* and, although she thought Rita overemotional on occasions, had a warm regard for her energy and devotion to principle, and was profoundly saddened by her untimely death.

The lively, often challenging contents of her 'Notes' highlighted the fact that even in her eighties Margaret's humour, political perception and curiosity about outlandish facts were undiminished. She notes, for example, that the Gettysburg Oration was not delivered by Lincoln but by the Chosen Orator, one Senator Everett! She questioned the role of the Poet Laureate — in her view he was a 'Court Jester', and the role an anachronism — and with equal aplomb expressed delight in the beauty of Kuala Lumpur and 'its surviving smell of Somerset Maugham'.

Whenever appropriate, she would defend the Webbs in her column, re-emphasising, for example, that their 'Minority Report laid down the essentials of the Welfare State'; but above all, anecdotes and facts of Labour history flowed from her pen. After the death of Herbert Morrison, a few weeks before that of the LCC 'which he did so much to create', she observed that

> Only a few can remember how great and how surprising was the 1934 victory of the London Labour Party . . . or, in thirty years, how much the LCC has done for London . . . from building a new Waterloo Bridge to creating the Royal Festival Hall . . . a great deal of that achievement was due to the tight party discipline Morrison imposed.[9]

Inaccurate tributes to friends always riled her. She castigated *The Times* for the obituary notice they published on Kingsley Martin of the *New Statesman* (whose 'only equal as an editor was Orage of the *New Age*') for omitting any reference to Dorothy Woodman:

> How could anyone imagine one could make sense of a character with such emotionally sensitive antennae as Kingsley . . . without taking any account of his life-long companion and colleague (herself so considerable a person in her own right) brings me all up-standing,[10]

she wrote. In contrast was the quiet, almost tender note on Arthur Skeffington MP, a fellow Fabian and sometime County Hall colleague, who died in 1970: 'Without the existence of a good many people like Arthur — hard working, knowing how to play, devoted without being fanatical, friendly and reasonably optimistic — there would not be any Labour Movement at all.'[11]

Margaret's last column was typically astute:

> [Today] . . . we see two things which idealistic predecessors did not . . . how easily material things once thought luxuries are turned into necessities, and how much more simple greed there is

in ordinary humans than our forefathers allowed for . . . We don't do more as a nation than clamour about those less fortunate than ourselves . . . (hard luck, we argue in private) . . . but we must preserve our own differentials . . . make sure that nobody gets a rise that will put them more nearly on equality with ourselves . . . we're all right, thank you.[12]

As she so often reiterated, pioneers of the Labour Movement — Morris, Blatchford, Keir Hardie — had persistently overestimated the altruism of man. This, her final contribution to *Socialist Commentary*, was still full of verve, and as G. D. N. Worswick, Director of the National Institute of Economic and Social Research, observed, 'the column was always astonishingly youthful and up to date, and might have been written by someone half her age'.[13]

One lesser-known facet of Margaret's journalism was as a contributor to the obituary columns of *The Times*. Insistent that fair recognition be accorded to distinguished personalities, she wrote many a witty, anecdotal appreciation of friends high and humble. *The Times* former obituary editor, Colin Watson, recalled her impeccable standards: she was a 'good deliverer' who 'always did what she agreed to do, and on time'. She could nevertheless 'be most forthright, and never failed to point out factual errors with the utmost frankness, which could be most disconcerting'.[14]

Frequent references in her *Socialist Commentary* columns to current publications, prose and poetry, proved that Margaret was still an inveterate reader. She was also an excellent book critic, as evidenced from her frequent reviews in *The Listener* and *Tribune* during the sixties, and for *Books and Bookmen* in the seventies. She had mellowed greatly from the days when an early literary editor of *Tribune* recalled her as being 'abrasive, almost rude, in defence of her copy being cut'. Indeed, Cis Amaral, editor of *Books and Bookmen*, echoed Colin Watson in admiring Margaret's 'sheer professionalism' in finding her 'scrupulously punctual, meticulous over proof reading, and invariably correct about facts'. Margaret's power of total recall and her good judgement show how she, literally, had lived history, and explains why Cis Amaral did not like having 'any issue without something from you in'.[15]

The best reviews provide informative sketches of personalities Margaret knew and merge into a panorama of Labour history. For example, in dealing with a biography of Victor Feather, a former

General Secretary of the TUC, she could 'personally testify' to the 'remarkable authority' which Sir Walter Citrine (his predecessor), with 'his precise, controlled manners and shorthand notebook at the ready . . . came to exercise in discussion . . . He made the TUC a power by the time the second world war was over.'[16]

Margaret knew almost everyone who had contributed to contemporary political life, from Annie Besant and Mrs Bernard Shaw to Arthur Henderson ('the best Foreign Secretary for years') and Lady Vi (Violet Bonham Carter), whose 'crisp writing and salty descriptions' in her book about Winston Churchill Margaret warmly approved; even though in the review she assessed Winston as 'at the highest a glorious buccaneer, with an independent self-made mind, a tremendous gift of phrase, and a passion for military enterprise, forlorn hopes, and non-Party government.'[17]

Her judgement was rarely clouded by prejudice, indeed Margaret's balance and fairness in reviews are evidenced in her writing on, for example, Professor Harold Laski, who had little love for the Coles. Laski was 'by far the most prolific with pen and tongue of all LSE contemporaries' and she warmly acknowledged his 'wide ranging kindnesses' to students. However, she pinpointed his two main weaknesses as 'telling tall stories with little basis in fact', and the complete misjudgement of his role in Labour politics. The former was not of great import because the tales, 'practically never malicious', were intended to exhibit Laski as being in closer touch with more distinguished persons than was in fact the case, 'so the result to the historian is chiefly one of inconvenience'. More serious was the second tendency, for Laski to see himself either as 'an *eminence grise* dictating policy from behind the arras', or 'as leader of the Labour Party laying down policy'. His attempt to dictate to Attlee about policy at Potsdam, Margaret observed, evoked 'understandable resentment' and, not surprisingly, when Laski suggested to the Prime Minister that he might be appointed Ambassador to Washington, he received a dusty answer! Laski's real misfortune, Margaret concluded, was that

> his streak of megalomania prevented his genuine generosity and genuine socialist faith from making the impact on Labour thought that they might have done. Nevertheless, he was a teacher of remarkable ability, and could make a very favourable impression on his contemporaries.[18]

In view of Laski's former spitefulness over Margaret's work on the Webbs, which she must at least have sensed, this review emphasises her characteristically generous lack of rancour.

Possibly the most important of all her reviews are two sensitive essays in *Books and Bookmen* on Professor 'Harry' Tawney of LSE, author of *The Acquisitive Society* and a pillar of the WEA. An absent-minded, untidy, shambling man, he 'wrote like an angel' but as the discussions over the Webbs' biography had shown, could be obsessive, petulant and narrow-minded. The quality of his 'beautiful and memorable English' accounted, in Margaret's opinion, 'for a great deal of the admiration not to say devotion which he excited in his lifetime', and won for his books 'their secure place in literature as well as in the history of British political thought'. Yet Tawney had to be bullied or forced to write. 'I myself more than once reproached him for withholding from posterity books which would have been of great value,' Margaret wrote. His only reply was that he wasn't ready, or that the book would not have been good enough.

> The self deprecating nature of the excuse is curious when one considers how eagerly what he did publish was received . . . but he was singularly unassertive [and] had an almost morbid contempt for pretentiousness of any kind which he applied to himself as ruthlessly as he did to others. He possessed to a very big degree true humility.

After Tawney's death she commented that many spoke of him as a saint, including Hugh Gaitskell, who described him as 'the best man I have ever known . . . lesser mortals thought him irritating, perverse and prickly — qualities not unknown to some official saints of the church, but nevertheless did not attempt to deny his distinction'.[19] It is a measure of her loyalty to old colleagues that Margaret revealed little of Tawney's sluttishness to the world, and that Cis Amaral could write to her, 'You give a vivid idea of Tawney the man, and what he stood for.'[20] Yet about the same time that she wrote these reviews she told Robin Page Arnot:

> Tawney was an odd phenomenon — I don't know what psychological need forced him to be such a physical slut. Did he find it necessary to make that kind of protest against the Acquisitive Society? His kind of polished writing, I find, doesn't appeal to many of the young today, but I still think it more pleasing than Mother Fucker or Pig.[21]

If any book particularly pleased Margaret, she would not only express that pleasure in a warm review, but also (whether reviewing it or not) would often write to congratulate the author personally. Such was the case, for example, with the MacKenzies' *The First Fabians*, with Cecil Woodham Smith's work on the Irish famine — *The Great Hunger* — which 'I should like everyone to read,' Margaret wrote, 'for the future as much as for the past', even though she found its 400 pages over-long.[22] Margaret herself once commented that book reviews reveal more about the critic than the author. And certainly this could be true in her case. For her warmly informative, well-written pieces often exposed a generous attitude to colleagues and friends, her impatience with slovenly scholarship, and, above all, appreciation of a good book.

Margaret, an inveterate letter writer, both to friends and to the press, was regarded by C. H. Rolph, no mean scribbler himself, as a correspondent without equal. On one occasion, after receiving a letter full of reminiscences about Ezra Pound, he wrote to her, 'I've always thought you ought to make a charge for your letters . . . if I were a publisher I should be camping on your doorstep!'[23] Privately, Margaret was entertainingly shrewd over contemporary events and warmly sympathetic about personal grief. Publicly, since misrepresentations of fact or misrepresentations of history rarely escaped her, she could be both acid and witty — from a protracted correspondence in *Encounter* with Canadian Professor George Feaver, defending the Webbs against allegations of racialism (although Margaret did concede they were elitist) to an amusing brush in *The Times* with Bernard Levin who was flogging, in her view, 'moribund horses'. She agreed with him that it was aggravating when personages claimed 'they were the voice of the people when patently they were not', but 'there is nothing very new about this form of effrontery', and she quoted from a document in her possession written by a Victorian university vice chancellor protesting to a railway chairman against a proposal to run trains on Sunday from Cambridge to London. ' "Rest assured that such an innovation will be as displeasing to the Almighty God as it is to the Vice-Chancellor of the University of Cambridge" . . . I think the sentiment leaves Mr Levin's enemies at the post.'[24]

Some years later, *The Times* declared its intention of announcing her eighty-fifth birthday on the Court page. She wrote to the Thunderer, not ungratefully, but pointing out that apart from the status such an honour conferred it also provided a great deal of unwanted advertising . . . to name some recently received: three adjurations to be kind to elephants (of which there are few to be seen in Ealing), an invitation to purchase a pet crocodile (where should I keep it?), and a suggestion that I put up a patio (although living in a first floor flat)![25]

Research

An unflagging interest in research was woven into Margaret's literary work and her journalism, yet, although the Webbs and to a lesser degree Douglas were her mentors, her own exacting standards pre-dated them both. For, 'when I first went up to college I was informed that the motto of my university was "verify your references" ', she wrote. Facts always demanded respect.

You must spare no pains to check and re-check . . . and a fact which did not fit the picture must not be ignored . . . You must investigate and give it weight . . . No reader of Marx or Engels can fail to realise that they themselves kept this standard continuously before them.[26]

Because research was integral to so much of her and Douglas' work, and aimed to contribute to the totality of knowledge, Margaret cared deeply about the presentation and quality of material. A review she wrote of Julius Braunthal's *History of the International* (Volume 2) indicated the standards she respected. The author, she noted approvingly, had made every effort to check his sources against others, even though he did use some that were biased. She found the book 'a quarry of facts', praised its 'sheer readability', and above all commended the thorough documentation, the full bibliography and the footnotes 'with references for those who might want to check statements or pursue stories further'.[27] Her personal attitude she had summed up in a letter to Kingsley Martin:

I take note of your hint not to be fussy. I feel, though, quite strongly that in writing for print, and therefore for posterity, one has a duty to 'verify your references', so as not to give error permanent record. I am continually shocked by the laziness of would-be historians (and some not so would-be) in checking facts. You will remember what trouble H. G. Wells took, in collecting and and actually printing criticisms of his *Outline* [*of Modern Knowledge*].[28]

Margaret was unfailingly generous in time and expertise to researchers world-wide. It was, she considered, 'the proud position of scholars to help would-be scholars, and I would not wish it to be otherwise'. Even so, she and Robin Page Arnot once discussed the practicality of charging for the inroads upon their time and knowledge that 'research consultancy' made.[29] In fact they wrote to *The Author*, but their letter evoked no action. Once convinced of a scholar's seriousness of purpose, Margaret took infinite trouble to clarify and confirm. For an American, Arthur Mitzner, working on a biography of Ford Madox Ford (*The Saddest Story*) she compiled a detailed list of people who possessed paintings by Stella Bowen. She supplied observations and corrections about the life of Kingsley Martin which his biographer, C. H. Rolph, 'greatly appreciated' ('Kingsley was inaccurate — and I am pedantic . . . he thought it was pedantic to be accurate,' she told him)[30] and gave Norman and Jeanne MacKenzie careful comments on their draft of *The Time Traveller*, about H. G. Wells. She was also deeply interested in the definitive life of George Bernard Shaw, on which Michael Holroyd was working. In the course of a revealing correspondence about the great man, she expressed her dislike of ponderous tomes and hoped that Holroyd would not

> make the book very long . . . Enormous biographies even if authorised, are bad for the reader . . . Of course you could easily make Shaw write it all himself! Though not with perfect accuracy . . . I don't think Shaw's life is important in detail, unlike the Webbs: what is important is what he wrote and said . . . so don't please expend too much space in Freudian poking into detail! The risk you run of course is that extensive quotation from Shaw invites comparison with the writer's own, which generally comes off worst!

Adding later:

> There were at least two Shaws: one who could work quite hard at rather humdrum jobs, as on the old St Pancras Vestry . . . and the other, an irresponsible advertiser, as in the case of Roger Casement (see the Webb Diaries, 1912–1924).[31]

It was by no means only established scholars to whom Margaret gave help: she was genuinely interested in encouraging and assisting less sophisticated overseas students. An Indian college lecturer, (Dr) K. I. Sharma, researching in Delhi for his PhD thesis on Douglas, wanted to visit England 'to gather more fruitful material'. His persistence and patent sincerity appealed to her for he was determined that 'my eight long years of study on Professor Cole should not go to waste . . . the Doctorate is my only ambition in life'. Promptly Margaret sent advice over sources and contacts at Nuffield, and ultimately Dr Sharma's plans came to fruition. After visiting Oxford (and Margaret), he wrote from India that his university department was celebrating its silver jubilee and 'I have initiated a move for it to be named after Professor Cole . . . I am really thankful for the help you gave me. Keep care of your health, I need you much for years.'[32]

She also had a charmingly uninhibited correspondence with a young Ghanaian, the son of a cocoa farmer — 'my mother who is younger, produces foodstuffs' — also anxious to study in England. He wrote to her out of the blue when she was 84.

Hi Maggie . . . I very well like your article in the *New Statesman* and thought of taking you as a pen friend . . . I am a boy aged 19 pursuing a sixth form course which leads to University. I hope you will respond to this letter, without considering age . . .

This she did, promptly, and a charming correspondence ensued. The young student, delighted at Margaret's 'remarkable achievements' which he found listed in *Who's Who* of 1960, told her, 'I can boast of it when I am with friends . . . that I have a pen pal who has written so many books and articles.'[33] In reply to his request 'for one of your books . . . because any time I read your letter I feel delighted in the English and the way and manner you use to write', she responded, and he wrote delightedly, 'Good Dame . . . your precious gift was handed to me yesterday . . . I cannot tell you how much I appreciate it, until you receive something from me.'[34] Sadly, there was no further correspondence.

Overseas students were by no means the only applicants for Margaret's attention. She seems to have provided facts and bibliographical details to scholars world-wide. From requests for help over a dictionary of British radicalism from Detroit, to booklists on workers' control for a London Polytechnic lecturer, she dealt with almost any request in patient detail, though she did repulse a threat from a student anxious to submit a 400,000 word thesis on George Holyoak, the early British Co-operator! On balance, however, she liked being asked and was always ready to advise and inform.

Although Margaret's reaction was usually to be generously helpful, there was nothing she scorned more than the slipshod academic. One unfortunate university lecturer drew upon his head her most scathing strictures for a book on Fabianism in which he generalised from ill-substantiated unauthoritative material. 'I am amazed that anything quite so casual could come from a professed historian,' she wrote, and accused the hapless man of making endless 'snide remarks' because of 'your dislike of Fabianism'. After castigating him for lack of evidence and writing half truths, she concluded acidly:

> Part of your trouble is that you cannot take the word of any really good historians who were contemporaries and knew at the time whatever was happening. Men like Halévy, Trevelyan, Barker you despise, and believe that they did not know what they were talking about . . . Whereas a small paragraph in an obscure paper or a minute, written up in a hurry, is gospel truth. This is not being a scholar; this is being a goose . . . Your Woolwich and Erith chapters are good![35]

Margaret had firm views about methods of research and was sceptical about the value of historiography which consisted of 're-producing either literally or in summary what a number of writers had said about a contentious subject, in the belief that study of such works would elicit the Truth'. There was nothing new, Margaret observed, in the fact that value judgements on people and events varied from age to age, but it was essential to know the work and the academic standing of authorities quoted. Nevertheless she was delighted when Dr Malcolm Thomis, in his book *The Town Labourer and the Industrial Revolution*, exonerated the Hammonds from accusations of economic ignorance, of being sentimental and selective in their books *The Village Labourer* and *The Town Labourer*. They had been excoriated for making moral judgements because they had analysed and decried the beneficial effects of the Industrial Revolution. 'It is a pleasure to one who never thought it right to exclude value judgements from history or day to day comment,' she wrote, 'to find that his [Dr Thomis'] judgement comes firmly down on the Hammonds' side.'[36]

She also loathed 'horrid bits of psychological jargon' and foot-notes which ought to have been included in the text. She chided writers who incorporated large extracts without evaluating the authors cited, and distrusted the current practice of tape-recording the oldest inhabitant, and regarding what was said — 'oral history' — with deep reverence: 'accepting such recollections uncritically is not really the way to write good and lasting history'.

Margaret was also dubious about the 'commendable practice' of giving research grants. She considered that it could foster the inability to omit from published results any fact which the researcher had discovered. And whereas she conceded this was understandable — since 'researchers wished to prove to their bene-factors that all available authorities had been properly consulted' — it did not make for a satisfactory end product because

> To stud the pages with numerical references to notes . . . or . . . to break up pages with huge footnotes . . . makes reading an obstacle race, and it blurs the picture which the writer is trying to convey. The great historians . . . were not guilty of this kind of fragmentation.[37]

Moreover, contemporary historical biographers should assume that readers already knew a good deal of the circumstances in which their characters had their being. It was singularly unlikely that any-one stout hearted enough to embark upon reading, for example, the massive two-volume biography by Yvonne Knapp of Eleanor Marx — 'a vast tombstone . . . to an attractive, charming, vigorous woman' — would need to be informed that 'B. Potter was not the creator of Peter Rabbit'.[38]

Although always sensitive to the qualities of good writing, Margaret regarded Gibbon as the historian without peer, and con-sidered Bertrand Russell 'the supreme master of English style'. His writing was

> the most perfect for lucidity combined with force and happy phrasing, one would venture to say, since Jonathan Swift . . . In these days of jargon and endless tortuous sentences (which completely lack rhythm and often seem to lack meaning as well) . . . [his] writing is always clear and nearly always a joy to read.[39]

Socialist Records — Archives and Artefacts

If Margaret was somewhat critical of the method and content of certain contemporary research, she was constructive in planning to preserve records and memorabilia of the Labour Movement. Her practical approach was exemplified by her role in creating the *Dictionary of Labour Biography* and in her support for the Museum of Labour History.

She was deeply committed to the *Dictionary*, which is a unique publication, edited by Professor John Saville and Dr Joyce Bellamy of Hull University. This continuing work, which has already encompassed seven scholarly volumes and is likely to reach a baker's dozen, interprets the lives of men and women, humble and high, who built socialism. A monumental achievement, listing factual biographies and definitive bibliographies of every entrant, it owed its genesis to the joint vision of Douglas and Margaret. Indeed, in 1948 Margaret had hoped that 'one day our Movement will itself produce its own Biographical Encyclopaedia'.[40] But as John Saville explained in his Introduction to the first volume (rightly dedicated to Margaret and in memory of Douglas):

> The idea originated with G. D. H. Cole. After his death Margaret offered a number of manuscript volumes which G. D. H. Cole had been putting together for many years. They consisted of hundreds of names with a few lines of biographical information attached to each,

but were potentially invaluable. Largely because of Douglas' association with the Institute of Social History at Amsterdam, and through the good offices of Margaret and Professor Julius Braunthal, the Institute made a research grant available. Thus a most prestigious work was launched.

The first two volumes were widely praised for their scholarship and scope.

> The compilers dug far deeper than the top layer of national personalities in Labour history to encompass those men and women who stood for the integrity and self respect of the downtrodden . . . The work attracted some marvellous writers . . . particularly Dame Margaret Cole.[41]

That view was echoed by E. P. Thompson, who considered that

'Dame Margaret goes from strength to strength as an historian as she grows older . . . writing on George Lansbury, Raymond Postgate, Edward Pease and the Webbs . . . Her information is enlivened by asides, sometimes humorous, sometimes waspish.'[42] Margaret, delighted with the enterprise, wrote in *Socialist Commentary*:

> although the original spark came from G. D. H. Cole and myself, the result is far more impressive than we could ever have imagined . . . One gets the impression of looking at a world apart from that of the ordinary biographical dictionary — An underwater world, as it were, inhabited by strange fish and coral insects.[43]

Apart from the high standard of scholarship, she also admired the technical care exercised in production, and wrote to John Saville, the joint editor with Dr Joyce Bellamy:

> I would like to congratulate you particularly on your printers and on your proof reading. I am enclosing a few cases of misprint or slight error . . . I daresay there are a few more, as I don't pretend to have read it all closely, but they are really astonishingly few — the actual entries are mostly very good indeed . . . though not all equally good, of course.[44]

From time to time Margaret would send suggestions for future entries or for new methods of presentation. It seems likely that she was an irritant to overburdened editors, and certainly on occasion John Saville found that she could be both 'bitchy and tough'. Wisely, however, he sidestepped anger, fully recognising her worth, and recalled that 'Her own contributions were the only ones on which the editors never did any editorial work.'[45] Their merits, however, lay in more than accuracy. As Professor Saville assured Margaret, her entries were unique in that

> No-one else has the range and depth of recollections that you have . . . They really are important additions to our knowledge of the history of the Labour Movement in the last half century . . . I hope that we can continue to press you for further contributions since there is literally no one whose historic understanding and knowledge is more important . . . You have the kind of

memory and recollections that undoubtedly add a new dimension to our understanding of the personalities of the past.[46]

As a Labour historian Margaret was always eager to preserve documents and socialist memorabilia. 'No other country has a Labour and radical past anything like ours,' she wrote, recalling how in the early twenties she and Douglas, when visiting Colchester Castle, had found

> lying on a heap of ancient papers about to be burnt, a copy of a very rare original edition of the 1842 Report on the *Health of Towns*. We salvaged that one; afterwards kept a steady look out, so far as two private people could, for other valuable historical documents.[47]

When therefore the idea for a Labour History Museum was mooted in the early sixties, she and (Professor) Asa Briggs gave it their enthusiastic support, and Margaret became a vice president of the Trade Union Labour Co-operative Democratic History Society (TULC), which was working to build up such a centre.

Writing in *Things* (later *Visual History*), the society's journal, she argued the case for preserving artefacts and for 'stopping the drain of historic treasures'. Between the two wars valuable documents had been sold for waste paper, and now a greater menace threatened, she warned:

> American libraries, some none too scrupulous in their methods, have shown themselves willing to pay good dollars for historical books, manuscripts, letters . . . and people trying to get themselves doctorates (to be in the running for better-paid jobs) have been writing theses on English social and industrial history and have snapped up — sometimes by plain pilfering — historical documents which are a valuable part of Britain's cultural heritage.[48]

The concept of a Museum of Labour History grew from the vision of Walter Southgate, who as a boy had purchased a first edition of Thomas Paine's *Rights of Man* (now in the Museum) for sixpence. From 1963 Southgate worked closely with a like-minded enthusiastic trade unionist, Henry Fry, who, with his wife Betty, helped to assemble and house the embryonic collection in their home at Reigate, Surrey. Later the collection was moved to Florence Willard House, also in Reigate, which all too soon was 'bursting at the seams'.

Margaret fully appreciated the need for new premises. Praising the unstinting efforts of a few devoted enthusiasts who had made the moves within Reigate possible, she was

> impressed by the amount of Labour history there . . . kept in cupboards and drawers, on tables and in trunks . . . impressed by their single-minded devotion . . . [but] horrified by the thought that the very life of the collection depends on the energy and dedication of a very few people.[49]

Typically practical, she urged the need to create a 'real Foundation' so that valued possessions could be kept 'in a permanent centre, on permanent display, with someone on hand to show and interpret'. Portable exhibitions designed for publicity helped to generate interest, but raised little financial support. Enthusiasts such as historian Stan Newens MP and Paul Beasley, then leader of Tower Hamlets Borough Council, were scarce. Even the TUC gave no encouragement to a TULC delegation (which included Margaret and Asa Briggs) urging sponsorship for a specific centre.

As a keen protagonist of this idea, Margaret angrily countered Bernard Levin's derisive dismissal of the embryonic Reigate collection as 'idiotic detritus'. 'I can assure him', she wrote to *The Times*, 'he will find there a serious conspectus of the past history of a large part of his fellow citizens, and I hope he will apologise to them.'[50] Victory for the TULC was not far distant. The Council of Tower Hamlets, formed from the boroughs of Stepney and Poplar, areas rich in socialist tradition, advanced a solution. Clement Attlee had been Stepney's first Labour mayor and was elected MP for Limehouse (then part of Stepney) in 1922, which he represented for nearly thirty years. Attlee was interested in Labour history, so it was wholly appropriate that part of the vast old Limehouse Town Hall (now in Tower Hamlets) should be offered at peppercorn rent to accommodate the Museum. 'The Council officials and staff were real comradely and helpful,' Henry Fry told Margaret, 'and everyone representing TULC was delighted with the offer which we accepted with gratitude.'[51] So in September 1974 the Museum moved into the Town Hall and was officially opened the following May by the Prime Minister, (Sir) Harold Wilson.

The spacious premises, draped with often enormous, and always handsome, pictorial trade union banners made years ago by hand and sewn with love, provide a splendid background for a unique collection of visual history. Today the Museum occupies the entire Town Hall, a far cry from the Frys' small front room, and a growing collection of 'Things', with libraries, documents and photographs of British working-class history, has been built up. Exhibitions are arranged and lectures for schools on social and political history are provided. The Museum, now a registered charity with financial support from local authorities, individuals and the wider Labour Movement, seems well established. Of course, there is never enough money, but a vision has been realised. Margaret really wanted working-class people to understand their history. She wanted the documents and the artefacts cared for, and above all she wanted the Museum to be seen. And this indeed has come to pass.

The Society for the Study of Labour History, which was primarily though not exclusively for academics, also won Margaret's support. With her brother Ray and Professor Tawney she had been present at the initial meeting in 1960, when (Professor) Asa Briggs had launched the organisation, and was an assiduous participant at all London meetings. She was always attentive and useful in discussion, John Saville recalled, and 'obviously regarded the Society as an important new development for the more vigorous study of Labour history'.[52] Margaret was also a lynx-eyed reader of the Society's *Bulletin*, contribruting to it personal experiences and commentating on factual accuracy. Exploding the theory that the General Strike was not taken seriously, she cited Professor Mowat's relevant (and excellent) chapter in *Britain between the Wars* and explained:

> The impression of 'light heartedness' arose from the enormous uplift given to local organisations when it was decided first that the whole Movement must unite to stop the rot and secondly that it was up to local union members to conduct the struggle by their own organisations in their own towns. The spirit thus generated was comparable with that of the country as a whole after the Fall of France . . . In many districts the surrender was simply not believed.[53]

Among her other contributions was a spirited defence of Guild

Socialism. This arose from a review concerning several reprints of Douglas' books in which a critic had regretted that it was the last edition of *The World of Labour* that had been republished. 'Only a fool', Margaret observed caustically, 'would have stuck irremovably to what he had written in 1913,' when Labour was little more than a pressure group, and before the economic results of the war conditions had so deeply altered the powers and aspirations of the unions. She doubted whether this critic had realised 'the enormous effect of the scarcity of labour intake during the war years', which had accounted for the conversion of so many trade union leaders to Guild Socialism, 'as it also accounted for its collapse when that scarcity vanished overnight in the post war slump', and concluded:

of course I agreee that Guild Socialism had as mystic a faith in the abilities of shop stewards and union branch secretaries as the collectivists had in civil servants. Later experience has made us sadly conscious that both groups [were fallible] . . . and also of the dangerous possibility of a developing trade union bureaucracy — hardly on the cards sixty years ago . . . but what conclusion is drawn from that? That the Guild Socialists were visionaries who should never have been listened to? The revived interest in workers' control which has called for these reprints does not suggest it.[54]

Similarly Margaret encouraged *History Workshop Journal*, a left-wing publication for Labour historians, based at Ruskin College. Raphael Samuel, one of the editorial team, remembered Margaret as an 'honoured, supportive figure of the *Journal*', who wrote to its Editorial Collective congratulating them on a reprint of the *Martyrdom of the Nine* which she considered 'of great value'. She also once contributed a spirited defence of historical novels for children, suggesting that there were many books which children could still enjoy. 'Not all were like G. A. Henty or Manville Fenn,' and she cited

The Cloister and the Hearth, Kipling's *Puck O' Pook's Hill*, and *Rewards and Fairies* . . . and the various novels of E. Nesbitt . . . Of course the earlier books don't have a proletarian setting or a good socialist moral, but children should learn to discount that if the writing is good.

She considered the editorials were 'very good so far as they go', added a final plea for the inclusion of maps in the *Journal* and concluded, 'I congratulate you heartily on the production generally.'[55]

The Good Food Guide

As a frivolous footnote to Margaret's more serious activities must be included *The Good Food Guide*, which grew from the Good Food Club founded by Raymond in 1949. It first appeared in 1951 under his editorship and was based on reports and assessments voluntarily submitted by family and friends. For a long while Margaret was one of several unpaid inspectors, who, unheralded and unidentified, would dine at, and report upon, restaurants throughout Britain. She liked good food and wine, and relished these investigations, but even more she enjoyed producing the *Guide*, which in its youthful days owed a good deal to the collaboration of her sister-in-law Daisy. Early on 'the Guide was largely compiled by the efforts of volunteers crawling over her living room floor armed with pens, scissors and bits of paper'.[56]

Margaret helped nurse the new publication and later, when Ray was seriously ill, found much of her time taken up in its production. She recalled writing in great haste 'twenty seven reports for the GFG — a dreadfully finnicky, messy business', but it was a job she gladly tackled.[57] Initially the *Guide* was viewed sceptically: with time, however, it became profitable financially and gastronomically authoritative. Not without reason was Raymond dubbed Public Stomach Number One!

After ten years Ray sold the *Guide* to the Consumer Association, but continued as editor until 1969. 'He made the *Guide* above all readable,' Christopher Driver, his successor, wrote. 'His editing was firm and pernickity but he did not suffer fools gladly whether they held a pen or a soup spoon!'[58]

Notes

1. M. I. Cole to Robin Page Arnot, 20 July 1969 (CFP).
2. *Time and Tide*, 30 September 1921.
3. M. I. Cole, *Books and the People* (pamphlet, Hogarth Press, London, 1938).
4. Moons earlier Margaret had written to Gilbert Murray 'after slanging in a review the *Cambridge History of the British Empire*' that

it makes me wild with rage to see what English professional historians call history: battles and diplomacy, diplomacy and battles i.e. technicalities and scandal . . . 37 pages for literature and social conditions to 1783 — all of it — and 13 for Shelbourne's wriggle before the Treaty of Paris . . . how long are these creatures to go on choking young minds with grit? (Gilbert Murray Papers, 23 July 1929, Bodleian Library, Box 56, fos. 20–6)

5. M. I. Cole, *Makers of the Labour Movement* (Longmans Green, London, 1948), Introduction.

6. Gilbert Murray Papers, 3 October 1948, Box 99, fos. 116–17.

7. Naomi Mitchison to M. I. Cole, 14 September 1971 (CFP).

8. M. I. Cole to Robin Page Arnot, 20 July 1969 (CFP).

9. *Socialist Commentary* (March 1965).

10. Ibid. (April 1969).

11. Ibid. (March 1970).

12. Ibid. (November 1978).

13. Letter to author, 25 June 1982.

14. Colin Watson, letter to author, June 1982.

15. Cis Amaral to M. I. Cole, 28 July 1975 (CFP).

16. *Books and Bookmen* (June 1975).

17. *Tribune*, 9 May 1965.

18. *Books and Bookmen* (February 1978).

19. Ibid. (November and December 1974).

20. Cis Amaral to M. I. Cole, 26 September 1974 (CFP).

21. M. I. Cole to Robin Page Arnot, 4 September 1974 (CFP).

22. In correspondence Cecil Woodham Smith told Margaret that she

took out some 40,000 words . . . because I was anxious to keep the price down. I do hope you think the book good value at thirty shillings — I wanted as many people as possible to read it, as a contribution to Anglo-Irish understanding. (8 December 1952 (CFP))

23. C.H. Rolph to M. I. Cole, 16 November 1976 (CFP).

24. M. I. Cole to *The Times*, 8 May 1971.

25. M. I. Cole to *The Times*, 20 January 1978.

26. 'Truth and Politics', *Political Quarterly* (July 1943).

27. Society for the Study of Labour History, *Bulletin* (Autumn 1968).

28. M. I. Cole to Kingsley Martin, 17 August 1966 (University of Sussex Library).

29. M. I. Cole to Robin Page Arnot, 5 May 1969 (CFP).

30. M. I. Cole to C.H. Rolph, interview/notebooks, 10 May 1971.

31. M. I. Cole to Michael Holroyd (probably June 1977, in the possession of Michael Holroyd).

32. Dr K. L. Sharma to M. I. Cole, 1 May 1977 (CFP).

33. Letter from Ghana, 13 December 1976 (CFP).

34. Letter from Ghana, 24 May 1977 (CFP).

35. November 1967 (CFP).

36. *Books and Bookmen* (April 1975).

37. Ibid. (November 1976).

38. Ibid. (April 1977).

39. Ibid. (July 1977).

40. Cole, *Makers of the Labour Movement*, Introduction.

41. Robert Taylor, *New Society*, 5 September 1974.

42. *Guardian*, 15 August 1974.

43. M. I. Cole, *Socialist Commentary* (August 1972).

44. M. I. Cole to John Saville, June 1972 (CFP and Hull University Library).

45. John Saville, letters to author, 30 September 1982 and 27 February 1983.

46. John Saville to M. I. Cole, 5 September 1973 and 13 September 1973 (CFP and Hull University Library).

47. M. I. Cole, *Things* (Winter 1968).

48. Ibid.

49. Ibid. (Spring 1970).

50. *The Times*, 10 March 1973.

51. Henry Fry to M. I. Cole, January 1973 (CFP).

52. John Saville, letter to author, 17 December 1984.

53. Society for the Study of Labour History, *Bulletin* (Autumn 1971).

54. Ibid. (Autumn 1974).

55. M. I. Cole, letter to *History Workshop Journal*, 31 August 1976.

56. M. I. Cole, *The Times*, 30 April 1971 (in obituary of Daisy Postgate).

57. M. I. Cole to Robin Page Arnot, 20 October 1968 (CFP).

58. *Guardian*, 30 March 1971.

PART FOUR:
DAME MARGARET COLE

13 ONE GOES UP AND DOWN

'Forty Years is Forty Years'

Margaret possessed abundant resilience, and after Douglas' death coped stoically with the attendant loneliness. 'I know it's better that he died . . . and I don't find anything awful to reproach myself with,' she wrote to Agnes Murray, 'but forty years is forty years. He was good, you know . . . All the things that people said in their letters were perfectly true.'[1] She missed him intensely, 'not being able to turn and just make a remark (even if the only answer was "I hate")'.[2]

In the immediacy of Douglas' death, Margaret appreciated the support she had from both Humphrey and Agnes, but was profoundly anxious not to be a burden to either. 'It would be awful to be a nuisance,' she confided to Agnes, 'I hope I haven't grumbled too much.'[3] Humphrey cheered her greatly. 'Last weekend we worked quite hard packing up glass and other stuff for Jane,' she wrote, and afterwards

> we took our lunch to Kew and it was lovely. Bluebells all over the place, quantities of azaleas and lilac. And birds singing like anything. 'Are they larks' asked my ignoramus. Larks in Kew! He had on a new suit and looked really elegant.[4]

After deliberation, Margaret decided to move, although 'I am just wilting at the thought of what has to be done — nobody else to do it and nobody to do it for.'[5] However, only fleetingly prone to self-pity, she faced yet another uprooting, after finding a charming house in Hampstead Garden Suburb. It had a small garden in which she delighted, roses bloomed all the year round, and it was close to her old friends Lance and Taffy Beales. Unlike Douglas, to her possessions mattered little. Margaret resolutely disposed of yet more chattels and by early autumn was writing almost cheerfully to Agnes, 'I think the house is attractive and I like to come back to it . . . but one goes up and down.'[6]

Margaret always had the capacity to assess her own limitations, and even before she was widowed admitted that it's pretty grim to be getting so deaf, and to have what a foreign friend called a 'herringade' — sounds like a loathsome new temperance drink! If I can't get it right I shall have to chuck 'public work'. It ought to be possible to vaporise yourself when your usefulness has come to an end![7]

She wrote Agnes again in a similarly melancholy mood:

Growing old is certainly the root cause of much trouble in oneself, and there really isn't an answer. I do wish people would not send me books to review about *Old People in Bethnal Green*, how lonely they can be, and how useless they feel! *I feel*, don't you, that having as one hopes been of some use for the middle of one's life it will be appalling to be none later on. What do the people who go on to 100 . . . think they're doing? And what a fool old Rabbi Ben Ezra was![8]

After Douglas' death Margaret did not remain low-spirited indefinitely. She was determined to continue with some public work, though with what she was for a time uncertain.

Not paid work because age and hearing do come in . . . but I am a good home nurse . . . a good chairman and administrator, and a good letter writer. But no one is going to pay me for any of that — and I shan't get far by reviewing for *Tribune*![9]

In fact she resumed working along several familiar channels — for the Fabian Society, for London education, and substantially extended her writing and journalism. As Richmond observed, Margaret's powers of adaptability and readjustment were remarkable.

If over the years Margaret gave much to London, the LCC and other public activities gave much to her. For the various responsibilities and contacts which fanned out from further education generally helped immeasurably to enhance her sense of usefulness while the companionship of Council colleagues diminished loneliness, even though occasionally she did weary of too much shop. 'I wish County Hall was a little less closed in. I am interested in public education, but I don't want to think and talk about it only.'[10]

A little-known aspect of Margaret's public service was her

membership of the Staff Side of the Civil Service Arbitration Tribunal. She had been appointed to this as far back as 1943 with (Lady) Barbara Wootton, Leonard Woolf and Harold Laski. The only previous woman member had been Madeline Robinson (a friend from the days of LRD), so this feminine invasion created something of a precedent.

The function of the Tribunal was to arbitrate on matters concerning conditions of employment, hours of work and discipline. Membership was not onerous, the composition of tribunals was fixed by rota, and Margaret was greatly interested. She had always enjoyed prodding behind the facts to find out how a service worked, and over the years until 1965 proved a valuable member. Stanley Mayne, former General Secretary of the Institution of Professional Civil Servants, a union which regularly used the Tribunal, considered that the Civil Service had much to thank her for:

> The practice in her day was for each side to submit a written statement of case, then to argue the points before and with the Tribunal. Margaret's incisive mind made her a particularly valuable member, because her questioning often elicited aspects of the case that had not been sufficiently emphasised. She was never in any doubt that while her function was quasi-judicial, she was a Staff Side nominee.[11]

The Honours of Age

By the late sixties Margaret's public work had contracted. She left County Hall in 1967 (although retaining various governorships) of her own volition, but regretfully. For it was at a time when the Tories had swept the political board, and she wrote to Francis Meynell that

> The crash of the London elections has just deprived me of a part-time job [as Chairman of the Further Education Committee] which I was doing quite well and liking, of a desk and table I have occupied for seventeen years, and of a club of 'work friends' whom one met and conversed with casually without need to make complicated arrangements. So I was feeling very cold and lonely and it was lovely to get your letter just as the waters

of oblivion seemed to be closing . . . Nobody will remember the defeated for long.[12]

This 'defeated one', however, had not been forgotten, and in 1965 Margaret received the OBE in recognition of her public work for education in London. Congratulations flowed in, although not a few friends shared the opinion of Mary Omerod, a long-time colleague not given to flattery, who was

> seething with indignant protest . . . that a Labour Prime Minister [Harold Wilson] should give you a lower Order than I got from a Tory, for doing less in one field of activity against three in which you might well have been equally honoured . . . A life peerage would have been fitting, but the Labour Party is very ungrateful.[13]

Restitution came, however, in 1970, with what friends called her 'Damery': Margaret was made a DBE. This pleased her greatly, and petulant annoyance was often evoked if her 'title' was inadvertently overlooked. She carefully listed all the congratulatory messages received, and retained them as rich evidence of friendships long preserved. From early political days there materialised Otto Clarke, Lady Chorley, Arnold Toynbee and Julian Huxley ('You should have been honoured decades ago . . . the announcement brings back memories of you and GDH half a century back')[14] together with academics and administrators. 'I can't remember what Douglas thought of such things,' wrote Lord Redcliffe-Maud, 'but so long as there are honours I'm all for people like you accepting them.'[15]

The literary world, too, approved. David Higham, her agent, and Alan Hutt, editor of *The Journalist*, were delighted. 'The Dame part of the Order has, after all, always been kept worthy and exclusive,' Hutt wrote, 'dear old Sybil, Fonteyn, et al.' It was, however, Naomi Mitchison's note, simple and direct, amid the eulogies, which summed things up. 'I am so glad you have had one of those few decorations which hasn't been shop soiled. Dick would have been so pleased.'[16]

Later Margaret sent her own idiosyncratic account of the investiture to Francis Meynell:

I was bedamed on Tuesday . . . had to go up at the end of the

line and then (as you know) to sit for hours . . . while thick and
fast they came at last . . . one just has to stare at the yeomen and
wonder if one of them will wobble! Going up the stairs I nearly
laid hands on one of the attendant cuirassiers, forgetting that I
wasn't in Tussauds . . . Does one wear the DBE bauble on top of
the one earlier, or side by side? It doesn't say.[17]

Three years later, 'fit and spry', Margaret celebrated her
eightieth birthday with a splendid party at County Hall, which was
unexpectedly mentioned (to her great glee) in the Court pages of
The Times. Over a hundred members of family and friends of long
standing gathered to acclaim her: socialists from The Movement,
pillars of the WEA, Fabians, Members of Parliament, County Hall
colleagues, peers and peeresses, academics and administrators.
Affection and loyalty were paramount; the Prime Minister, Harold
Wilson, proposed her health, and the occasion delighted her. 'I was
touched and a bit embarrassed by the number of people who put
themselves out to come,' she told Nicolas Pease, 'and the nice
things that were said which I don't think I deserved.'[18] She did,
however, deserve them, as Ted Littlecott wrote her:

> Your birthday dinner was a splendid affair . . . I thought you
> were in great form . . . You looked good and you sounded good,
> and you pleased me at the end of your talk with your gracious
> reference to County Hall staff . . . It thrilled me to hear you say
> that your work in London Government had brought you so
> much personal reward.[19]

A formal recognition of Margaret's contributions to knowledge
came with her being elected a Fellow of the Royal Historical
Society in 1976. The proposal — initiated by Dr Brian Harrison —
gratified her although she was surprisingly apprehensive as to
whether or not she would be acceptable on grounds of age. In fact
she was elected, attended the President's party in her eighty-fifth
year, and was generally delighted at receiving this honour.

One of the last official tributes was Margaret's receiving an
Honorary Fellowship of LSE in 1977. This conferred certain
library privileges and implied the hope that those honoured would
support the annual dinner and various public functions. Because of
the School's association with the Webbs, the bestowal was a most
felicitous gesture.

More Travel

Unlike Douglas, Margaret was no xenophobe, and once admitted in *Who's Who* that her recreations included 'looking at my own and other countries'. In this she was able to indulge more fully after Douglas' death, partly because Jane and her husband — for professional reasons — moved around the world. Thus travelling provided a pleasurable means of maintaining family contacts and Margaret, immensely interested in her grandchildren, continued her visits, 'fading but dogged', when clearly unwell, until within eighteen months of her death.[20]

The Abrahams rarely seemed to live in countries that were politically stable, but Margaret would always observe and prod with interest into local situations. An early trip in 1960 took her with Jane to Cuba the night Fidel Castro seized power. 'I often wonder how that night of street shooting and the shrouded public rooms of the hotel seemed to her,' Jane recalled.

> We were the only guests, yet next day were able to take a perfectly normal tourist tour . . . Perhaps this helped her to realise that life just goes on, amidst the bombs, revolutions and coups which we encountered later . . . Our next point of call was Mexico. We explored Mexico City together, saw its art treasures and the pyramids of the Aztecs . . . We took a hair-raising bus ride to Taxco . . . then on to Acapulco where she enjoyed her first swim in tropical seas and rum drinks served out of coconuts . . . She later said that while our peripatetic way of life prevented her from living with us, it did enable her to visit many places she would not otherwise have seen.[21]

During the sixties Margaret stayed with Jane on Long Island, and camped with the family in Canada on several occasions. She helped with the cleaning, coped with family crises (on one early visit Anne drove her car into a ditch, and the boys lost their canoe) and once received the press who 'discovered her clutching an extremely dirty, smelly baby!'

Another major trip abroad was to Kuala Lumpur, Malaysia, in the spring of 1969. Margaret's health was not then of the best, and she had an infection of the lymphatic gland, but she never allowed her ailments to deter her from doing as much as possible. The family took her to the mountains where she saw tea growing and

enormous tree ferns. She loved the food and at one Chinese cele-
bration ate raw fish with enormous relish. She was deeply upset by
riots which took place shortly after her visit, and hated 'to think of
all those smiling faces slaughtering each other'.

Margaret visited Addis Ababa in Ethiopia in 1972. There she met
an old Girton friend, Christine Sanford, 'who had a very English
looking farm at the top of a 3,000 foot cliff', and enjoyed the
English food and the fresh coffee ground from beans grown in the
garden. She and Jane also found the grave of Sylvia Pankhurst,
whom Margaret regarded as 'much the preferable' of the three
Pankhursts.[22]

During the early seventies there were more visits to America and
Canada. Margaret was much upset by the news that Anne was
having treatment for cancer and anxiety was aggravated by her
daughter's being a bad correspondent, so she went to find out for
herself. Mercifully her fears were allayed; Anne made a good
recovery and subsequently heartened her mother by a late marriage. Margaret revelled in a family gathering at Cambridge,
Massachusetts, over Christmas 1974 to which Susan, Jane's daughter, brought her first-born. Later she explored New England towns
with Jane, delighting in the white churches and village greens. She
especially liked Concord for its associations with Walt Whitman
and Emerson.

Indomitability

Although Margaret was becoming frail, she refused to relinquish
her commitments. She continued to attend governors' meetings just
so long as she could get around, where others less stoic would have
contracted out long ago. During October 1971 she had moved into
a pleasant airy flat in Ealing to be near Humphrey and Hilda, but
she never came to terms with having to leave Hampstead Garden
Suburb. 'I like my house and garden here . . . I've already cut
myself down to size in possessions, so another move will be a
bleeder,' she wrote before the change, adding with practical
honesty, 'I've run downhill in ability to look after myself and to get
about — and I agree I must live nearer (so long as I do live) to my
son and his family. So there it is.'[23] Moving into an area that she
did not know, soon after the deaths of Raymond and Daisy and
several long-standing colleagues, produced a 'great feeling of

lonely survival'. Transport was not good, she felt isolated from friends, and would make tortuous journeys back to the Suburb to visit them.[24] Her mobility was becoming slow, but she persisted.

Dr Brian Harrison recalled an interview with Margaret in 1975,

> during which she held an unlighted cigarette for much of our conversation, and occasional smiles modified a rather severe way of speaking . . . She was indeed very interested obviously in the history of politics . . . [and] was much on top intellectually during my brief encounter . . . but rather crusty.[25]

At 84 she was still being consulted over Fabian matters, which cheered her. 'The financial straits and the over-elitist behaviour by the Executive Committee', she wrote to Jane, 'take a lot of time, and people assume I can do what I can't. I don't control Shirley Williams, the NEC or the Labour Party.'[26] Early in 1978 she went on a deputation to the DES to try to save Sidney Webb from being closed down within the Polytechnic. 'We were received very kindly, even fulsomely, but nothing doing.'

During the following months she took Leila Campbell (later chairman of the ILEA) to the London College of Printing celebrations, attended the National Trust birthday jamboree ('rather a waste of time') and went with Dorothy Fox to a Mozart concert. All this when her home help was *hors de combat*, so 'I've had to crawl around doing housework and shopping . . . while at the same time there is a complicated row going on at the Polytechnic in which the Chairman has . . . succeeded in libelling the Head of the Law Department.'[27] It was understandable why in spirits she went up and down like a jack-in-the-box, but Margaret's sense of humour rarely departed, and with a hint of her old gaiety she wrote to Jane:

> Don't you believe that the British are all starving . . . there is quite a lot of money about for all but the worse off . . . someone the other day paid £120 for a pair of Queen Victoria's drawers with a royal monogram. Can't think what a purchaser will do with them — hang them up or put them in a glass case? You can hardly wear them, especially as the legs are divided as was the case with Douglas' Aunt Emma, when her pants came off at a wedding breakfast . . . Of course, there is a lot of public moaning . . . and everyone saying to everyone else, 'it's your fault'.[28]

Although understandably resentful of her physical impairment, Margaret was never overly self-pitying. She did, however, come to rely heavily upon friends, some of whom found her excessively demanding. Nevertheless, she retained her alert outlook on the world, and continued to write stimulating articles. She also remained the outgoing matriarch, as deeply interested in the progress of her grandchildren as of her own children, and especially proud of Humphrey, a high-powered senior economic adviser in the public service.

Jane at long distance and Humphrey nearer home must have agonised long and often over what was best for their mother's health and comfort. There were, inevitably, protracted family deliberations over the advisability of Margaret's visiting Bolivia, where the Abrahams were then living, high up in the Andes, in La Paz, amid snow-capped mountains. 'You will talk to Will, but please don't pressure him,' Margaret wrote more than once to Jane. 'I very much don't want to be a burden but obviously cannot promise that I won't.' Later she suggested that

> I'd better come to you this year if I am to come at all . . . I am distinctly more feeble, especially as regards walking and standing, than when I was in California with you . . . I am better when I have company . . . so do talk it over again with Will.[29]

In the event Margaret did go. Although not well enough to do much sightseeing, she sat happily in the Abraham's garden, 'absorbing the sunshine and loving the rioting roses, geraniums and the galaxies of summer flowers'. They were, she said, her 'memories'.[30] In spite of her health Margaret found La Paz delightful, and evoked its colourful bustling atmosphere in letters of sharply observed detail:

> The women of Indian race or descent (about one-fifth) wear high crowned trilby hats in various colours with widish brims, a blouse with a big shawl pinned across their bosoms, and what appears to be four or five skirts worn on top of one another. In such a rig they can't ride bicycles as the men do, and nobody gives them lifts, so they stagger along on foot carrying great heavy bags and quite often with a baby slung on their backs as well!

This letter concluded, three days later, 'We were told not to go out in the city as there had been a coup d'etat — one branch of the military ousting another — so we stayed around here, with reports of large demonstrations, but no killings to date.'[31]

Although she was so mentally alert, Margaret's health was giving cause for increasing concern. The altitude of 12,000 feet proved to be bad for her, and in spite of excellent medical care the visit had to be curtailed. She returned home just before Christmas 1978, immensely appreciative of the forbearance Jane and Will had shown her, and wrote thanking them 'wholeheartedly for being so kind . . . I was very conscious of being a nuisance and wouldn't have come if I had known, but still I cannot be really sorry that I did.'[32] And neither was Jane, as she wrote after Margaret's death, 'I would not have undone that visit. I loved my mother very much.'[33]

During the early part of 1979 Margaret was in and out of hospital where, she related, conditions were almost Dickensian. She certainly was not the most placid of patients, and could be extremely ungracious to the nurses, but St Mary's in the Harrow Road (not the great teaching hospital of Praed Street) does seem during her sojourn to have been a place lacking in compassion. Certain employees went on strike, so the regular nurses had to do their work for them, which made them 'take it out' on the patients. Margaret reported to Jane, presumably with dramatic licence:

> They often leave you waiting for a long time . . . I was 1½ hours sitting on a chair in an empty corridor waiting to have an X-ray . . . The general impression . . . is that one is in a concentration camp — we started those in the South African war — or in a Victorian workhouse. I am constantly reminded of a poem Jack Squire wrote in December 1914, when the Lambeth Guardians had just decided that the Workhouse Child could not be allocated an egg at Christmas. It ended, 'I am sorry Jesus dear, I don't deserve an egg this year, Peace on earth and mercy mild, and Christ forgive a workhouse child.' Last night we didn't get any supper except a cup of soup.[34]

The 'concentration camp' to which Margaret was consigned did not effect any improvement in her health, so 'having struggled against hospital authorities I got let out', she told Jane in late February. Soon after, she was taken to the North Middlesex Hospital, which 'had a lot of room, a small stream running through the grounds, and an atmosphere less unpleasant than in the Paddington one'. Here Margaret had one major complaint, 'They won't let you smoke,' she told Jane, 'I tried to pinch some cigarettes and matches from Humphrey, but he was all law-abiding and Civil Service and refused me them!'[35]

By Easter the Wilful One was back home at Ealing, busily dealing with a subscription-to-the-*Economist*-muddle for Jane, and sorting out papers. She was, however, becoming increasingly dependent on the family, her loyal helper from the Hayes and Harlington Labour Party, Ruth Belcher, and various district nurses to whom she was often rude. '[They] come in to wash me at times, though I never know when . . . However, the weather has improved . . . and the neighbourhood is full of wild almond, broom, forsythia and wild cherry. The beeches are not yet showing.' Although outwardly cheerful, she was well aware of her disabilities, but she wrote to Jane, 'I do get about a bit and go to some meetings,'[36] which must have taken great determination. A friend, Mrs Crane, recalled meeting Margaret — then in her mid-eighties — in a crowded Tube train during the rush hour. She was returning from a meeting in Central London and standing (with a stick in a crowded carriage) until a seat was given to her, on Mrs Crane's insistence.

Even though she continued to read exhaustively, Margaret's pattern of life was becoming steadily more circumscribed. The necessity to move from a flat which had become burdensome was obvious. Since no living-in companion could be found, supervised accommodation seemed inevitable, and this view Jane shared with Humphrey when she came over later that year. Margaret, of course, resisted such an idea, until Providence intervened when she broke her leg. This enabled Jane to settle her mother into a bright, cheerful nursing home she had found at Goring on Thames, 'with as many reminders of home as I could get in'. Margaret had a spacious room from which she could watch the river and identify the various birds hopping around in the lush grounds. She was, and looked, well cared for, although she grumbled about the food and still behaved wilfully. Indeed, she had to be remonstrated with severely for trying to cajole visiting friends to dress her and take her out for a walk in bitterly cold weather.

Margaret died peacefully and without pain on 7 May 1980, just after her eighty-seventh birthday. This had been spent happily reminiscing with Naomi Mitchison, and with Humphrey — so like

Douglas to look at — in affectionate attendance. Margaret once said, after Mrs P had died, that she would not have wished her to linger any longer. She was wise enough to have felt precisely the same about herself.

Notes

1. M. I. Cole to Agnes Murray, 27 January 1959 (at Menton) (all letters to Agnes Murray cited are in the possession of Beryl Hughes).
2. M. I. Cole to Agnes Murray, May 1959.
3. M. I. Cole to Agnes Murray, 21 June 1959.
4. M. I. Cole to Agnes Murray, 16 May 1959.
5. M. I. Cole to Agnes Murray, 3 April 1959 (at Exmouth).
6. M. I. Cole to Agnes Murray (probably October 1959).
7. M. I. Cole to Agnes Murray, 24 April 1957.
8. M. I. Cole to Agnes Murray, 23 December 1957.
9. M. I. Cole to Agnes Murray (possibly May 1959).
10. M. I. Cole to Agnes Murray, 5 May 1959.
11. Stanley Mayne, letter to author, 14 January 1983.
12. M. I. Cole to Francis Meynell, 29 April 1967, Meynell Papers, Cambridge University Library.
13. Mary Omerod to M. I. Cole, 2 January 1965 (CFP).
14. Julian Huxley to M. I. Cole, 16 June 1970 (CFP).
15. Lord Redcliffe-Maud to M. I. Cole, 16 January 1970 (CFP).
16. Naomi Mitchison to M. I. Cole (possibly June 1970) (CFP).
17. M. I. Cole to Francis Meynell, 8 December 1970, Meynell Papers (privately held).
18. M. I. Cole to Nicolas Pease, 14 May 1975 (CFP).
19. Ted Littlecott to M. I. Cole, 20 June 1973 (CFP).
20. Margaret had seven grandchildren in all. Jane had three sons, Stephen, Roger and Charles, and one daughter, Sue. Humphrey had one daughter, Nina, and two sons, David and Richard.
21. Jane Abraham, letters to author, July 1982.
22. Jane Abraham, who contributed much to this section (interview and letters to author).
23. M. I. Cole to Robin Page Arnot, 30 August 1971 (CFP).
24. Molly Bolton, interview, and M. I. Cole to Robin Page Arnot, 23 November 1971 (CFP).
25. Dr Brian Harrison, interview.
26. M. I. Cole to Jane Abraham, 11 December 1977 (CFP).
27. M. I. Cole to Jane Abraham, 24 March 1978 (CFP).
28. M. I. Cole to Jane Abraham, 17 April 1978 (CFP).
29. M. I. Cole to Jane Abraham, May 1978 (CFP).
30. Jane Abraham, letter to author, June 1982.
31. M. I. Cole to Rosemary Beresford, 23 November 1978 (in the possession of Rosemary Beresford).
32. M. I. Cole to Jane and Will Abraham, 25 December 1978 (CFP).
33. Jane Abraham, letter to author, June 1982.
34. M. I. Cole to Jane Abraham, undated (CFP).
35. M. I. Cole to Jane Abraham, 20 February 1979 (CFP).
36. M. I. Cole to Jane Abraham, July 1979 (CFP).

14 A VERY INTERESTING OLD LADY

Through seven decades, happy, purposeful and creative, Margaret had striven for socialism. She had planned and organised, written and argued for a just and compassionate society, never forgetting that politics concerned people. Neither introspective nor deeply philosophical, her socialism derived from a belief in equality and democracy: that all men are born equal, with an equal claim to certain fundamental rights, and that social control and organisation within society are necessary for social rather than for individual ends. This was not to imply that men and women were equal in all respects, but it did mean that 'their equal humanity is more important than their differences'.[1] Margaret was, like Douglas, a socialist on grounds of morals, decency and aesthetic sensibility.[2] As she once said in a rare emotional generalisation, 'I don't think there is anything particularly scientific about socialism. It is a faith.'

As popularisers and teachers, the Coles worked in harness, through a range of political bodies, from Guild Socialism to the Fabian Society: Margaret as organiser rather than thinker. She it was — at least in her younger days — who, as Lord Elwyn-Jones recalled, 'could not wait upon events, but expected immediate results from her activities'.[3]

In no way did this imply a belief in revolution. Indeed, she recognised that because of consensus politics 'time and again the British elite has given way to preserve their own position in the face of surges of public opinion . . . so a good deal of social change has come about without violent physical struggles.'[4]

Margaret's deepest commitment was to education. She hated its prevailing inequitable, inadequate structure, and considered that Britain's class-ridden society — as reflected in its schooling — exacerbated social inequality and wasted vast reserves of latent talent. Her experiences in adult education fortified these views and, later, on the LCC Education Committee, she channelled her energies into extending educational provision (and therefore extending opportunity) and generally helping in the 'eradication of accumulated educational slumdom'. She also believed passionately in the need for public discussion about education — of 'what we want to achieve and how it can be effected'. She was also alert to 'the inevitable attempts of public schools to perpetuate their existence and their class', and in her eighty-fifth year was urging the importance of

> working out a new shape and policy for education . . . It is going to be difficult because so many cling emotionally to the ideal of elitism and the old school tie [but] . . . after some experience I am much afraid that the absence of agreement about aims and methods may turn out to mean stagnation and argument as the various interests say nothing and sit around.[5]

Legislation, particularly that effecting social change, operates slowly. Yet even so, looking back from a peak of optimism in the late forties, Margaret acknowledged the fundamental improvements in social habits and in living standards — for which she and Douglas had worked — that had taken place in her lifetime, albeit within a capitalist framework. Women's clothing had become both sensible and unhampering, people ate better food, were adopting wiser eating habits, and with extended motor transport and the advent of holidays with pay, opportunities for the 'common man' to travel widely were opening up. There were also other more basic innovations. Free medical care, introduced for the whole nation, meant that good health was no longer to remain the preserve of those with the ability to pay. The school leaving age had been raised; secondary education for all was made a reality, and university education — especially at Oxford and Cambridge — was no longer accepted as the prerogative of the 'gilded rich'. The most radical of all changes, however, was in the development of a comprehensive scheme of social security, conceived initially by the Webbs, to lift the fears of poverty.

In her youth, Margaret recalled, there had been no sort of social security whatsoever.

> I was at school when the first Old Age Pension Act became law . . . [Previously] those who fell sick or out of work had nothing but private charity . . . or the cruel mercy of the Poor Law to fall back on.[6]

The Poor Law, that is, which decanted husband and wife into

separate institutions when, frail, ill or impecunious, they fell on hard times. In 1948, with an optimism that then in no way seemed illusory, Margaret wrote from her heart, 'the social security system is complete. The Poor Law is dead': she did not live to witness the extensive and deliberate dismantling of the welfare state.

Characteristically Margaret remained critical of the glaring extremes of wealth that persisted, and would caustically highlight any precise evidence of ostentatious opulence, both in her conversation and in her columns of political comment. Yet she was also a realist, well aware of the greed and selfishness that lurked within the average human being, of the attitude that supported claims for steeper wage differentials 'providing they do not reduce mine'. These tendencies, she considered, had been as underestimated by the founding fathers of socialism as the altruism of man had been exaggerated.[7]

Margaret, while optimistic, admitted the need to define and defend democratic principles. Society must still find answers to profound questions of government. 'How much inequality, and of what kinds, could a society contain and yet be fundamentally equalitarian? How much authority, how much leadership should be found in a society calling itself democratic?' This challenge, thrown out four decades ago, is as relevant today as the concluding passages in her autobiography.

> If a democratic technique for running society cannot be evolved, society will either disintegrate, destroy itself in war, or, as I still think is the more probable, resort to armed and dreadful tyranny, or to a crawling and exasperating bureaucracy . . . to do the job for it.[8]

If the socialist beliefs that Margaret strove to establish have been temporarily bruised and battered, her personal achievements stand secure. 'A lady who wrote with a sparkle', she is an historian of the Labour Movement whose books and articles bear the hallmark of veracity, scholarship and wit, and whose foresight helped preserve the artefacts and archives of socialism. As a research worker of repute she gave as generously of her expertise to international scholars as to the inexperienced novice. She also was an effective administrator and a convinced (though no loudly protesting) feminist. She extended every encouragement to, and made opportunities for, young women (and men) keen to participate in public affairs or to progress in the professions. Her kindnesses to people at all levels were legion. Yet in no sense was Margaret only a cerebral socialist. She was a warm, if sometimes waspish, human being to whom William Morris' Fellowship of Common Purpose was all important. Affectionate, if undemonstrative, towards a family held dear, she was deeply caring of Douglas. Indeed, as an old friend remarked, had Margaret been less his protective prop, her own output might well have been far greater.[9]

She remained as loyal to old friends as to causes, yet was tolerant of new ideas. 'One should keep one's mind open and try everything once so far as age and infirmity permit', she wrote,[10] for it was not in her philosophy to oppose change merely because it might alter the political flow. On the contrary, she considered that the Labour Movement needed strong left wingers if the body politic was to move forward.

For all her intellectual agility, Margaret could be devastatingly if unintentionally rude. To some she seemed acidulated, even frightening, to others a 'putting-off' if not 'putting-down' lady.[11] In all fairness she was largely unaware of these reactions, and hated to hurt anyone's susceptibilities; but, like Douglas, she could never suffer fools gladly. With the onset of age and her 'Damery' an element of imperiousness surfaced: she would batten on to certain friends, and her behaviour could be highly wilful.[12] Yet until her final years that wilfulness was leavened by a bubbling irreverence. Margaret possessed that rare quality of gaiety and the ability to take neither life nor herself too seriously: although unwavering in her convictions, she was no ideologue. 'For Margaret,' H. D. Hughes wrote, 'politics was essentially a matter of fun and friendship rather than of ideologies and sects.'[13]

For all her high ideals and her sense of history, Margaret was not the *grande dame* of British socialism which the *Guardian* suggested in her obituary. This accolade she would have been the first to insist was for Beatrice Webb. Yet Margaret was assuredly far more than that 'very interesting old lady' of Susan Lawrence's dictum. Throughout her happy, rounded and useful life, for all her exacting standards and passion for reasoned scholarship, she never forgot the significance of Blake's 'Minute Particulars' or the import of the 'poorest He that is in England'. Her compassion was ever present.

In a memorable testament contributed to a book of essays, *What I Believe*[14] when well over seventy, Margaret listed four fundamental convictions that had been her 'unfailing guides' in life. These she preferred to express in (not always precise) quotations:

> The first is verify your references; the second, I beseech you gentlemen, consider in the bowels of God that you may be mistaken; the third, that we hold these truths to be self evident that all men are created equal and that they are endowed by their creator with certain inalienable rights; and the fourth, that fellowship is heaven and the lack of fellowship is hell.[15]

To her four basic beliefs Margaret added a fifth, which she considered was the best precept for living in the world. It was her own interpretation of the prophet Micah, 'that gentlest of Old Testament prophets' —

> And what shall be required of Thee? To do justice, love mercy, and walk humbly according to the light in thee.

No mean epitaph for a Labour historian who, as Professor Asa Briggs said succinctly, 'presented socialism with a human face'.[16]

Notes

1. M. I. Cole, *Tribune*, 22 July 1966.
2. Professor Asa Briggs, *The Listener*, 20 October 1960.
3. Lord Elwyn-Jones, interview.
4. M. I. Cole, *Socialist Commentary* (September 1977).
5. Ibid. (September 1978).
6. M. I. Cole, *Growing Up into Revolution* (Longmans Green, London, 1949), p. 216.
7. M. I. Cole, *Socialist Commentary* (November 1978).
8. Cole, *Growing Up*, p. 216.
9. Bernice Hamilton, interview.
10. *Tribune*, 22 July 1966.
11. Dorothy Fox and [Enid] Jeeves, interviews.
12. Dorothy Fox, C. H. Rolph and others, interviews.
13. Society for the Study of Labour History, *Bulletin* (Autumn 1980).
14. Contributors to this symposium — *What I Believe* (Allen and Unwin, London, 1966) — included Lord Boothby, John Bratby, Malcolm Muggeridge, Naomi Mitchison, Norman St John Stevas and others. It still reads well.
15. M. I. Cole, *Tribune*, 22 July 1966.
16. Professor Asa Briggs, interview.

BIOGRAPHICAL NOTES

ALLEN, Clifford (Lord Allen of Hurtwood) (1889–1939). Fabian socialist Member of ILP. Pacifist and conscientious objector (absolutist).

ARNOT, Dr Robin Page (1890–). Margaret Postgate's 'first boss'. Associate of G. D. H. Cole and William Mellor in Fabian Research Department. Founder member of the Communist Party of Great Britain. Major historian of the Miners' Federation and of the mining industry.

ATTLEE, Clement (Lord) (1883–1967), MP for nearly three decades. Deputy Prime Minister to Winston Churchill during the Second World War. In 1945 became first Labour Prime Minister with majority government. A greatly underestimated politician and administrator.

BEALES, H. L. (Lance) (1889–). Reader in Economic History at LSE. Founder member of SSIP. Active in WEA and Tutors' Association. Close neighbour and friend of Margaret and Douglas Cole.

BENTWICH, Helen (1892–1972). Friend and much-travelled colleague of Margaret Cole's. Chairman of LCC Education Committee. Later chairman of LCC. Her husband Norman, Professor of International Relations at Jerusalem University, distinguished lawyer and scholar of Jewish affairs, was Attorney-General, Government of Palestine (1920–31). Her brother was Hugh Franklin, long-time member of LCC Education Committee, and protagonist of comprehensive schools.

BEVERIDGE, William Henry (Lord) (1979–1963). Author of Beveridge Report. Director, LSE, and later Master of University College, Oxford.

BEVIN, Ernest (1881–1951). From drayman at Bristol to National Organiser, Dockers' Union: became General Secretary, Transport and General Workers' Union. MP (1940–51), Minister of Labour during Second World War; Foreign Secretary (1945–51).

BOLTON, Molly (Ivy Schmidt). Worked before her marriage as Beatrice Webb's secretary. Active in early days of LRD. Member of LCC (1934–64), of which a former chairman.

BOWEN, Stella (1895–1949). Close friend of Margaret Cole. Australian and a talented painter. Official war artist in Second World War. Author of *Drawn from Life* (1941).

BRAILSFORD (Henry) Noel (1873–1958). Widely regarded as the greatest journalist of his generation and an outstanding political writer. Prolific author and pamphleteer.

CARR-SAUNDERS, Professor Sir Alexander (1886–1966). Statistician and population expert. Booth Professor of Social Science, Liverpool University. Later Director, London School of Economics.

CHESTERTON, Gilbert Keith (1874–1936). Poet, journalist, author. Creator of detective-priest Father Brown. His *Song of the Wheels* (1911) Margaret Cole considered 'the best English poem ever written about a strike'.

DALTON, (Edward) Hugh (1887–1962). Fabian, economist. Chancellor of Exchequer in Labour's 1945 government. Life peer.

DAVIES, Emil (1875–1950). Honorary treasurer of NFRB and Fabian Society. Alderman LCC (1936–47), and sometime deputy chairman. Labour Party's authority on finance. City editor, *New Statesman* (1913–31).

DRAKE, Barbara (1876–1963). Beatrice Webb's favourite niece. An active Fabian. Writer, author of seminal *Women in Trade Unions* (1920), LCC Alderman and member Education Committee. Advocate of equal pay for equal work.

DUGDALE, John (1905–63). Private secretary to C. R. Attlee (1931–9) and Parliamentary Secretary when Deputy Prime Minister. Member LCC; MP, held office in 1945 Labour Government.

Married George Lansbury's daughter.

DURBIN, Evan (1906–48). Member of Cole Group; of SSIP, and with Hugh Gaitskell assistant honorary secretary to NFRB. Economist: author of *The Politics of Democratic Socialism*. MP 1945. Drowned tragically while on holiday.

ELWYN-JONES, Lord (Frederick) of Llanelli and Newham (1909–). Attorney-General (1964–70). Long-time friend/colleague of Margaret Cole and Naomi Mitchison. Lord Chancellor of Britain (1974–9).

FARINGDON, Lord (Alexander) Gavin (1902–77). Pacifist. Active Fabian, member of Executive Committee (1943–69). Main interests international and colonial affairs. Chairman of Fabian Colonial Bureau. Member LCC. His Buscot Park home housed many Fabian conferences and seminars.

FORD, Ford Madox (1873–1939). Author, novelist and critic. Companion of Stella Bowen.

GAITSKELL, Hugh T. N. (1906–63). Member of Cole Group and NFRB, WEA. Extra-mural and university lecturer. Elected MP 1945. Leader of Parliamentary Labour Party, 1955.

GALTON, Frank Wallis (1867–1952). Abandoned engraving trade to become Beatrice and Sidney Webb's devoted secretary and research assistant. General Secretary to the Fabian Society (1920–39).

GOLLANCZ, (Sir) Victor (1893–1967). Publisher and writer. Instigator of the Left Book Club. Great Jewish humanitarian. Founded various political-philanthropic organisations, including War on Want.

GRIFFITHS, James (Jim) (1890–1975). Miners' agent. MP Llanelli for 34 years. Member of Labour Party NEC and sometime chairman. Minister National Insurance (1945–50). Secretary of State for Colonies. Later Secretary of State for Wales.

HAMMOND, J. L. (Lawrence) (1872–1949). Joint author, with

his wife Barbara, of *The Town Labourer, The Village Labourer* and *The Bleak Age*, which set history in a social and economic context. Honorary Fellow of St John's College, Oxford; Barbara Honorary Fellow of Lady Margaret Hall, Oxford.

HENDERSON, Arthur (1863–1935). 'Uncle Arthur' entered Parliament in 1903. Treasurer, then long-time Secretary of the Labour Party, whose organisation was largely of his building. Home Secretary in first Labour Government and Foreign Secretary in the second. Close friendship with the Webbs. Made great effort to bring peace to Europe; President, until its final failure, of the Disarmament Conference (1932–4).

HOBSON, John Atkinson (1858–1940). Radical pacifist economist and internationalist. Author *Work and Wealth, Imperialism*, etc. Anticipated much of Keynsian economic theory, but received inadequate recognition.

HOBSON, S. G. (1864–1940). Author, journalist, socialist. Early Fabian, often at odds with Shaw and the Webbs. Colleague of A. R. Orage on *New Age*, and leading Guild Socialist. Believed that the collectivism advocated by the Webbs would leave the workers unaffected.

HOGBEN, Professor Lancelot (1895–1975). Zoologist. Great populariser of science and mathematics. Author of *Mathematics for the Million* (1936) and *Science for the Citizen* (1938).

HORRABIN, J. F. (Frank) (1884–1962). Guild Socialist, Fabian and member of ILP. Briefly an MP. Close colleague of Ellen Wilkinson. Cartoonist, cartographer, journalist. Drew maps for *Empire* (journal of Fabian Colonial Bureau) and *News Chronicle* (plus cartoons). To Margaret Cole he looked 'exactly like the Mad Hatter — but is neither mad nor bad, but sweet all through'.

JOAD, Professor C. E. M. (1891–1953). Head of Philosophy Department, Birkbeck College, London University. Prolific author and broadcaster, notably in the BBC's Brains Trust.

JONES, Arthur Creech (1891–1964). Organising Secretary, Workers' Travel Association. Founder member and chairman of

Fabian Colonial Bureau; private secretary to Ernest Bevin during the war. Parliamentary Secretary of State for Colonial Office; then Secretary of State for Colonies (1946–50). Governor of Ruskin College, Oxford. Widely travelled in British colonies.

KEYNES, John Maynard (Lord Tilton) (1883–1946). At Peace Conference, 1919. Author of *Economic Consequences of the Peace, General Theory of Employment, Interest and Money* (1936), etc. Treasury adviser (1940–6).

LANSBURY, George (1859–1940). Lifelong socialist and pacifist. Editor *Daily Herald*. MP for 20 years. Led Poplar Guardians in their strike (and imprisonment) over refusal to collect poor rates and their campaign to equalise burden of poor relief over London. And they succeeded. Leader of PLP (1931–5). Resigned over pacifist issue. His daughter Daisy married Raymond Postgate.

LASKI, Harold J. (1893–1950). Professor of Political Science, University of London (LSE) (1926–50). Member of Fabian Executive Committee and of Labour Party NEC (chairman 1945–6). Prolific author; notably *Grammar of Politics*.

LAWRENCE, (Arabella) Susan (1871–1947). Initially a Conservative/Municipal Reformer, became the first Labour woman member of the LCC in 1913. Later Alderman (LCC), and Poplar councillor. Imprisoned with colleagues for refusal to pay poor rates. Active in National Federation of Women Workers. Member of Fabian Executive Committee, also Labour Party NEC, of which first woman chairman (1930). MP (1923–4), and, with Margaret Bondfield, first Labour woman to take her seat. Re-elected 1926. Parliamentary Secretary to Minister of Health (1929–31). An excellent debater. 'Drank in statistics as some do whiskey!'

L'ESTRANGE MALONE, Leah (d. 1951). Member and Alderman LCC: served on Public Assistance and Welfare committees. Chairman Education Committee. Devotee of theatre, ballet and opera.

LLOYD, (Charles) Mostyn (1878–1946). Fabian, life-long socialist. Founder member of NFRB. Head of Department of Social Science, LSE. On staff of *New Statesman* for many years.

MacARTHUR, Mary (1880–1921). A dynamo among trade unionists. Secretary of Women's Trade Union League, then of National Federation of Women Workers. Chief campaigner against sweating and *causa causans* of the Trade Boards Acts. 'A bright light that burnt herself out too soon'.

MacDONALD, James Ramsay (1866–1937). Labour Prime Minister (1924 and 1929–31). The Prime Minister in National Government until 1935.

MALLON, Dr J. J. (Jimmy) (1875–1961). Secretary Anti Sweating League. Prominent protagonist of Trade Boards Act 1909. Warden of Toynbee Hall (1919–54). A Fabian. Covered much ground work for Ellen Wilkinson's Hire Purchase Act (1938).

MANSBRIDGE, Albert (1876–1952). Founder of the WEA (1903). Member of numerous national committees on higher education and religious matters. Founded also National Central Library and Seafarers' Educational Service.

MARTIN, (Basil) Kingsley (1897–1969). A brilliant journalist, editor *New Statesman* (1931–60). Companion of Dorothy Woodman.

MASEFIELD, John (1878–1967). Poet Laureate and author.

MELLOR, William (1888–1942). Secretary of Fabian Research Department (1913). Worked on the weekly *Herald* and later edited the *Daily Herald*. Subsequently first editor of *Tribune*.

MEYNELL, (Sir) Francis (1891–1975). Printer, designer, founder of the Nonesuch Press. Poet and author.

MITCHISON, Gilbert Richard (Dick) (Baron Mitchison of Carradale) (1890–1970). Joined socialist movement in early thirties. Undertook social research for Beveridge's Manpower Survey and later for G. D. H. Cole's Nuffield Reconstruction Survey. MP 1945, QC 1946. Life peer 1964. Front Bench spokesman on local government matters, and later on science and technology. Parliamentary secretary in Ministry of Land and Natural Resources.

MITCHISON, Naomi (Nou) (1897–) Margaret Cole's closest friend. Mother of five. Argyll county councillor (1945–65). Author of over seventy books: fiction, non-fiction, drama for children and adults. Also a poet. Tribal adviser to Bakgatla, Botswana. Sister of Professor J. B. S. Haldane, geneticist and scientist.

MORRIS, William (1834–96). Poet, translator, author (*News From Nowhere*) and creative craftsman: designer, artist, illustrator. A socialist who believed that in a decently ordered society all work should give pleasure to the doer, and combine beauty with utility in the thing made. Founded Socialist League (1884) and the Kelmscott Press.

MORRISON, Herbert (Lord Morrison of Lambeth) (1888–1965). Member of LCC (1922–45). MP for nearly 30 years. Able organiser and administrator. Home Secretary/Minister of Home Security (1940–5). Member of War Cabinet. Deputy Prime Minister and later Lord President of the Council.

MURRAY, (George) Gilbert (Aimée) (1866–1957). Professor of Greek, translator of Euripides. A devoted internationalist and pillar of League of Nations.

NEEDHAM, Dr Joseph (1900–). Biochemist, sinologist, internationally distinguished scholar and author.

ORAGE, A. R. (1873–1934). Key exponent of Guild Socialism; editor of *New Age* in which published writings of Hilaire Belloc, G. K. Chesterton and Arnold Bennett. Made his paper the brilliant spokesman for Guild Socialism and contemporary dissident causes. Later embraced Social Credit and 'a form of spiritualism'.

PARKER, John (1906–). MP Dagenham (1945–83). General secretary of Fabian Society, of which chairman, vice president and president. Honorary secretary Passfield Trustees. Father of the House (1979–83).

PEASE, Edward R. (1857–1955). A founder member of the Fabian Society. General secretary of the Society between 1889 and 1914, and its honorary secretary both before and after that date, retiring finally in 1939. Author of the *History of the Fabian Society*.

PEASE, Nicolas (1894–1984). Son of Edward Pease. Rubber broker. Life-long Fabian. 'Knew all prominent Fabians and Socialists from about 1906'.

PUGH, (Sir) Arthur (1870–1955). General Secretary, Iron and Steel Confederation and British Iron, Steel and Kindred Trades Association. Chairman of TUC.

RECKITT, Maurice (1888–1980) Guild Socialist. Active in LRD. Friend and admirer of G. D. H. Cole since their undergraduate days, and collaborator in satirical verse and political revues. 'Distinguished in croquet and Christian Theology!' His sister Eva founded Collett's bookshops.

ROBSON, Professor W. A. (1895–1980). Professor of Public Administration in London University (LSE) (1947–62). Founder, joint editor of *Political Quarterly* (1930–74). Chairman Passfield Trust. Writer, lecturer of international repute.

ROLPH, C. H. (Bill Hewitt) (1891–). Former Chief Inspector, City of London Police. Member of editorial staff of *New Statesman*, specialising in police, legal and humanitarian matters. Broadcaster and prolific writer, almost always under name of C. H. Rolph.

SHARP, Clifford Dyce (1883–1935). Fabian and journalist. Editor of *New Statesman* from its foundation (1912) until 1931. Married daughter of Hubert Bland, treasurer of Fabian Society.

SHAW, George Bernard (1856–1950). Music critic, dramatist, socialist. Early member of Fabian Society to which he introduced his life-long friend, Sidney Webb. Editor of (first) *Fabian Essays*. The Fabian Society's 'most brilliant pamphleteer'.

SHEARMAN, (Sir) Harold (1896–1984). Resident Tutor, then National Education Officer, WEA (1946–61). Academic Adviser for tutorial classes in London University. Member of LCC Education Committee of which chairman 6 years. Alderman then councillor (Deptford) LCC, of which chairman. Also first chairman GLC and of ILEA, on which he remained until 1970. Wrote and lectured extensively on education.

SKEFFINGTON, Arthur M. (1909–71). MP from 1945, nearly 20 years. Member of LCC, active Fabian. Member of Fabian Executive Committee, of Fabian Local Societies Committee and of NEC, Labour Party. Held various parliamentary posts. Concerned with conservation long before a popular issue.

SMITH, Charles (Lord Delacourt-Smith) (1917–72). General Secretary, Post Office Engineering Union. Worked in NFRB. Member of Executive Committee of LRD. MP (1945–50). Life peer.

SQUIRE, J. C. (Jack) (Sir John Collings) (1884–1958). Literary editor, *New Statesman*, and acting editor (1917–18). Later editor and chairman, *London Mercury*. Prolific writer, critic and poet.

SUTHERLAND, Mary (d. 1972). Chief Woman Officer of Labour Party (1932–60).

TAWNEY, Professor R. H. (1880–1962). Professor of Economic History, University of London (1931–49). Taught for Tutorial Classes Committee, Oxford University. Executive Committee, WEA (1905–47). Author of *The Acquisitive Society* and *Equality*.

WALLAS, Graham (1858–1932). Socialist. Lecturer at LSE. Author of *Human Nature in Politics* and *Our Social Heritage*. With (Sir) Sidney Olivier, G. B. Shaw and Sidney Webb, comprised the 'Big Four' of the early Fabian Executive.

WARWICK, Frances, Countess of (1861–1938). Wealthy aristocrat and friend of royalty. Converted to socialism by Robert Blatchford, and remained life-long active supporter: the 'Chatelaine of Easton Lodge'.

WEBB, Beatrice (1858–1943) and WEBB, Sidney (1st Baron Passfield of Passfield Corner) (1859–1947). Writers, historians and research workers. Sociologists, Labour propagandists and politicians. Inseparable in their monumental work for the Labour Movement.

WELLS, Herbert George (1866–1946). Author, scientist, internationalist.

WOOLF, Leonard (1880–1969). Ex-Ceylon civil servant. Author, founder of Hogarth Press. Editor of various reviews, including the *Political Quarterly* (1931–59). Long-standing Fabian, active in International and Colonial Bureaux. Married to Virginia Stephens.

SELECT BIBLIOGRAPHY

Allen, Bernard *Memior of William Garnett* (W. Heffer, Cambridge, 1933)

Blunden, Margaret *The Countess of Warwick* (Cassell, London, 1967)

Bowen, Stella *Drawn from Life* (Collins, London, 1940; reprint, Virago, London, 1984)

Briggs, Asa and Saville, John (eds.) *Essays in Labour History* (Macmillan, London, 1960), vol.1

Burrows, John *University Adult Education in London (1876–1976)* (University of London, Senate House, London, 1976)

Carpenter, L. P. *G. D. H. Cole, An Intellectual Biography* (Cambridge University Press, Cambridge, 1973)

Cole, G. D. H. *The Crooked World* (Gollancz, London, 1933)

—— *The World of Labour* (G. Bell, London, 1915)

—— and Cole, M. I. *The Condition of Britain* (Gollancz, London, 1937)

—— and Postgate, Raymond *The Common People (1746–1938)* (Methuen, London, 1938)

Cole, M. I. C. *Beatrice Webb* (Longmans Green, London, 1945)

—— (ed.) *Beatrice Webb's Diaries (1912–24)*, vol. 1 (Longmans Green, London, 1952)

—— (ed.) *Beatrice Webb's Diaries (1924–32)*, vol. 2 (Longmans Green, London, 1956)

—— *Books and the People* (pamphlet, Hogarth Press, London, 1938)

—— 'Comprehensives in London', special supplement in *Plebs* magazine (NCLC, London, April 1967)

—— *Growing Up into Revolution* (Longmans Green, London, 1949)

—— *Life of G. D. H. Cole* (Macmillan, London, 1971)

—— *Makers of the Labour Movement* (Longmans Green, London, 1948)

—— *Marriage* (Dent, London, 1938)

—— (eds.) *Roads to Success* (Methuen, London, 1936)

—— *Servant of the County* (Dobson, London, 1956)

—— *The Story of Fabian Socialism* (Heinemann, London, 1961)

———— (ed.) *Twelve Studies in Soviet Russia* (Gollancz, London, 1933)

———— (ed.) *The Webbs and their Work* (Frederick Muller, London, 1949)

———— *What is a Comprehensive School?* (pamphlet, London Labour Party, 1953)

———— (ed.) *Women of Today* (Nelson, London, 1937; 1946 edition)

———— and Drake, Barbara *Our Partnership* (Longmans Green, London, 1948)

Crossman, R. H. S. (ed.) *New Fabian Essays* (Turnstile Press, London, 1952)

Devereux, W. A. *Adult Education in Inner London, 1870–1980* (Shepheard-Walwyn, London, 1982)

Ford, Ford Madox *Parades' End* (Bodley Head edn, London, 1963)

Haycroft, Howard *Murder for Pleasure* (Peter Davies, London, 1942)

Kenney, Rowland *Westering* (Dent, London, 1939)

Martin, Kingsley *Editor* (Hutchison, London, 1968)

MacKenzie, Norman and Jeanne (eds.) *The Diary of Beatrice Webb* (Virago, London, in association with the London School of Economics and Political Science, 1982, 1983, 1984 and 1985), vols. 1–4.

————, ———— *The First Fabians* (Quartet, London, 1979)

Meynell, Francis *My Lives* (Bodley Head, London, 1971)

Mitchison, Naomi *You May Well Ask* (Gollancz, London, 1979)

———— *Vienna Diary* (Gollancz, London, 1934)

Mowat, C. L. *Britain between the Wars (1918–1940)* (Methuen, London, 1955)

Muggeridge, Kitty and Adam, Ruth *Beatrice Webb: A Life 1858–1943* (Secker and Warburg, London, 1967)

Parker, John *Father of the House* (Routledge and Kegan Paul, London, 1982)

Postgate, Margaret *Margaret Postgate's Poems* (printed for the *Herald*, London, 1918)

Pugh, Patricia *Educate, Agitate, Organise* (Methuen, London, 1984)

Radice, Lisanne *Beatrice and Sidney Webb* (Macmillan, London, 1984)

Reckitt, Maurice *As It Happened* (Dent, London, 1940)

Rolph, C. H. *Kingsley: The Life, Letters and Diaries of Kingsley*

Martin (Gollancz, London, 1973)

Todd, Margery *Snakes and Ladders* (Longmans Green, London, 1960)

What I Believe (a Symposium) (Allen and Unwin, London, 1966)

Woolf, Leonard *Downhill All the Way* (Hogarth Press, London, 1967)

Wright, Anthony *G. D. H. Cole and Social Democracy* (Clarendon Press, Oxford, 1979)

INDEX